A MOUNTAIN TO CLIMB
ON TIMOR

A MOUNTAIN TO CLIMB ON TIMOR

DR MICHAEL EARLE

Matador
9 De Montfort Mews
Leicester LE1 7FW, UK
Tel: (+44) 116 255 9311 / 9312
Email: books@troubador.co.uk
Web: www.troubador.co.uk/matador

ISBN 978 1906221 829 (paperback)
978 1906221 867 (hardback)

A Cataloguing-in-Publication (CIP) catalogue record for this book
is available from the British Library.

Typeset in 11pt Stempel Garamond by Troubador Publishing Ltd, Leicester, UK
Printed in the UK by The Cromwell Press Ltd, Trowbridge, Wilts, UK

Matador is an imprint of Troubador Publishing Ltd

To the memory of my parents:
Rose Edith Stock Earle (1923-2003)
Maurice William Earle (1922-2007)

CONTENTS

PREFACE

I have known there was a story to write about my adventure on Timor ever since I returned in 1977. When my mother died in 2003, I realised that I should wait no longer. She held the key that opened the door to the garden of my forgotten childhood, where I could reclaim pleasing facts and anecdotes about my early life, even truths about my personality. Suddenly, that part of me had gone forever. More than this, it was now too late to capture one side of the family history for future generations.

So I set about the task of writing this memoir in tribute to my dear mother and as a legacy for my own family. In addition to the journal that I kept of my trip to Timor, I had squirrelled away diaries, photographs, letters and boxes full of memorabilia going back forty years. And when I sat in the loft of my London home and dusted them off, I set free a genie bigger and more powerful than I had anticipated. Timor is an adventure story within a longer journey that I made in my formative years.

A Mountain to Climb on Timor is about the metamorphosis of a person and his life, a transformation brought about by free will, determination and chance. It documents a journey of personal exploration and discovery that other people take at some time in their lives. Yet vanity leads me to believe that my particular story is worth telling, and I hope it will encourage others to see that change is not only possible but also necessary if dreams are to be realised.

Driven by a need to prove my worth, I changed my attitude, behaviour and priorities to rescue myself from certain failure as judged by my parents and the society in which I lived during my teenage years. Ultimately, I took risks; I shunned friendships and romance; and I pushed myself to mental and physical limits to achieve what I desired. At crucial moments I duelled with the shadow within and conquered negative thoughts of giving up; and in so doing, I influenced my destiny and attained the self-esteem that I sought.

I owe a debt of gratitude to my parents and to all the friends with whom I shared such worthwhile and fulfilling experiences during the period 1967 to 1980, especially Ruth, Sarah, Iain, Max, Nick, Bernie, Rob, Greg and Brian.

London

November 2007

FREEWHEELIN'

FREEWHEELIN'

WILDERNESS ROAD

I had a Webley air rifle that fired 0.77 calibre lead pellets and was accurate only up to 20 feet. For targets further away, I had learned to aim high to compensate for lack of power, and could hit unsuspecting birds sitting in trees or flying over the back garden at home. Whereas the birds had a sporting chance to escape, passing lorries presented a much easier target, though the possibility of retribution was greater. One driver whose vehicle I hit did stop and knock on the door of our house. By a stroke of good luck, my parents were away, and my dear grandmother swore that she was the only person living there.

The Battle of Black Bridge was on a different scale altogether, and the outcome rather more serious. In March 1967, a group of us took our guns to a crossing of the River Avon about half a mile beyond the edge of town on the disused railway line connecting Chippenham and Calne. Splitting into two groups, our gang took up positions about 120 feet apart behind the stone abutments on both ends of the bridge. We exchanged pot shots for a while, and then the battle really hotted up when Willy Mann came out from cover and ran across the bridge to storm the other side. Midway, a pellet hit him in the groin and put an end to his bravado. He dropped his weapon and fell on the track, both hands clasping the precious genitals.

"Arggh. You bastards, you bastards," Willy shouted, sounding more aggrieved than injured.

His trusty Levi's had taken the brunt of the force and no blood had been spilled, so our initial shock and disbelief gave way to relief and hilarity. Susan was not so fortunate. A pellet from a powerful 0.22 calibre rifle hit her in the neck, and penetrated to within an inch of her jugular vein. The boys dispersed and the other girls took Susan to the hospital. When the full story came out at the police station, I was named as a participant. In due course, several of us appeared before the Juvenile Court in the Market Place and each were charged and convicted of being in possession of a gun 'which was not so securely fastened that it could not be fired.'

"You're a disgrace to my name, what will people think of me?"

This was not the first time, nor would it be the last time that my father would utter those sentiments. Described as '...extremely well known throughout the West of England' in a local newspaper, Maurice William Earle was an imposing figure who stood nearly 6 foot 2 inches tall and had jet black hair swept back and constantly held in place by Brylcreem. In addition to building a successful business across the region, his achievements were many, as cricketer for Plymouth in his youth, as Mosquito pilot in the war, as rally driver with a display cabinet full of cups and medals, and as a director of Swindon Town Football Club. Various commitments occupied him seven days a week, and his hard work and business acumen enabled our family to live a comfortable existence in a huge detached house in virtual seclusion from the neighbours. As a proud man, a product of pre-war society and a well-respected figure in the community, it must have been a great disappointment and irritation that his only son was such a wayward character.

Youth counterculture made small beginnings in the 1950s with the beat generation in America and the teddy boys in London, and then blossomed in the 1960s to the point when a conservative backlash began against the drugs and provocative music scene of the hippies. The Monterey Festival, Jimi Hendrix, and the Sgt Peppers album all made news in 1967 as the Summer of Love happened in San Francisco, Los Angeles, New York and London. On the other hand, Nixon, Reagan and George Bush appeared on the scene!

4

I was not a hippie, but this was my generation, a generation emerging from the shadow of a World War, a generation that eschewed continuity with the past. No longer would a son unquestionably follow his father into the family business or farm. We had different values and aspirations, and said to society 'Let us be different', though at times we had to be defiant, even shout or protest to be heard. Indeed, 1968 was to be a year of student protests around the world, as well as demonstrations against senseless carnage in Vietnam. It was also a year in which 4,600 Russian tanks extinguished democracy in Czechoslovakia, and black civil rights leader Martin Luther King was assassinated for advocating equality in the land of the free.

Though the drama of world events would intrude on television screens and in newspapers, it was remote and peripheral to my concerns and preoccupations. Now aged fifteen, I had been on the road of discovery and expression of my independent self for about three years. It was to be a long and often lonely journey and only accomplished by developing the discipline to defer instant gratification, to accept sacrifice and to tackle problems, as this story relates.

As soon as it reopened after the Christmas break, I spent my main present in the record shop and rushed home clutching a new acquisition under my arm. Ripping off the cellophane wrapper in haste and removing the album from its sleeve, I placed the record on the deck and carefully lifted the stylus onto the spinning vinyl disc to play the first track on the old mono record deck that was sitting on the floor of my bedroom. *Blowin' in the Wind* was the first track and it begins:

How many roads must a man walk down
Before you call him a man?

I played the entire *Freewheelin'* album over and over again in the retreat of my bedroom that Christmas and New Year holiday. It was sensational, astounding and magnificent, and Bob Dylan's songs became a powerful and habitual influence that helped shape me and sustain me through the difficult years of my adolescence. The incisive and biting social commentary of the lyrics was foreign to the comfortable, tame society in which I lived, and served to sustain the detachment towards it that I felt. Without an ambition in life, I was drifting at school: I had no direction that would stimulate hope or engender the determination to go forward with the persistence to succeed. I knew only of influences, distractions and desires, and the horizon of my daily world extended no more than 25 miles in any direction from home, encompassing a small area of the West Country between Bristol and Marlborough, Salisbury and Malmesbury.

However, growing up in a small market town in Wiltshire during the 1960s did not mean that the world passed me by. Chippenham experienced the era of the Mods and Rockers with full force, though I preferred freedom of expression in the way I dressed and was not tempted to emulate or join either sect. My non-allegiance was apparent from my appearance out of school. My hair was long and I wore Levi's jeans, Ben Sherman shirts and desert boots or Kickers. In comparison, the Mods sported butch haircuts, and fur trappings on their huge parka coats, whereas the Rockers had long hair and wore studded leather jackets and hilarious pointed shoes. Rockers had a serious propensity to be violent. I well remember the tense atmosphere of nervous anticipation as the town waited for them to ride in on their motorbikes from neighbouring Melksham and Trowbridge to confront the Chippenham Mods and thrash them with knuckle-dusters, metal pipes and chains.

There were pugilistic elements in Chippenham too, including a boy of diminutive stature known as Dapper Capp, Dapper because his speciality was 'dapping', or head-butting, anyone who annoyed him or was just in the vicinity as an innocent bystander during his testosterone-fuelled displays. One night, at the summer fair on the Bath Road, I witnessed an unprovoked attack on my friend Ross Henning when Dapper calmly walked up and took a mighty leap into the air to plant a head butt on Ross's nose. To be fair to Dapper, Ross was a very tall boy and therefore had set himself up as provocative target.

My long hair had been the first visible sign of my need to be recognised as an entity with the power of personal choice. I hated the ritual butchery every time I was forced to get the regulation 'short-back-and-sides' haircut at the barber's shop. A desire to be identified with the patently free and rebellious rock bands I admired, especially the Rolling Stones, also motivated me to want long hair. But it was also a way to look older than my years, perhaps to be more attractive to girls. For whatever reason, my long hair became a symbol, a banner advertising and confirming my right to be in control.

I was thirteen years old when I started to make a serious stand against having my hair cut. My father was emphatic in his opposition to long hair, threatening all sorts of reprisals.

"You are a disgrace to my name," he said, "no boy of mine is going to look like that."

And in the sixites it was strictly against school regulations to have long hair, when long meant any length over the ears or touching the collar. It constituted a stand against prevailing authority, it showed lack of conformity, and short hair was linked with society's need for a distinct and visible segregation of gender.

At times, I was subjected to immense and unfair pressure. After weeks of hectoring and threats, the authoritarian geography teacher Mr Perkins brought in a pair of scissors and chased me around the classroom. I was also in trouble with the headmaster, who threatened to throw me out of school. But it was all to no avail because I was determined not to succumb. Mr Perkins did not catch me, the Headmaster eventually suspended me, but only for a day, and my father gradually toned down the attacks to mere taunts that I looked like a girl.

Being so noticeable brought problems for a boy who

embarrassed easily, but the principle of being independent was more important than suffering occasional social discomfort, and eventually I overcame this problem to enjoy the notoriety of being recognised as different.

DISTRACTIONS

In January 1968 the Christmas break ended with the distant voice of my mother calling from the bottom of the stairs.

"Mike. Mike. Mike, it's time to get up for school, come on."

I had spent much of the holiday with Elizabeth, at Elizabeth's house, taking Elizabeth to the pictures, and sitting talking with her in The Galleon coffee bar, making a single cup of tea or frothy coffee last for hours so we wouldn't get thrown out onto the street. Elizabeth was a shapely and attractive thirteen year old with long blonde hair and a distinctly sultry look. She seemed to be unattainable as the central figure in a clique of three devilishly attractive girls who determinedly avoided hopeful suitors, of which there were many at the school. However, after we started dating, I found that Elizabeth had a shy, gentle and considerate nature, and I enjoyed being in her company.

My diary entries for January record the routine of going to school, which I found tedious and boring, and the importance of Elizabeth, music and my social life:

Mon: School. No Elizabeth today. Macbeth homework. I love Elizabeth.
Tue: School. Elizabeth on bus. Hockey. Geography revision.
Wed: School. Elizabeth lunch. Galleon. Bob Dylan.
Thu: School. Saw Elizabeth in theatre and on bus. Homework. Dylan.
Fri: School. No Elizabeth. Con's Club dance. Miss Elizabeth.

Another morning. The bedroom door opened.

"Mike, get up, I'm not going to tell you again. Your breakfast is ready, hurry up please."

I opened one eye and focussed on the pale grey sky through

the veil of condensation on the bedroom window. It was cold in the room and I was loathe to get up, but there was an obligation to my mother and an imperative to catch the bus in time to avoid questions and excuses if I arrived late at school. And I wanted to see Elizabeth.

Chippenham Grammar School was on the northern side of town off the Malmesbury Road. Housed in the grounds of a former Saxon estate known as Hardenhuish, the school was an unfortunate mish-mash of architectural styles and building materials, including the vulgar new dining hall that had an octagonal shape and a grey, white and apple green exterior. It didn't sit comfortably next to the pre-war pre-fabricated blocks, but at least it was well away from the more pleasing architecture of Hardenhuish Manor, the Sixth Form building, and the small 18th Century church built in classical Georgian style.

The town itself was not a Mecca for devotees of grand sights, period architecture or great engineering feats. True, it had a profound claim to fame, but not one that led people to flock to the town, perhaps because the town didn't care to exploit or profit from the opportunity. In May 878, King Alfred and his makeshift army of men from Wiltshire and Somerset fought the marauding Danish Vikings under their leader Guthrum, and secured an agreement that the invaders would pull out of the stronghold in Cippenhamme, which had been seized earlier from King Alfred. Alfred expelled the Danes from his kingdom of Wessex and, to our great fortune, saved the nascent English kingdom and language from certain extinction. That is why he is 'The Great', a title not bestowed on any other English monarch, not even Henry VIII or Queen Elizabeth I. True, Chippenham straddled an important crossing of the River Avon and had been on the main route between London and Bath since at least the 14th Century. True, it lay on the fringe of truly magnificent tourist attractions such as the Cotswold Hills to the north, and the two world heritage sites of Stonehenge on the chalk uplands to the south, and the stone circle at Avebury to the west. True, the beautiful Roman and Georgian Heritage City of Bath was only twelve miles distant, but all this historical and natural splendour merely served to highlight the enormous contrast with Chippenham.

To me, Chippenham was a sleepy, bland and uninspiring place in the 1960s. It was a market town serving a predominantly rural community preoccupied with pig and dairy farming, horse riding and foxhunting. Almost 18,000 citizens lived in the town. Many of the men folk were employed by the Westinghouse Brake and Signal Company, which occupied a vast site deliberately adjacent to the railway station. A loud hooter blared out at the works at five o'clock every weekday, and was the signal for a seemingly endless throng of cyclists wearing flat caps to exit the main gate and return home. Nestlé occupied a former silk factory next to the bridge in the centre of town and produced condensed milk. My father's Ford Main Dealership on Cocklebury Road was probably the next largest business in the town, employing about 50 staff. And that was about it.

On Sundays the town came to a standstill. Church bells rang and dogs took their humans to the park. This was the worst day of the week for me, especially with the ritual of the family lunch. With luck, I would be able to arrange a meeting with friends in Monkton Park or, if I had any money, I would take Elizabeth to the cinema. Failing this, I took refuge in my room and listened to records.

There was nothing about Chippenham to interest a restless teenager, though what entertainment could I have afforded when I was constantly short of money for even my simple needs? The precious £6 I owned at the start of the year dwindled to nothing by mid-January. It was not that I never received any money, it was more that I couldn't save it. Hand-rolling tobacco, cups of tea or coffee in The Galleon, and the occasional purchase of records left me broke.

On Sunday 14th January, I celebrated the second 'monthiversary' of my courtship of Elizabeth, but days later she told me she no longer wanted to go out with me. In those days I was painfully slow with girls, shy and hesitant. We had kissed, but I had not progressed matters beyond this stage. Our relationship lasted sixty days, which was an achievement considering that each of my seven previous girlfriends had lasted between one and four weeks.

A devilish Irish girl named Cathy was my first girlfriend. She was mad about Davy Jones, the baby-faced English-born singer with The Monkees, America's attempt to cash in on the success of The Beatles. Some people thought that I looked like Davy Jones, so perhaps there was a connection for Cathy? Whenever I went to her house, she seemed to be playing *Last Train to Clarkesville* or *I'm a Believer*. Cathy lasted thirty days and didn't even get a kiss. We would sit together in the darkened cinema while I counted to ten to pluck up enough courage to put my arm around her, the essential precursor to kissing. On the count of ten, my arm would twitch a little and then relax as I began the countdown once more, or abandoned the process to gather the determination needed for the next planned attack. Why was it so difficult? Where had I picked up the idea that the boy had to make all the running and take matters progressively to test the reaction of the girl? Still, it was evident even to me, that my first romantic liaison was at an end when I stumbled on Cathy and a friend of mine shagging in a bedroom at a party.

Yes, but that was more than a year ago when I was only fourteen, and things had moved on since then. By the time Julie from Melksham finished with me in June, I was up to 4 on the scale of 1 to 10 that I had devised to measure progress. At Level 4 I had ventured beyond the stage of unclasping brassieres and was touching under knickers. The next goal would be to have the girl touch me, but for this development, I had to wait until Angela from Corsham.

All through February I mourned the loss of Elizabeth, and to comfort myself I ate too much, too frequently, a correlation between unhappiness-boredom and snacking-overeating that would stay with me for life. To make matters worse, I was penniless. This unhappy situation continued unabated and there were no girlfriends in March or April, and never more than £1 in my pocket.

Yet in other ways, my situation *was* changing. I was approaching a major crossroads in life, the significance of which I only dimly perceived at the time. No amount of advice or warning from the adults around me seemed to register the need for change. Summer Term began at the end of April, and I was facing the onset of exams starting in May and continuing over five weeks to the end of June, just days after my sixteenth birthday. At the end of this ordeal I could leave school having taken General Certificate of Education (GCE) Ordinary Level examinations, or could continue into the Sixth Form for two years and take GCE Advanced Level exams at eighteen, and A levels were the passport to a good job or even university.

My mock exams began in March with French dictation. Yet the day before, I passed the time trimming my hair a bit, cutting the lawn for my father, and going to The Galleon with friends. Indeed, I spent much of the Easter holiday wandering about the town, sitting in The Galleon coffee bar or canoeing on the River Avon in Monkton Park, as if I didn't have a care in the world. But I did, and the stress of the period manifested itself in my behaviour and affected my health. A persistent and very itchy rash developed over my groin, and despite the embarrassment, I told my mother about it and we went to see the doctor in the week before exams started.

I planned my periods of revision according to the exam timetable, but revision was interspersed with much socialising and other distractions, more than usual, in fact. Tall, dusky Diana from Lacock was girlfriend for ten days, ginger-haired Julie from Melksham for twenty, and there was time for repeated flirtations with blonde sisters Carol and Deborah in company with my constant companions Willy Mann, Mike Comley, Rodney Acourt and Anthony Byrnes. However, this circle of friends faded away within weeks of the last exam, precipitated by an argument with Anthony Byrnes over my fickle behaviour towards the girls in the crowd. Most of these friends were a wider circle of older youths who had left school but who I knew from my frequent nights out in Chippenham and neighbouring towns like Melksham and Calne. Their defection was hurtful, but probably beneficial for me in the long term.

I slept most of the weekend following the last exam. The end of term was still three weeks away, and at school it was a period of introduction to the courses that I had decided to take at A level, assuming, of course, that I passed enough exams to be allowed to continue at school. And the anxious wait for the results began.

THE SYSTEM

In the 1960s the school system in England was straightforward if unfair by modern values. At the age of 11, most children either failed the 11+ examination and went to a secondary modern school, or passed the 11+ and went to a grammar school. Alternatively, if your parents were well connected or rich you could go to a fee-paying public school, irrespective of your ability.

This tripartite system seemed logical to me and the choice was easy. I didn't want to live away from home in an all-male environment just to be buggered, bullied and beaten, so that ruled out public school, even if I had been in a position to go, which I was not. Of the two remaining possibilities, passing the 11+ was a gateway to greater things, such as university, success, respectability. Failing it led to classes in woodwork and technical drawing at the Secondary Modern school, and a destiny as a factory worker, lorry driver or builder's mate. In Chippenham at least, few inmates escaped from secondary modern across to the grammar. There was a huge open playing field between the two schools, but there might as well have been a barrier of barbed wire, a moat full of piranhas, and manned observation towers for all the chance there was to cross to the better side.

When taking the 11+ examination I knew I was required to pass, but its significance as a major watershed in life had not fully penetrated my conscious mind. I was coasting along in life at my own pace, content to play at every opportunity at school and at home. I was never going to be a top achiever, and so it was a stroke of good fortune that I was required to attend an interview for a place at the grammar school. It meant that I was a borderline case and competing for the last few places. Passing or failing during the ten-minute interview became akin to tossing a coin: heads or tails would decide my path through life. Headmaster Mr Stephens asked what I liked to do in my spare time.

"Watch television", I replied.

A less honest, more astute boy would have said that he was interested in building refracting telescopes, or reading about ancient civilisations, or collecting rare species of beetles – anything at all that would have improved his chance of winning a place – but I was neither dishonest nor astute.

Yet I won a place at the grammar. I was allocated to Class 1R, where R stood for Ravenscroft, the surname of the French woman who was head of the class. In the first year, all pupils were treated equally, and the outcome of the exams at the end of the year would enable the school to stream the pupils. From Year 2 the pupils were placed in five streams: Upper and Lower Science, Upper and Lower Arts, and one stream of two classes for those who showed no particular aptitude in either direction or, perhaps, no aptitude at all. I came 27th/28 in the class examinations at the end of the first year and was put into the bottom stream of Year 2. Come Year 3 and I dropped chemistry and physics. After Year 3 I dropped history; or was it that history, chemistry and physics dropped me?

For whatever reason, leading up to the milestone of O levels, I had no specialisation at all, not in science, not in humanities, not in languages. Quite literally, I was in mid-stream, taking English language, English literature, mathematics, French, geography, human biology, art and metalwork. This was not the best combination to build a platform for eventual entry to Cambridge University and on to a career as Strategic Management Consultant with McKinsey.

A patchy performance in term examinations gave crumbs of comfort after I achieved top ten performances in French, English and geography. *'He has ability and with consistent effort could do quite well'*, the English teacher opined in my School Report. *'Has some ability, but is disinclined to use it'* ran another clever one-liner, and I earned the comment *'His attitude to work is far too complacent'* from the Maths teacher. This was a constant theme in my school career. Although I had been in second or third position in class during my early years at primary school, my teacher Mrs Volker nevertheless penned the most accurate insight into my character when she wrote the following summary in my final report in 1961, just before I moved from Seend to Chippenham at the age of eight:

Michael is an able little boy, who will waste his opportunities in life by an assumption that he will get on without any effort on his part.

AWAKENING

Summer 1968 was the first year that I did not go away with my parents in the school holidays. Instead, I went on trips to London and the Cornish seaside resort of Newquay with Max Hoare and Iain Sim, two new school friends I had met after the barrier of the ability streams was removed near the end of the term. Max and Iain were much more studious than I was, yet still able to have outside interests and a sense of humour. Like me, both were committed Dylan fans who could interject one-liners from his songs into the conversation at appropriate points, and this was a significant factor that brought us together in the first few weeks of meeting. Iain was a brainy boy with a talent for various sports, while Max was a cheerful lad who more than closely resembled comedian Tony Hancock. He had moved around a lot in the wake of his father's career in the RAF, and was soon to disappear to Episkopi in Cyprus.

To pay for the trip to Newquay, I found a job and worked for two weeks at Stephens Plastics in Hawthorn, a blot on the landscape on the outskirts of Corsham. Stephens Plastics manufactured synthetic rubber membranes for pools and tanks. Manual labour handling hot and smelly rubber sheets did not appeal to me, but I needed the money, and with overtime had amassed £15 by the end of the ordeal. This promptly reduced to £7, however, following a visit to the pub that Saturday night and the purchase of two more Dylan albums, *Blonde on Blonde* and *Another Side of Bob Dylan*.

On Friday night after work on the first week, I went into the little town of Corsham and met Angela. We embarked on a relationship that lasted all summer and into the next term at school, setting a new record of sixty-seven days. Angela enchanted me and was rather sexy, hence the progression to Level 6 referred to earlier. One Sunday afternoon we lay on the grass in a secluded area of Monkton Park and I got first-hand experience of a second hand.

Like most of my girlfriends before and after, Angela was slim, had brown eyes and long brown hair. She resembled Mick Jagger's girlfriend Marianne Faithful and her distinguishing feature was a small gap between her two front teeth, a condition I found inexplicably alluring. Angela was enjoyable to be with and certainly aroused my interest in sex. However, her sexual forwardness and strong local accent marked her out as a little bit 'common' in my judgment, because to some extent I viewed Angela through the lens of values received from my parents and peer group at school. My interest waned and I eventually sacrificed the pleasure of her company.

I went to South Wales with Iain and Max in a party of helpers intent on renovating a derelict cottage into a centre for outdoor activities for the school. Buying the cottage was the brainchild of teacher 'Geography Jones', who led the trip and drove the minibus. Tylemorgrug cottage perched on a steep hillside and stood alone at the end of a rough track more than a mile from the main road, if there was such a thing as a main road in Wales.

Tiring manual labour, cold nights in sleeping bags, blisters searing with pain, and a constant diet of food badly cooked did nothing to dent my fascination and enjoyment. In fact, I felt moved by the remoteness and natural beauty of the area and was stimulated to write poems about the insignificance of my existence and all human activity in the context of immense natural forces and endless time and space.

DIRECTION

I passed three O levels and was greatly disappointed. Such was the expectation and emphasis on scholarly achievement in my community, that I felt practically useless. Six would have been a reasonable haul, and the best pupils had passed in eight or nine subjects. If I left school now it would confirm that I was a failure, since I could not expect to get a decent job and might as well have failed the 11+ and gone to the Secondary Modern. So, lightly armed with passes in English language, geography and human biology & hygiene, I decided to stay at school and go into the Sixth Form to re-take some of the subjects on the way to A levels.

I stayed and discovered a vocation, and became driven by a newly found interest that made me determined to succeed in that field. I chanced upon geology through the serendipity of a discussion with Max, whom I had met in the run-up to the end of the Fifth Form. At the time, geography was my favourite subject, and I was definitely going on to take it at A level, along with economics and history.

"If you like physical geography, you should take up geology as one of your A level choices", Max said. "It's all about rocks and minerals and fossils and very interesting." Max was a credible source because he had studied geology at O level, and so I promptly dropped history and enrolled on the course.

In the first term of Sixth Form, I was making more effort and my next school report accurately reflected the change. In geography, Mr. Perkins commented that *Michael has made a very good effort, and has tackled his work with determination.'* The geology master Mr Jones wrote that my work was *'of a high standard and he shows interest and some enthusiasm for the subject.'*

Now, I had a direction in life instead of just interests, and a strengthening ambition to pursue a career in geology. Geology released me from the personal and local issues of my daily existence; it endowed my imagination with new dimensions of thinking; it extended my awareness of past time from hundreds of years to billions; and it pushed the horizon of my thinking to a planetary scale.

It was a time of great discovery in the science, and I became entrained in the excitement caused by the emergence of the theory of plate tectonics, which was a coherent body of knowledge that established a new framework for understanding the entire science of the study of the earth. It boggled the mind to know that 200 million years ago all the continents of today were one landmass, a supercontinent named Pangaea. Dispersal of Pangaea created the Atlantic Ocean, and caused India to drift across the equator and crash into Asia and push rocks to rise five miles into the sky. Surely, humanity was rendered insignificant, art and literature irrelevant, and politics futile, when compared to the history and wonders of the planet.

Of course, we were not at the leading edge of understanding at Chippenham Grammar School! Geology was a subject of negligible importance on the curriculum, and taught by a geography teacher. The availability of recently published material was nil. Our standard text was the thousand page tome entitled *Principles of Physical Geology*, written by the brilliant English geologist Arthur Holmes. In 1927, Holmes made a giant contribution to the theory by postulating that dissipation of heat from radioactive processes deep in the earth causes convection currents to form, and that the force of the currents causes continents to break apart and 'drift' across the globe. But in 1968, so much was not understood about the theory and consequences of plate tectonics that the lack of full information and clear explanation was an integral part of the fascination of geology. I wanted to know more; I wanted to travel along a road going to an unknown but clearly exciting destination.

RUGBY

At the start of the school year, I was chosen to play in the First XV. Rugby was the premier winter sport in West Country towns and schools, to the extent that football was not played at all at the Grammar, and the fortunes of the rugby team were highly newsworthy and had an appreciable effect on the school's self esteem.

I had been accepted into an exalted position at school and it gave me a feeling of belonging to something worthwhile. True, the rugby team was identified with the school establishment, which I did not care for, but it bonded me to a worthy cause and to the players at a crucial phase in my life. There was camaraderie during training and on the field of play, and endless singing and hilarity in the changing room after a match and on the coach after away fixtures. Friendships were nourished during school hours with endless talk about victories and the heroics and blunders of our team mates or the opposition. And these friendships overflowed naturally into my social life, so that my closest friends during the last years at school had some involvement in the squad of two teams. Rugby now joined geology as a motivating and stabilising force at the centre of my world.

Tonk, Wild Man, New Boy, Scratch, Leech, Nose, Pheasant, Podge, Scab, Mouse, Dave the Rave, Lung, Sid and I were the regular players in the team. My nickname was Bubble, a reference to the physical outline I had sported in my early teens. A sturdy boy named Nick Brewer was our able Captain, and became a good friend. Nick had been in the rugby team since playing for the Colts, the under 15s, and he later took the school team into the Bath 7s competition. Nick was the fastest runner in the school and completed the 100 yards race in 10.8 seconds.

Season 1968-69 began with a 0-6 defeat against Bristol Kingswood, but we won the next match 41-3 against Devizes Grammar and followed this with a succession of good results. There were easy wins against Park, Kingswood Bath, Lackham Agricultural College, Chippenham Technical College and Bath Technical College, and hard-won victories against Marlborough Grammar, Keynsham, Bristol Commonweal, Bristol Headlands, and Midsomer Norton. It was a packed season, with all but one match played before Christmas. We won fifteen out of twenty matches and scored 342 points, which easily beat the previous record of 261 points, established in 1952. Only 64 points were scored against us.

Resurgence of the team was due to the recent arrival of George Squires, a games master who knew how to motivate the players and who introduced a hard regime of discipline and fitness from the beginning. It was a refreshing change from the reign of the partisan and aggressive previous master.

I played hooker in the middle of the front row of the pack, supported in set scrums by props Tonk and Wild Man. I was a fast and agile hooker and in set piece play I was difficult to beat, even winning a high percentage of balls put in by the other side. But this was the only skill I brought to the game. It was fortunate for me that a hooker did not need to be an eighteen stone giant who could knock over a concrete post yet accelerate faster than a Ferrari. Indeed, it helped to be on the small side because the hooker had to be lifted off the ground by the props to be able to swing for the ball, a practice now prohibited.

A highlight of the season was the 6-6 draw achieved against Marlborough College, the well-known public school in the town of the same name. Such a good result meant a great deal to the Grammar boys, and Marlborough knew it, because they falsely claimed to have fielded a 2nd XV against us, as a way of showing their superiority and simultaneously ensuring that they would not be embarrassed in the event that they lost.

ROCK AND ROMANCE

Romance dropped out of the picture during the autumn term. My new-found interest in rugby and the additional effort at schoolwork meant that I had less time and inclination to attempt amorous pursuits. However, I did find plenty of time to listen to Bob Dylan in my bedroom at night to feed a growing dependency.

By the winter of 1968 I had acquired most of Dylan's albums, and I was also listening to Captain Beefheart, Leonard Cohen, Cream and The Rolling Stones. I had followed the Stones from the early days – as far back as August 1964 when I went to a Stones concert played on the steps of Longleat House, the stately home of Lord Bath. I was just twelve years old at the time, and I was so gripped by the raw rock and roll and biting lyrics that I bought a copy of their latest single, *Not Fade Away*. Now, I had all the singles and my other favourites were *It's All Over Now, Get off My Cloud, The Last Time, I Can't Get No Satisfaction, Paint it Black, Play With Fire, We Love You,* and *Let's Spend the Night Together*. Incredibly, the USA was still strongly puritanical, and many radio stations did not play *Let's Spend the Night Together*. As a result, the song only reached Number 55 in the charts, whereas the 'B' side, *Ruby Tuesday,* became a number one hit!

Mixtures of rhythm and blues plus rock and roll music were becoming mainstream, and the Stones concert was a major factor in my awakening. Beat music and groups from Liverpool had become popular in 1963 on the back of the spreading fame of The Beatles, replacing, mercifully, 1950s and early 1960s chart-topping favourites such as Elvis Presley, The Everly Brothers, Cliff Richard, and others whose music seemed to belong to an older era. I didn't like beat music, for it smacked too much of 1950s teddy boys. The new music that I listened to really came to prominence in the summer of 1964, when The Animals topped the singles chart with a raw rendition of Dylan's *The House of the Rising Sun*.

It was a different scene in the local clubs on Saturday nights. Motown and Soul music from America outdid British music in popularity because it was great for dancing and smooching with girls. However, most of the songs had a faraway, 'foreign' feel and were about romance and love, so I did not buy any of the records, despite the enormous catchy appeal of songs by Otis Redding, Aretha Franklin, The Four Tops and The Temptations.

I went to concerts as often as I could. My local venue was The Pavilion in Bath, where many excellent groups appeared on Monday nights. Pink Floyd, The Yardbirds, The Who, Jeff Beck, The Walker

Brothers, The Move, The Small Faces, and a host of other top acts appeared there in the late sixties. Ticket prices were affordable at about six shillings, though adding the cost of taking the train from Chippenham meant that I could not always afford to go.

Nor could I often afford to pay 30 shillings for an LP. However, I had a growing collection of first rate albums, including *Rubber Soul*, *A Hard Day's Night* and *Sergeant Pepper* by The Beatles, this despite not liking their singles, with all that effeminate sentiment about wanting to hold hands or wanting to be your lover, baby. It was the haunting and stark lyrics of Bob Dylan that above all other artists I found appealing. His songs were about contemporary issues, such as racial injustice, social deprivation, and the distinct possibility of a nuclear war, which in some measure was responsible for the 'live today' attitude of youth in the early sixties that flowed into the hippy era that crystallised in 1967.

To earn some extra cash for my simple pleasures, I worked for a week delivering post in the pouring rain, but otherwise the Christmas break passed uneventfully. Our Sixth Form Party at school was a big bore, and because I had no-one to take to the annual school dance, I agreed to serve on the soft drinks bar. I did not end up with a date, and the last entry in my diary for the year read, '*I need Elizabeth*'.

Fran was my next love and we dated for a record eighty-two days through the spring of 1969. My eye had been on Fran for some time and her name had appeared frequently in my diary many weeks before we eventually dated. I was waiting for the right moment to ask, but Nick Brewer just went ahead and arranged the first date for me. Because of the lengthy build-up to this occasion, Fran and I already fancied each other very much, and the relationship got off to a quick start and we were inseparable.

I spent weekends at her parents' house, and we also went to the Folk Club in town, and to the cinema, and saw each other most days at school. In appearance, she was a typical Mike Earle girlfriend: slim, pretty and with brown eyes and dark hair. I especially liked her innocence and lack of pretence. It meant a lot to me that she was sexually inexperienced because it gave me confidence that her feelings towards me were genuine and sincere. But in a curious way, I became uncomfortable with the emotions that surfaced during our petting sessions. She slipped into a vulnerable state, seemingly transported to another place, a place I could not share with her and where my presence was almost incidental. It was as if anyone could have aroused her to such heights. The heavy breathing, the flickering eyelids and darting eyeballs, and the proclamation that 'I love you' possibly meant that she only loved what was happening to her. And even if she did truly love me, I questioned, it was evidently not enough to be bothered to monitor the way I was responding and try to please me. At sixteen, I was still shy and not mature enough to talk to her about my feelings. Naively, I believed that love should be a spontaneous journey of discovery without the need for explanation; to speak of it and to try and define it would likely destroy it. I found that I became emotionally detached during our heavy petting sessions, more of an observer, and the relationship eventually lost its special significance.

Fast approaching was the annual ritual of examinations. I re-sat French, metalwork and English literature O level exams, and took geology O level for the first time. Mocks were in March and exams were in June. In between, there was an eight-day trip to Tylemorgrug cottage in Wales, the first of three that year. It was a more comfortable experience this time, more lively, more drunken and more musical. And there was the possibility of romance because Brenda was there.

Brenda was an appealing and buxom girl with long brown hair. She brought a guitar and there was an evening of folk songs, western-style by the gate of the cottage. Brenda succumbed to my charms on the night that our group went to a pub. In Wiltshire vernacular, I knocked her off. Knocking someone off was often no more than snogging and romantic chat, ideally with some minor groping thrown in. Knocking off Brenda was being unfair to Fran and was a dilemma for me, and when I returned from Wales I wrote to Brenda. In the letter I reassured her that my feelings were genuine but explained that I was dating Fran, and I thanked Brenda for the enjoyable time we had spent together; she wrote back.

When I got back to reality, I thought that the whole thing never happened, that it was all a beautiful dream. You made me very happy, and I shall always remember that week. If ever you feel down, and want someone to talk things over, remember I'll always be willing to listen and pleased to help.

I finished with Fran the following day and started dating Brenda, yet two days after that I wrote in my diary: *'Fran my love, I'm a fool'*. But I did not like to go back on a decision; onward, onward with sadness but not regret. Brenda lasted twenty-two days.

GRAN'S CAR

Granny Earle started driving before there was a driving test in England. The pinnacle of her driving career was a journey to the outskirts of London in her youth. Born in 1887, she was now more than eighty years old, and when she drove, she was a danger to herself and other road users. Cataracts had given her tunnel vision, and she drove straight down the centre of the road guided only by the white lines. With her peripheral sight now confined to seeing straight ahead, it was nothing short of miraculous that she survived unscathed on roads that had no lines at all, like many of the country lanes leading into and out of Seend, where she lived. Of diminutive stature even in her prime, she had now shrunk to the point where casual observers at best caught a glimpse of her hat of the day as the car sputtered past. She sensibly agreed to abandon driving on the sage advice of doctor and family, and in August 1968 I became the lucky recipient of her car.

My car started life as a black Ford Prefect 100E with the rare registration number of OMR 1, but became 530 EMW and dark green when my father sold the registration plate and had the car re-sprayed after a major effort to remove a multitude of rust-infected areas on the ageing vehicle. In common with other British-built cars in the 1950s, it came with a catalogue of endearing qualities, not least a tendency to leak rainwater through the windscreen, which caused the velvet trim to go mouldy and smell. A vacuum pump powered the windscreen wipers, and pressure dropped progressively as the car was driven faster and faster. Driving in the rain became somewhat hazardous at speed because the wipers would stop completely. Nevertheless, this acute handicap did not concern me unduly, because my overriding priority was speed not visibility, and I compensated by leaning forward close to the glass and squinting. Indeed, there was little point in trying to observe speed limits because the speedometer needle swung relentlessly from side to side like a metronome: one moment you seemed to be going at 60mph, the next moment 100mph. This didn't matter so much because getting caught was nigh on impossible. Speed limits had been introduced on open roads in 1965, but there were no cameras or radar traps, and police cars were a rare sight in the district.

After the First World War, my grandfather Maurice Stafford Earle abandoned his trade as a carpenter and started the family's garage business that spread across the West Country after my father took over. The workshop and forecourt were joined to, and inseparable from, our house in Seend, and were among the most intriguing parts of my playground in the village. Quite literally, cars and motoring were in my blood, but perhaps owning a car at sixteen was a little premature when the legal minimum age was seventeen. My father kept the vehicle off the road at his business in Cocklebury Road, but occasionally allowed me to drive it in the grounds of the Cattle Market opposite, which operated only on Fridays. I needed no encouragement to turn the Cattle Market into a rally course, darting in and out of the buildings and around the animal pens going sideways and making the tyres squeal like the frightened little piggies that came to market every Friday.

This arrangement worked for a while, but only for a while. I had the rare distinction of being convicted simultaneously for driving under-age, driving without a licence and driving without road tax. It felt unfair in the circumstances, because I was not even in the car when the offence was discovered, and I had only driven it half a mile from the garage. It was parked outside the Liberal Club on Station Hill and I was inside at a dance. A passing policeman noticed that the vehicle was not taxed, and Nick, who was in the back of the car snogging his girlfriend, had to come into the club to fetch me.

At the court appearance at 10 o'clock on 16th June, the magistrates handed down a conviction on all three offences. I was fined a total of £8 and told that two endorsements would appear on my first licence. Three endorsements would have resulted in disqualification, so I was a little lucky there. Only my grandmother knew that I had driven her car around Seend village a few times when I was 15 years old!

Dad was not at all pleased, especially as he had to pay the fine. Once again, his pride took a serious knock.

My seventeenth birthday was six days after the court appearance and I drove seventy-five miles in the Prefect with my father alongside as passenger and instructor while we cruised at speed along country roads. I had an excellent awareness of the width of the car and was comfortable driving within a whisker of nearside objects such as kerbs, hedges and parked cars, or offside objects such as oncoming vehicles. My father's anxiety was palpable, but he persisted with lessons over the next week or so, and I drove in several different cars to places as far apart as London and Southampton. My spirits were so high after I passed the test that I drove a hundred miles just for the fun of it, including a trip to pay the homage due to my especially proud grandmother.

SUMMER MOODS

The summer of 1969 was a hot one. It had been sweltering since the first week of June. I sunbathed at home between exams, or played my guitar and composed songs. This hot spell followed some odd weather, notably snow late in February and a flood in July the previous year, when it had taken me four hours to get home across the partially submerged River Avon bridge in the centre of town.

My morale was as unpredictable as the weather. Definite high points of the summer were passing my driving test, trips to the cottage in Wales, a holiday in Spain, buying a Spanish guitar, and winning 3rd place Discus and 2nd place Javelin prizes at the School's Annual Sports day. Definite low points I recorded in my diary for June through September were:

Sad because of Elizabeth.

Life often boring, especially at home.

My life is slipping away.

Depressed over Elizabeth.

Tons of schoolwork to do.

At the end of June, I went to Tylemorgrug cottage in Wales for a week's geological field trip. It was a project for my A level course, mapping an anticline in the rock formations of the Carboniferous period that outcropped on the hill behind the cottage. Most of the class went to the New Inn at Cefn Rhigos on the last night for a bit of underage drinking, accompanied by Geography Jones driving the van. I drank two whiskies, two pints of Whitbread bitter and a half pint of Mann's, a dark beer. This was not a beneficial mixture. I became rather dizzy and out of sorts. On leaving the pub, I picked up my duffle bag, which was sitting on the window ledge behind me. A group of local lads looking for a fight with the English followed us out of the pub.

"Hey, that's my bag you've got there," said the weasel-faced one.

'No, I don't think so," I said, lamely.

A tussle for the bag developed into a pitched battle in the car park. Poor Mr Jones was attacked by two fellow countrymen and got kicked a few times in the shins before he managed to calm the situation.

The last week of term followed, and then I returned to Wales on another trip to renovate the cottage. In this particular week, the work was very physical and tiring because the main task was to dig a drainage ditch to divert water away from the cottage as it filtered down the hillside. The task fell to Iain, Bernie Jones and me. A formation named the Millstone Grit formed the bedrock around the cottage, and it was full of boulders that jolted my arms and shoulders whenever the pickaxe clanged into one. It was hot, it was balmy, and everyone worked in shorts and stripped down to the waist – except Angela, my ex-girlfriend who had joined us on the trip. On the Saturday night we chatted outside in the moonlight, leaning against the gate on the south side of the property, and then embraced and kissed; I was still fond of her and it was a sweet experience.

On Sunday night a group of us decided to go for a drink. In fear of another fight, going to the New Inn was out of the question, but it wasn't easy to find an alternative in the middle of nowhere. We struck across country to find a pub at Penderyn, a village we spotted on a map and that was two miles down a track and over the hill behind the cottage. Navigating on the return journey proved a trifle difficult after a few drinks and in the dark, and the leaders almost fell into a reservoir that should not have been there. Still, not to look a gift horse in the mouth, we all went skinny-dipping before wending our way back to the cottage.

All week long the radio played *Something in the Air* by Thunderclap Newman. It was number one in the charts and became a theme tune for the trip. Our trowels and shovels tapped and marched to the beat of the tune as we sang '*We've got to get together sooner or later/ Because the revolutions' here and you know it's right.'* In fact, there *was* something very special in the air, because the first men on the moon landed that Sunday night, the 20th July. In our Welsh retreat without television pictures, it was hard to get excited or be amazed just listening to the radio bulletin.

I saw Angela several times more after the trip to Wales. The weather was so good that we met at the public swimming pool in Monkton Park, but the casual bond was tenuous and broke as I prepared to go to Spain for three weeks with my parents. It was to be our last holiday together for many years.

PILGRIMAGE

'Come and help Bob Dylan sink the Isle of Wight' was the challenge issued by the promoters of the festival. Dylan had not appeared in concert in more than three years, and had not been to England since 1965. In fact, the festival would be his return to the stage after a motorbike accident in which he had broken his neck. He hadn't even performed at Woodstock, the definitive happening that took place in upstate New York two weeks before the Isle of Wight Festival. There were scare stories in the press that Dylan might not appear because the contract had yet to be finalised, but Iain Sim and I were going anyway, because it was too big an event to miss. The festival provided a unique context that could never be repeated, and it was a pilgrimage for many of the 150,000 fans. To me, it seemed to be a fitting culmination of the sixties, a climax, a musical firework display to see out the remarkable decade.

On Friday 29th August, I drove to Portsmouth in the Prefect with Iain, parked the car at the ferry terminal, took the boat to Ryde on the Isle of Wight and then walked to the site at Woodside Bay. A two-day pass cost 50 shillings and we manoeuvred into the best position that was available. No tent, just sleeping on the floor in our clothes and protected by our trenchcoats. Among the roll call were some of my favourite performers: The Who, The Moody

Blues, Pretty Things, Family, Joe Cocker, Nice. And among the audience were John Lennon, George Harrison and Ringo Starr of The Beatles, plus Keith Richard, Bill Wyman and Charlie Watts of The Rolling Stones. *That's* how influential Dylan was, and that's how big was the occasion.

Poor organisation delayed Dylan's appearance until 11 o'clock on the Sunday night, and he played for an hour instead of the three hours that were promised. He came on stage in a white suit that made him visible from afar. He stood like a beacon or even Messiah of the generation, guitar in hand, voice rasping out the well-known lyrics clearly into the cool night air. His voice and the musical arrangements were different to the recorded songs, which heightened the sensation that I was experiencing a rare moment. Dylan broke his three-year silence with *She Belongs to Me* and sang fifteen more songs, including the all-time greats *Like a Rolling Stone* and *Mr Tambourine Man*.

Experiencing the live event was a truly moving occasion and my immediate disappointment at the sudden ending turned to satisfaction in a definite afterglow.

DENIAL

No sooner had the festival ended an eventful summer than the Autumn term began at school. For me there was the exciting prospect of a new rugby season, geology field trips, and maybe some romance. I was entering the final year at school and gearing up for the A level examinations, and was now the owner five O levels, having added geology and English literature through the summer examinations. Though it was a more respectable total than three, crucially, I still lacked maths and decided to start classes and take the exam at the end of the year.

I took part in the rugby trials during the first week of term and was chosen for the First XV to play in the first match of the 1969-70 season. It was against Kingsfield in Bristol, and after a hard-fought game, we won 16-10, starting a run of thirteen straight victories in another record-breaking season, including the trouncing of Marlborough College 36-6.

Elizabeth was still often in my thoughts. I was trying to get back with her. Though she was dating a friend of mine, one Monday evening I took her to see Nice in concert at The Pavilion in Bath. However, the rendezvous did not go well, and at school the following day I sensed that she avoided even looking at me. I was so depressed. I loved her deeply, and for several weeks I was too distraught to think about anything else.

All this was to change on 15th December when I knocked off Ruth at the school dance. She was the chirpiest, sweetest and prettiest girl in the school. I had noticed her a few weeks before the first date, and since then we smiled and glanced sideways and meaningfully at each other whenever we passed. It was the age of the mini-skirt and Ruth had a perfect bum and fabulous legs that in one direction ended in regulation dark blue knickers that could be glimpsed as she walked up various stairways around the school. And she had a pale blue, tight-fitting angora jumper that threw her voluptuous breasts into pleasing relief. Her fair hair was cropped short on top and she wore an irregular fringe above her large grey-green eyes. She enchanted me, and our romantic relationship developed into my first long-term partnership.

We spent Christmas together and then New Year's Eve in the Three Crowns, when I got home at 3am. It was a definite advantage to have a car. We could spend hours outside her house after I drove her home, chatting and smooching. There was none of that bother with planning our dates around a bus timetable, or worse, waiting to be collected by Mum or Dad. Even more fortunate for the relationship, her mother approved of me and allowed Ruth to stay out late and not be questioned too hard about where she had been.

During the first months of the courtship, I saw Ruth most evenings during the week and at weekends as often as possible. We spent evenings at my house, watching television until my parents went to bed and then petting on the sofa into the wee hours. Ruth and I went out a lot too, often to the cinema or drinking with friends in the Rose and Crown. Sometimes I arrived home at 5 o'clock in the morning and then slept in late the next day, missing lessons at school. Some days I didn't even bother to go to school. In truth, I didn't care, because at last I had found a girl who I felt 'right' with, a girl I wanted to sleep with. All thoughts of Elizabeth perished in the flames of my romantic desire for Ruth. It seemed to me that seventeen and a half was relatively late to be losing my virginity. There had been no lack of sexual drive or opportunity over the years, certainly not, but my conscience and the feeling that I should wait for the right girl and the right moment bridled my passion. Yet it had not been without periods of reflection or regret for the enjoyment I had forsaken.

Regarding my future, the path would be determined over the next seven to eight months by the results of my exams. I applied for a place at university through the centralised application and clearing system known as UCCA, but was rejected by four of the five choices. Though I wanted to read geology, Hull University offered me a place to read economics, an offer dependent on my examination results, and Hull was my only hope in the run-up to the exams in May and June.

There continued to be self-imposed obstacles in the way of success. I was still not working hard enough or smart enough to ensure a place at university. My aversion to mathematics was a big handicap, and I did not turn up for the exam. It was stupid behaviour. I believed that it wasn't right to sacrifice my adolescence to the god of social achievement on the altar of schoolwork. In fact, I was more distracted than ever before. I was playing chess at school, I discovered an interest in Russian history and literature, and I was going through a creative period of writing poems and composing songs to play on my guitar.

I suppose it was the angst of youth that drove me, and I composed for my private pleasure, though I had poems published in successive school magazines. I wrote poems about three of my four important preoccupations: romantic love, the natural world that I was discovering through geology, and a critical awareness of society's problems arising from becoming increasingly 'politicised', for which music and especially Bob Dylan was the principal catalyst. I composed late at night whenever I entered a particularly strange mood that brought forth intermittent streams of words that I dumped onto paper without much conscious thought, reflection or correction.

One of the first was a poem entitled *Island Hermit*, in which a boy encounters a wizened, shaggy-haired old man who is living alone on a small island. They come face-to-face and recognise each other as young self and old self. The Hermit tries to strangle the boy, but dies in the struggle against the youth. It was a poem about glimpsing the future and realising that destiny is not prescribed. Another perspective is that in the struggle between parent and child, the child can vanquish the control of the parent to win freedom of self-expression. *Screaming* expressed my frustration that time was taking my life away and that I was struggling to find answers to the meaning of my existence in the endless dimension of time. And, in *A Country Life*, I described a walk through a world destroyed by pollution, a walk that ends when I find my body burning in an open grave in the middle of a lifeless landscape.

Conversely, most of the songs were about love and girlfriends. I composed and played in my bedroom late at night into the early hours, on a six-stringed Spanish guitar, later with the option of giving it hell on a second-hand electric guitar that I bought. I accepted that the lyrics were simple and the songs too short, because my song-writing abilities were negligible and after one was written I moved on to the next one without making improvements. Song writing was no more than a need to exorcise a particular mood. When singing, I tried to mimic the gritty, anguished cries of Dylan but sounded more like a tomcat on a promise on a hot night.

It was the start of term in January 1970. I arrived at school on time, for a change, saw Ruth in the lunch break and gave her a lift home after lessons. In the evening, I did some geology homework and then settled down to continue reading about the Russian Revolution. Instead of solid revision leading up to the crucial exams, my waking time consisted of a gregarious diet of schoolwork, seeing Ruth, socialising and broadening my mind through reading and music. The popular music scene experienced a 'big bang' in the 1960s and there were now so many great bands and albums to discover and play endlessly at night. Neil Young was an emerging favourite of mine, as well as Crosby Stills and Nash, The Moody Blues, and even some of Donovan's 'psychedelic' music.

Parties were also on the list of distractions I could not resist. The most notorious party I went to was staged over four days at Nick

Brewer's house in the village of Kington St. Michael. Nick came to my house on the Friday morning ten days before my first exam, and the two of us sat in the kitchen to do geography revision. Saturday through Tuesday was spent at Nick's house with a constantly changing group of friends and a constant supply of alcohol, which was replenished by frequent visitors and by emergency missions to the village pub. Mercifully, the weather was fine and warm and the party often overflowed into the garden. Inexplicably, a boy not even on the fringe of our circle of friends turned up at the party. Edward Ponting was a short, studious boy who wore thick glasses and had a high-pitched voice that we found irritating, and to deal with this audacious intrusion we decided to stake him out in the midday sun. Ponting was stripped down to his underpants, then tied down to wooden stakes on the lawn. We covered him with sugar and let the ants do the rest. Sadly, after a while we had to let him go because the neighbours complained about the pleas and cries.

There was no shortage of events and other distractions just before and during the period of the examinations. Four days before the first exam, I learnt of my father's affair with a secretary at work, and the possibility that my parents would get divorced. On the day of the first exam, I went to see *The Graduate* in the evening, to celebrate six months of dating Ruth. A General election was in prospect on 18th June, but in common with many Englishmen, I was more interested in the Soccer World Cup. I watched Brazil beat England 1-0, England beat Czechoslovakia 1-0, and Germany beat England 3-2 in the week leading up to the final four examination papers. Polling Day coincided with the last exam and next day the country woke to a surprise victory by the Conservative Party under the ill-fated leadership of Ted Heath.

DRIVING LESSONS

Cars and motoring featured strongly in the summer break. I

sometimes secretly took out my mother's Ford Capri after my parents were asleep, and went for long drives to enjoy the exhilaration of commanding a fast, modern car on empty roads and daring to take corners at high speed. I was careful to watch the fuel gauge to avoid suspicion, though my mother got her petrol free from our garage and seemed unaware of the consumption. My favourite journey included a mix of fast straights and blind but fast bends along the Marshfield Road to Ford or Castle Coombe.

After the M4 motorway opened between Bristol and London, I had an alternative journey, one I could drive flat out all the way. On one occasion, coming back from a trip to Heathrow Airport 80 miles away, I fell asleep going at full speed in the outside lane, and woke to find myself driving over gravel on the hard shoulder and about to careen up the embankment at 95mph. This kept me awake for the remainder of the escapade.

Courtesy of my father, I now had a new car, a pale yellow 1962 Ford Anglia 105E. The Anglia was an odd-looking car. It featured tail fins, so beloved of American automobiles of the time, but was a model distinguished by its raked back window. I felt lucky to have a faster car and four forward gears at my disposal instead of the three on the Prefect. And the inclusion of full synchromesh on the gearbox eliminated the need to stop the car to get into first gear on steep hills.

I had been driving for just over a year and felt confident and skilled. However, on July 16th I learnt a valuable lesson the hard way, when the driver of a heavy lorry on the A46 at Cold Ashton failed to stop at the red light and crashed into the side of my car behind the driver's position. The force of the collision pushed the back of the car sideways and it executed two and a quarter rolls, coming to rest on its side some distance from the junction. I opened the door skyward and climbed out, shaken but uninjured. 132 PHT was a write-off. Dad took the loss stoically. He even lent me a year-old 1,300cc Mk I Cortina so that I could drive to Spain for a holiday with Bernie Jones and Nick.

This was my first foreign holiday with friends, and my first drive abroad. I had just turned eighteen and felt highly adventurous, not least because driving abroad was still uncommon in 1970. Bernie and I planned the route, and Bernie was to be navigator during the round trip of 1,800 miles in thirteen days. He was a lanky, skinny boy with a mop of thick black hair, possessed a triangular face, sharp nose, and some very peculiar mannerisms indeed. But he was a good friend and good company. Sometimes we referred to him as Bernie the Bolt after a character in a popular television programme, or, when we wanted to query his unusual statements and actions, we just exclaimed 'Bern!'

On August 2nd the three of us crossed the channel overnight from Southampton to Le Havre on a Thoresen 'Viking' car ferry. We paid £19 return for the car and £26 for the passengers, which was a lot of money but would have cost much more if we had taken cabins instead of sleeping below deck in the car at the risk of carbon monoxide poisoning. Our route across France took us through Chartres, Orleans, Limoges, Cahors overnight, then Toulouse and Perpignan on the Mediterranean coast the next day. Petrol in France was more expensive than in England and we were paying about 7 shillings and 6 pence a gallon compared with 6 shillings and 4 pence at home. We crossed the border into Spain and arrived at San Feliu to spend nine days camping in a pine forest near the beach, at night haunting Charley's Bar, Tiffany's and Maddox night clubs in Playa de Aro.

That Cortina didn't let us down once, despite me giving it a thrashing all the way there and back, flat out on those long, straight French cross-country roads. Driving on the opposite side of the road made no difference to my driving habits. At one point on the way down, I was going so fast into a corner that the car ran wide and two wheels went onto the gravel at the side of the road. It was all I could do to keep control and prevent the car rolling over into the field or crashing head-on into one of the trees that lined the road. Near Cahors, we had a race with a car full of French boys driving a weird-looking French car, though I thought that all their cars were weird-looking. They saw that we were English and the driver accelerated as I tried to overtake them. National honour was now an issue, of course, and I drove side-by-side with them for more than a kilometre. Nick, Bernie and I rocked forwards and backwards in our seats and shouted to make our car go faster, until this Citroen-thingy managed to pull ahead up a gentle incline. Merde!

Waiting in the post on my return was the letter containing my exam results. In their report before the exams, my three teachers had praised me for my attitude and work, but although I got a credible Grade B in geology, I only managed an E in geography. Economics I failed, getting an O level pass and contributing to the grand total of six O levels and two A levels. I needed a minimum of three A levels to win a place at university, backed up by good grades and preferably, at least for geology, passes in maths, physics and chemistry – subjects that I had not even taken. There was a clearing system that shuffled people around into university places after exam results, but going to university to study geology was completely out of the question for me, and my place at Hull to read economics was a non-starter. Thirty pupils at the grammar school had secured places at various colleges and universities, but I was not one of them. And what of my close friends? Bernie had a place at Plymouth Polytechnic to study geology and geography; Iain disappeared to live in east London and study town planning at college; Nick, very nobly I thought, decided to stop sponging off his parents and went looking for work.

"I've got a job in Chard", he said. Nick's parents came from Cornwall and he had a deep-felt connexion with the southwest corner of England. He spent summer holidays in the region, and the previous two years had worked on a farm in St Newlyn East, near Newquay. OK, so Chard is in Somerset, but it's within striking distance of Devon and Cornwall and the new job was the closest he could get, for the time being. "I'm going to work in the transport department of Allingtons, a company that transports milk products around the country." Nick had developed skills as a mechanic while helping his father restore a beautiful pre-war Alvis tourer – and from constantly having to repair his beloved and unreliable motorbike.

So I was losing Nick, Bernie and Iain, but I decided to return to school for a third year in the Sixth Form and re-take exams to improve my grades. This was definitely the comfortable option because the alternative was to find a boring, menial job. More than this, staying on would allow me to maintain my lifestyle and continue seeing Ruth, who was two years below me at school, and play rugby. And I would still have friends at school, because through rugby I knew boys from the year below me. Although it was the easy option, I felt that staying on was the best one because it kept me in with a chance of going to university the following year, however remote and improbable.

FINAL CHANCE

I finished with Ruth a few days before the start of term. My diary entry clearly records the effect it had on me:

At 3.21 this morning I left Ruth. I love her very much and it was the most emotional experience of my entire life. Dear Ruth, forever mine, I love you.

And I truly did love her, but dating required a huge commitment of my time. On the other hand, my relationship with Ruth gave me so much pleasure. It was a fundamental dilemma, one which would return again and again in life. Our separation lasted 17 hours. I called to tell her I loved her and wanted her back, and I can still hear the sound of her reply, spoken so sweetly.

"Don't be silly Michael: of course I want you back."

Ruth meant too much to me, so I would just have to continue juggling the conflicting commitments to career aspirations, rugby, social life and love life.

In the first week back at school I went with Ruth to see *2001: A Space Odyssey*, *101 Dalmatians*, and *A Man Called Horse*. I was a dedicated filmgoer. In 1970 I saw fifty-four films, some more than once because, in those days, having a ticket allowed you to sit in the cinema all day; I saw *The Graduate* four times at a single sitting!

Going to the cinema was usually a mid-week or Friday night activity. Saturday nights were spent in the Rose and Crown, the pub frequented by my friends. It had a little room at the back, with a single table large enough to seat up to ten people, at a pinch, and this was our favourite spot. But I was not a beer drinker. Apart from not liking the taste, I could not keep up with my friends in the race to sink as many pints as possible before closing time at 10.30pm. Where did all that liquid go? It defied reality, given the known yet admittedly approximate dimensions of the gut. Instead, my strategy was to drink spirits. Spirits took effect much more quickly, and I could impress everyone by making a double vodka disappear in the twinkle of an eye. And with vodka, I could get just as drunk as everyone else, but more rapidly. I took vodka with lime, since this prevented my head from shuddering involuntarily just after the drink hit the back of my throat, and perhaps observers would admire my fortitude at remaining cool and unaffected by a shot of high octane alcohol. Part of the performance was to hold up the empty tumbler and announce how many vodkas I'd drunk every time one was downed in rapid fashion. Eleven seems to be the record.

There were times when I got drunk so quickly that I missed most of the chatter of the evening, occasionally ending up under the table, incapable of self-support. But I was never sick – another point in favour of vodka – and I often recovered later in the evening, sufficiently to gaze around soberly at my drunken comrades. One night when Bernie got so drunk that he could not stand, Rob Noyes and I carried him out of the pub by the ankles and armpits, and lifted him into his Austin A40 so that he could drive the seven miles to his parent's home in Castle Coombe. Like everyone else I knew, Bernie was none too careful about the new drink-driving law, especially as there was virtually no chance of being stopped and breathalysed.

"There you go Bern", Rob and I said, in a way meant to convey that we had helped him and he should now be capable of getting home safely.

Though the rugby season of 1970-71 did not equal the heights of the previous year, it was a successful year nonetheless, with a run of ten wins after losing the first match. We played 17, won 11, drew 1, lost 5. Some of the local schools had hit on a way to increase their chances of winning against the formidable team from Chippenham Grammar: they opted to play on their home territory, and we played the last nine matches of the season on away grounds. Another tactic of the schools in fear of Chippenham was to cancel the match altogether, a distinction of Bath Kingswood, a public school side that we had beaten 72-0 the previous year. Those public school boys were so cowardly!

Ruth and I celebrated our first Anniversary, and two days later I went to the school dance in the Neeld Hall and afterwards recorded (in barely legible writing) that I had *kissed loads of girls*, though it was under the influence of six vodkas and an unknown quantity of sherry purchased from a pub across the road. I did more than kiss Holly. She was a friend, a humorous but patently neurotic girl who I saw a few times and kept occasional correspondence with for several years afterwards. From about November-time, we began writing a stream of amusing poems to each other. Her first ditty to me began thus:

When you read these noble words
Think not of other birds…

In *Ode to Michael* she wrote:
I have a job to keep awake
To write this letter for your sake
I've tried coffee, I've tried tea
How about you trying me?

And I did go further, but she told me in a letter:
The only reason I won't go to bed with you is that you are always comparing me with Ruth.

Whether or not this was a ploy to get me more interested, we did eventually go to bed together. I was drunk and unable to get a usable erection. At the time, I made an association between the two temporary disabilities and apologised to Holly that I was drunk.

Much later, I came to understand that the alcohol was not the culprit, but it was the presence of Ruth in my subconscious mind that had caused me to hold back.

ROME IS BURNING

For the past six months, I had known unofficially that my parents were talking about divorce, but I did not know why. Then my mother told my father to leave the house and he went on 5th January 1971, setting himself up in a bedsit in Cardiff to be close to his primary dealership – and his secretary, the erstwhile catalyst of his departure. I did not miss my father in the sense of an emotional loss. He had provided a comfortable existence for our family and I had the greatest respect for his achievements, but I could not recall that he ever spent time with me on father-son activities, and his attitude towards my long hair and general unruly behaviour had created a distance between us.

My mother and I moved in April to a much smaller house on the opposite side of town. I left many wonderful memories behind at Oakleigh, our beautiful 19th Century house at 132 London Road. It had been a wondrous place for me, even into my teenage years. Built on four floors, it had cellars, attics, seven bedrooms, plus a separate apartment occupied by my grandfather Arthur Fowles. I occupied a separate 'wing' with two bedrooms, a bathroom and attic, so had plenty of space for solitary pursuits. And I would play alone all day long in the gigantic garden, stalking birds through the dense cluster of evergreen trees on the northern border, or going down to the orchard to scrump apples and gooseberries, or climbing the great oak tree on the south side of the house.

Now, everything had changed. I had lost the home I had lived in since I was eight years old, the home of my late childhood and adolescence. The local council bought the house and converted it into an old people's home, despoiling the site by adding ugly new buildings in the grounds and removing the orchard to turn the back of the property into the front entrance, complete with concreted car pack where a dozen apple trees had once grown. Now, I could not even go back there to satiate my nostalgia.

Preoccupied with my own problems and agenda, I hardly noticed the plight of my dear mother, a devoted wife, mother and daughter to her parents. Her family responsibilities had extended to looking after her ageing parents through many years of invalidity and illness. Nanna and Gramps Fowles had lived in our home in Seend in the 1950s, occupying a self-contained area of the house. My mother Rose had cleaned, washed and cooked for them, as well as looking after herself and her family of three children and working husband. After Nanna's death and the move to Chippenham, Mum had taken care of her father until his eventual death in 1970, the year before.

Concerning my father's infidelity and departure, I was unable to comprehend my mother's loss and be empathetic, and she would have been alone with her problems but for the fact that my sister Tricia gave up her job in Italy and returned to help with the move and to live with us. Green Corner, the new residence, was situated on the Malmesbury Road opposite John Coles Park, handily close to my dear friend Rob Noyes but dangerously close to school. I spent even less time at school now that I didn't have to get up in time to catch a bus. And my busy social life continued unabated up to the last day of school. In fact, I was more active than ever, and nearly every evening between January and June I either had Ruth or friends at my house, or went to someone's house or a pub or coffee bar in town.

I began to stray a little from Ruth. I was restless. I flirted with Carol, Janice, Wendy and Rachel, and even saw Elizabeth a few times. There were times when the bond with Ruth was stretched and strained, but somehow our relationship held together.

Of note in the run-up to the end of spring term, 1971, my friends and I set a new record by cramming twenty five people into the coffee-making room; Jo Frazier beat Mohammed Ali; Apollo 14 landed on the moon; and Britain's currency changed from 240 pennies to 100 pence in the pound on Decimalisation Day. And tragically, a friend of mine named William Jolliffe was one of the first British servicemen to be killed in Northern Ireland since the conflict flared up the year before. His Land Rover was hit by petrol bombs. He was eighteen years old. His younger brother was still at the school, and a rather solemn memorial was held in the Assembly Hall.

My schoolwork was suffering. In the last school report I would ever have, my tutor 'Jock' Galloway had nothing more instructive to record than the following.

I do wish he could get to school on time, as his repeated lateness causes far too much administrative difficulty.

It was easy to be cynical and disinterested when the school put more emphasis on administrative compliance than scholastic achievement, or somehow saw a relationship between the two. In his official role as Careers Officer, Mr Galloway advised me that my only chance of employment was to get a job with the Forestry Commission. After all, the Commission had virtually no entry requirements and could provide a steady job to eventual retirement on a civil service pension. And with the Wisdom of Solomon, the nurturing of Florence Nightingale and the thoughtfulness of the Good Samaritan, the new Headmaster's comments perhaps said it all about the school's attitude.

Michael has reached a point of no return. He needs advice but he must make the effort to seek it.

So that was it. The teachers are not there to help children who can't help themselves or are too embarrassed or proud to seek support.

Even before the exam results, I was rejected by all five universities I had applied for through UCCA. After the letter arrived on March 12th, I wrote to some polytechnics and colleges. I failed two interviews and now had nowhere else to turn, and no other prospect except to get a job.

ENCOUNTERS WITH VIKINGS

In June, I received the most useful sum of £17 on my nineteenth birthday, sat a geography exam in the morning, sat in The Galleon in the afternoon and sat for dinner at home with uncle Albert Fowles and wife Aunt Marion, relatives on my mother's side who were over from Canada. Ruth turned up at 9 o'clock and stayed until three in the morning. Next day, I sat my last exam, went home, grabbed some clothes and made a rendezvous with Rob, Bernie and Greg, who was Bernie's younger brother. We drove two cars in convoy to Torquay on the English Riviera in Devon, arriving at 11 o'clock at night.

It was a week-long trip to have some fun. To preserve funds, we slept in the cars. But the local police were a bit sniffy about long-haired, scruffy vagrants, and we were moved on unceremoniously from several places where we had tried to park overnight. We slept in a field between Paignton and Brixham; we slept up side-tracks and lanes; we slept in a car park by Anstey's Cove. And we made an exceedingly interesting discovery. Torquay in the summer was full of foreign language students, and it seemed to us that most were blonde-haired girls from Scandinavia.

"Viking Hell", we exclaimed.

At the Paradise Castle on Friday night, we got friendly with a group of four Norwegian girls. We all met up again on the Saturday, going to the Cellar Bar in Torquay. On Sunday, we went to the cinema to see *Song of Norway*, a predictably dreadful film, but the girls had been insistent.

A few days after I returned from Torquay I started a summer job at Praesidium Products, the factory owned by Bernie's father. The purpose was to earn money for a trip to Scandinavia that Bernie, Rob, Greg and I had been planning for more than nine months. Meeting the Norwegian girls in Torquay was a happy coincidence, and meant making only slight modifications to the holiday itinerary so that we could meet them in their native environment. I earned about £20 a week doing piecework at the factory and laboured for six weeks right up to the departure date. My wages compared favourably with the national weekly average of about £23 for manual labour, though I was working shifts of twelve to thirteen hours.

I was fortunate to have such good friends as my close companions on the trip. Growing up with them and sharing formative experiences meant that the bonds were strong between us, and we were blessed with a common sense of humour. A deep thinker and interested in maths and astronomy, Rob had a frank sense of humour. His favourite party line of *Shall I get my knob out now?* when a new girl hove into view was hilarious, and Rob did not get embarrassed if the girl overheard the comment. He had acquired an ancient and clapped out motorbike-sidecar combo, an AJS in British racing green, and would clatter noisily around the streets of Chippenham with the tails of his black greatcoat flapping around, making him look like a latter-day Count Dracula off to find another victim.

Greg was also a deep thinker, but had yet to sort out where he was going. His nickname 'Donkey Kong', or simply 'Donk', alluded to the reputed size of his manhood and famed success in attracting girls and women alike. Out of our group, he and I in particular practised impersonations, notably of John Wayne, Tommy Cooper and Mr Champion, one of the faculty that taught French at our school.

Bernie, well, Bernie was just incomparably Bernie, the boy with the screwdriver in his top pocket, always ready to dismantle any item of electrical equipment that came within his reach, even if it did not belong to him.

As usual, my father kindly provided the car for the trip. SAM 633H was a white MkII Cortina 1.6 estate that we drove in and slept in for the next twenty-three days and nights. It didn't let us down once on the trip of 3,000 miles across Norway, Sweden, Finland and Denmark. On 16th August, I left home early in the morning, picked up Rob, Bernie and Greg and drove to Harwich, arriving after lunch. After a four-hour wait, the M/S Blenheim departed on the twenty-two hour overnight journey to Kristiansand on the southern tip of Norway. Most of the evening and a disproportionately large fraction of our cash reserves were spent in the bar and disco before crashing in our sleeperettes. On arrival in the morning, we headed west towards Stavanger, stopping overnight by a deserted lake in the middle of a forest.

Norway was one giant wilderness consisting of rugged mountains, vast pine forests, little glacial lakes and spectacular fiord coastline. It felt deserted and was such a contrast with the rolling countryside and mosaic of fields and villages of southern England. I fell in love with the tranquillity and natural beauty of the place.

Our plan was to go to Stavanger first and rendezvous with Christine, the girl I fancied. I telephoned her but she wouldn't see me. "Viking Hell", we exclaimed. Weeks later, I received a letter that explained that I had called too late, as she had to get up early the next day! It sounded suspicious, to say the least, and was a big disappointment, but she genuinely missed me and I continued to receive letters, cards and photographs from her for another two years. Perhaps her parents had seen a photograph of me and were against the encounter with an English ruffian, and had refused to let her see me when I was in Stavanger. Sadly, my first holiday romance had resulted in kisses and fond memories of a brief encounter with an exotic girl.

We packed up camp and drove back through Kristiansand to Andebu where we dropped off Bernie, who was going to stay at his girlfriend's house. Rob, Greg and I carried on to the capital, Oslo, situated at the head of the Oslofjord. We spent three days taking in the Vigeland Sculpture Park, the Kon Tiki Museum, and reeling at the price of beer in the bars.

Back in Andebu with Bernie, we stayed the night and shared floor space in a spare bedroom. We had been travelling and sleeping in the same clothes for a week and it was a relief to have a shower. Greg took off his jeans and hung them on a coat hook by the door. Stiff with grime, the trouser legs retained the striking curved stance of his own bandy appendages, defying the ridicule handed out to their owner as we got ready to settle down for the night. Breakfast was a strange affair consisting of open sandwiches with cooked meats and cheese on rye bread, or with cloudberry conserve, making quite a change from the typical English fare of cornflakes or Weetabix, or boiled eggs and toast.

To cram more adventure into our limited time, I drove during the night until reaching the outskirts of the next destination, usually a big city, then slept in the driving seat for a couple of hours before we ventured out to explore our new surroundings. To keep me awake on the journey the others plied me with cigarettes and opened the windows to let in the very chilly night air. But driving in Scandinavia at night was a hazardous activity. None of the roads had lighting or cats' eyes, even on E18, the international highway across Norway and Sweden. All too frequently when there was a sharp bend in the road, I nearly drove straight ahead into the primeval forest and a meeting with death at the trunk of a fir tree.

Just forty miles short of our objective to get to Stockholm, I felt I could not go on, and pulled off the road to take a brief rest. After what seemed like a minute, a tap tapping on the window woke me up. It was 6 o'clock in the morning. In the dark of night, I had parked on a bed of flowers in someone's front garden and, muttering English profanities, I hastily reversed out, slammed the car into first gear and sped off into the distance leaving behind an irate Swede muttering Swedish profanities. It was their fault for not protecting their property with a fence, and trapping unsuspecting tourists.

We spent most of the day in Stockholm before continuing to Kapellskar to catch the overnight ferry across the Baltic Sea to Finland, and set up Base Camp on the outskirts of Helsinki, the first time we had bothered to use the tent, and we spent the next thirty-six hours looking around the city centre. I knew that Finns were racially, culturally and linguistically different to Viking Scandinavians, and they certainly did look and sound different. Moreover, Finland lived under the shadow of Cold War communism. It bordered the Iron Curtain directly with the Soviet Union and the city felt different, somehow less developed, austere and not part of Western Europe. After looking around Helsinki for two days, we packed up camp and drove towards Naantali to catch the 10am ferry back to Sweden. Goodbye to the land of 10,000 lakes, none of which we had seen.

Reaching Stockholm at six o'clock the next morning, we set up base camp in a secluded and grassy spot behind a suburban railway station. My comments on Stockholm were summarised thus: '*No life, good shops but very expensive.*' The city had a pleasant aspect, but was a little too clean and sober for my liking. We stayed another two days, window shopping, and cooking our main meal of the day at the camp before going to a really good discotheque at the Tivoli.

We left Stockholm at seven in the evening and I drove 300 miles, stopping overnight ten miles outside Gothenburg. We continued on our way to Elsinore in Denmark via the ferry from Helsingborg, where we visited Kronberg Castle, immortalised by Shakespeare in Hamlet.

It rained heavily in Denmark, though I supposed it was only to be expected in September. I drove into Copenhagen and we gravitated to Central Station before going to a disco in the Tivoli Gardens until 4am. We were desperate to find a decent place to sleep, but couldn't find anywhere suitable, despite cruising around for ages, and finally parked outside the Law Courts in the centre of the city. Sure enough, a tap tapping on the window and the sight of two Danish policemen signified that it was morning and time to move on.

On the way out of Copenhagen, a stone smashed the windscreen of our car, it was pouring with rain, we still had four days abroad, and were 400 miles from home. A space blanket that Bernie was using to keep warm at night was redeployed as a makeshift cover for the hole whenever we parked. But while driving, we had to sit in the car wearing jumpers, coats, hats, scarves and anything else to try and keep warm and dry – which was a trifle difficult with bitterly-cold rain coming inside at high speed, horizontally.

And that was how the once in a lifetime trip ended. Back in Chippenham on the 7th September, I picked Ruth up from The Bear Hotel at the end of her shift in the bar. I was overjoyed to see her after nearly a month away, and she looked so inviting in the black skirt and white blouse of her work outfit as she ran down the stairs to greet me.

HARD REALITY

Chippenham had an industrial estate, situated off the Bath Road on the west side of town. 'Estate' was hardly the word for it, since it was little more than two factory units and a post office depot of some kind. Praesidium Products manufactured mouldings from a substance called melamine, a resin that was made from tree sap. Each week, the factory turned out thousands of ashtrays for pubs, as well as decorative teapot stands, trays and drinks coasters destined for high street shops.

I began working full-time at the factory one rainy Saturday in September 1971. I worked alongside Bob Sayers, George Cole and Jock, or sometimes a friend such as Rob or Greg. It was shift work, either 5½ days or 4½ nights a week. Nights were preferable, because the money was better and there were fewer distractions. To earn the most I could, I worked a thirteen-hour stretch without a meal break, but took numerous short stops for a cup of tea and a cigarette with the others. We took it in turns to make the tea, performing a time-honoured ritual in the preparatory stage.

'Nice cup of tea', Bob the Foreman would say, the signal that it was someone's turn to put the kettle on and prepare tea for all the workers.

'Lovely cup of tea' was the standard chorus from workers who were not due to perform the main ceremony.

Four moulding machines were at the heart of the business. Three were grey giants that stood like monoliths, arranged in a line backed against the partition wall in the middle of the building because the centre of the arched ceiling was the only place that could accommodate their great height. Inside each machine, a mass of cables, wires, electronic circuits and hydraulic pumps served to control the operation of a massive upper jaw that was driven down to generate 200psi pressure inside the highly polished titanium-plated mould. It caused a few scary moments every night, since hands could be crushed flat, but as long as I stayed alert I received only the occasional burn from the moulding platens that were heated to 200°C. All the men worked without the cumbersome protective guard that by law should have been fitted to the front of the machine to prevent the worker putting his hand in as the press came down. This was an arrangement that benefited the owner as well as the workers, and the guards were installed only when the government Inspector sent notification that he would be making his customary visit.

It was piecework and I earned a bonus if I produced above a minimum output for a shift, the minimum number depending on which product I was making. An unintended feature of the bonus system was that it encouraged us to produce as many as possible with scant regard to quality – usually just high enough to get past the quality control that would take place next day in the packing department. It was common practice to reduce the cycle times on the machines so that they would run faster. However, it was a fine judgment, and the whole batch got rejected if the melamine resin had not cured sufficiently. Mr Jones or his eldest son Michael would call the workers in for a serious reprimand, and punish the culprit or culprits by docking our bonus.

I enjoyed the solitude at night and the camaraderie at the factory, but felt out of place among the workers. They were older, they were married or divorced, and they seemed trapped in the job or had accepted they were going nowhere else. My expectations were different, however, and always at the back of my mind was the feeling that it was a temporary occupation until something better came along; but what, and when?

My family name was known to many inhabitants of Chippenham through my father's garage, his association with

Swindon Town FC, and The Stocking Shop, the lady's fashion accessory business that my mother owned and ran in the town centre. I had lived in a house that was many times larger than any of the neighbours', had owned a car since I was sixteen at a time when most working adults in the country could not afford one, and was privileged to have travelled to Spain, Italy, France and Switzerland for holidays. The Earle family was of working class stock but, because of my mother's upbringing and my Dad's money, I found myself in a solidly middle class environment surrounded by all the associated values and expectations. And I had been to the grammar school. In these circumstances, there was no way that I could feel comfortable or accept the possibility that my destiny was as a manual labourer.

Shift work and tiredness got in the way of my relationship with Ruth. Sometimes she would come to my house after school and I would be asleep or too tired to be sociable. At my suggestion, we split up, agreeing not to see each other for a week, but I thought about her so much that we were together again three days later.

The highlight of the autumn was on our second anniversary, December 15th. I left the factory after a night shift and went straight to school for a reunion and to play for the Old Boys in a rugby match against the school, which we won 16-14. Nick, Rob, Greg and I went to The Galleon coffee bar after the match, then I took Ruth out for a posh meal at a restaurant in Limpley Stoke, near Bath. It was a fantastic evening and I stayed up until 3 o'clock in the morning, thus ending a marathon session of being awake for thirty-five hours.

In 1971 I saw only thirty-two films at the cinema, far fewer than in 1970, and only three in the three months that I worked at the factory. Many were not memorable, except that I enjoyed seeing Mick Jagger in *Performance*, and Goldie Hawn in *Girl in My Soup*. For me, the year was more remarkable for the books I read, including works by Homer, Tolkien, Pushkin, Tolstoy, William Morris, Aldous Huxley and John Wyndham. A book that kept me enthralled from cover to cover was *The Lord of the Rings*, and it sparked my interest in books on Celtic, Icelandic and Anglo-Saxon mythology.

In the country, a state of emergency had been called over the Dock Strike in July, and the Miners' Union had voted to start a strike on 9th January. To top it all, the trade union movement voted against the terms of Britain's entry to the European Community. Britain was in a mess, and so was I. When 1971 ended, I was voluntarily out of work and had failed to get into university for the second time; my parents had separated, many of my friends were away at college or working in other towns, and there was no more rugby. I had no idea what the future would bring.

EARLE OF CHIPPENHAM

January 1972 began with a week's holiday with Bernie, touring Scotland in BUN 138B, the two-tone blue and white Anglia that my father had given to me two months previously. It served me well during the next three years, taking me more than 40,000 miles around the country.

As was the usual practice, Bernie and I slept in the car. While this was tolerable in the Lake District, where we spent the first night, it was unbearable on the second night, a further 300 miles to the north: Scotland in the depth of winter is not the warmest place on the planet. Etched in my memory is the night we almost froze to death at the foot of Ben Nevis, the highest mountain in the UK. Etched too, is the memory of the punch I got on the nose in a pub in Fort William while I was just standing there holding a beer. Was it that obvious that I was English? Our onward journey took us along the Caledonian Canal to Loch Ness, where we did not see any monsters, on to Inverness, and then south to Aviemore on pretty Speyside. We passed the third night sleeping soundly and comfortably in the warm surrounds of the Ardlogie Guest House.

Next day, Bernie and I lashed out £2 to rent ski equipment from Speyside Sports and went skiing on the slush and bare rocks on the slopes of Cairngorm Mountain. Without gloves, our hands became so cold that all feeling left our fingers, and we decided to call it a day, and went ice-skating at Aviemore Ice Rink. Edinburgh and its castle were the last places of interest on the trip before we sped the 430 miles back home in a little over six hours.

I dropped Bernie back at his parents' house in Castle Coombe and drove straight to Ruth's house, where I stayed until 5am the next morning. Ruth alone was able to comfort me; Ruth alone was a reason to get out of bed in the morning.

I signed 'on the dole' as unemployed, but I could not be bothered with the effort that was required to go every week and stand in a long queue, and never drew any money. In the event, a month later I started a part-time job at my father's garage in town, and I later moved to work at Temple Meads Motors, his dealership in Bristol. My main job was to clean new cars and make them ready for the showroom, keep the showroom cars clean, clean used cars for sale on the forecourt, and deliver and fetch cars. I cleaned a great many cars during my time in the business. I also made about fifty journeys delivering or collecting second-hand cars and vans, covering 7,000 miles between Chippenham and Cardiff, Bristol, Birmingham, Bournemouth and Southampton. There was a certain amount of camaraderie at the garages, though I was never at ease with the thought that the staff were being polite because my father was the boss. Still, the job provided me with a much-needed income and it kept me occupied during the day.

Though the job was not my idea of an ideal career, it could have been a way in to my father's business, and a route to comfort and eventual riches. My father and I talked about this.

"You will have to start at the bottom and learn all aspects of the business", he said. "Ford runs an apprenticeship management programme and you should go on this."

However, I could not see the romance or challenge in selling cars, retrieving spare parts from shelving, or in learning about accounts and administrative systems. I had set my sights on getting into college, though the odds against this were high. Even so, I was determined to prove myself by myself; this much was sacrosanct, and was my primary motivation.

LIGHT AND DARK

My determination not to give in achieved the desired result at the third attempt. Following an interview in April, and two days after I went full-time at the garage, Oxford Polytechnic made me an offer I could not refuse, and I accepted a place on the BA Social Studies course. Reading geology was not an option with my qualifications but, nonetheless, I would take the only chance I had to advance to a higher level in life. I would be reading politics, law, economics, sociology and quantitative methods in the first year. It suited me. It felt so good. Polytechnics were below the red brick universities in the academic league table, themselves below the traditional seats of learning in places such as Cambridge and Oxford. But at least I was going to college and could end up with a degree. By any yardstick, it was a worthy achievement, as only one in twenty-five people in the country went on to higher education.

I continued to work at the garage for three more months, and then took a break in August and September. My relationship with Ruth during this time turned into a roller-coaster ride now that it seemed likely that we would have to live apart or even end the relationship. Could the connexion be maintained and did we want it to be? My parents reunited and went on holiday in early June. Ruth stayed at my house the entire week and we made love every day, yet she finished with me two weeks later. In fact, we split up and got back together again five times in July, the most difficult period. And the tables had turned on me: Ruth began seeing Chris and Paul.

Ending the relationship was always going to be a serious emotional problem for both of us. Not only had we been dating for nearly three years, but we were virgins when we met and it was so much more special for that. True, I had flirted with other girls, but I had not slept with anyone else. I kept myself for Ruth. I loved her deeply, but could not let myself go completely and commit my entire being to her at the expense of my ambition. As I saw it, there was so much more to do in life before I could settle down. How could love and ambition be compatible?

We remained companions through the troubles, but our emotions were in turmoil. One Sunday in July we finished forever, or so we thought. On Tuesday she saw Chris. On Wednesday I drove her to an interview in London – then we talked and argued about our relationship in the car on the way home. On Saturday she dated Paul, and on Sunday she went with Paul to a motor race at Thruxton circuit before going out with Chris in the evening. What a week!

Some stability returned to our relationship late in the summer, and our lovemaking continued, despite Ruth telling me that she was now going out with Paul. I truly believed that Ruth could not give herself to two men and would not be sleeping with me if she had started sleeping with Paul.

Then came the holiday. I had booked a week's accommodation in Devon and Cornwall, centred on a beautiful country hotel in Chagford in Dartmoor National Park. Ruth kept changing her mind, but only a day before the scheduled departure said she was probably going. I packed that Friday night and next day went to pick her up at home. She said she was coming with me, but had to tell Paul, and would let me know at 12 o'clock. To avoid the embarrassment of fielding questions from my mother, I could not go home, so I drove to see my grandmother and waited for Ruth to call. But she didn't call, so I returned to her house, whereupon her brother told me that she had gone to Bournemouth with Paul. In a final attempt to persuade Ruth to come, the following day I went to the Bear Hotel where she worked, but to no avail, for she was not there as expected.

I was genuinely heartbroken, and so distraught that I felt pains in my heart and shoulder for the next few hours. I was a typical Cancerian, with a vulnerable interior that now needed protection by a hard exterior. I had been hurt in a big way and vowed it would be the last time I would let anyone get so deep inside me. But we were inseparable, and Ruth phoned me the next day. By Friday we were seeing each other again.

The following week we went on trips to Brecon, Bristol and then to see Ruth's mother, who now lived in Swindon after splitting up her husband a year earlier. Then two weeks later than planned, Ruth and I went to Devon and Cornwall for a week's holiday and stayed in a flat overlooking Brixham harbour. To say the least, life was a little bizarre.

It was now September 1972 and my last month of living at home. My awareness of being in a transitional period heightened. I made several trips to Oxford to view accommodation, to take possessions to my new digs, and to enrol at the college. Yet I still went out to the coffee bars and pubs in Chippenham that my social life had revolved around for years, and I still saw Rob, Greg and Ruth. She got a job as a nanny in a village north of London, a distance of 110 miles from Chippenham, as I found out when I took her there on 1st October for her first day with the family, before I drove to Oxford for the beginning of my first term at college.

ANOTHER SIDE OF...

DISCOVERY ROAD

I had found and opened a back door into a new world and crossed the threshold. It had taken three attempts and two years to get into college. I was twenty years old and believed I had left adolescence behind at home; and my first real love was many miles away, also starting a new life.

It was a world of unfamiliar norms and behaviours, and an awareness that life had changed was confirmed at the 'Fresher's Fair', where the Deputy President of the Students Union was wearing a multi-coloured poncho, topped by an empty cornflakes packet on his head. Welcome to student life in the hippy, psychedelic, whacky 1970s!

Oxford Polytechnic, 'the poly,' was in the suburb of Headington on the eastern fringe of town. It grew from roots in the centre of town as a School of Art established in 1865, and over the years had evolved into the Oxford College of Technology with the addition of architecture, science and engineering departments. Catering, design, construction, town planning and social sciences had been added in recent years. Its artisan and technical focus clearly distinguished the polytechnic from Oxford University, a world-renowned seat of traditional learning that occupied pride of place in the centre of town; indeed, the University *was* the centre of town. And it seemed to me that the functional, utilitarian 1950s design of the poly campus was designed specifically to provide a clear contrast with the glittering gothic spires of the University's ancient buildings, and pointedly emphasise the social distinction; it was unadulterated brand management.

One very fortunate by-product of the distinction was that the poly hosted the best social events in town. The university authorities controlled the city and did not see fit to allow discotheques or concerts on their campus or in town, as this might corrupt their charges, who were in large measure drawn from the well-heeled classes and therefore too feeble-minded to protect themselves against the uncultured proclivities of the proletariat. David Bowie, Genesis, Velvet Underground, Wishbone Ash, Procul Harem and Steeleye Span had all appeared at the poly in the previous year, courtesy of the Students Union. And there were more than 40 clubs and societies to join and enliven the mind at the expense of studying. What a temptation for me, what a distraction!

I started at college with a full social life, just as I had finished at school. A lax attitude to the course was aided and abetted by a Spartan sprinkling of formal but optional contact time at the college – a mere six hours of lectures a week, supplemented by eight hours of seminars. On the third day of term I went to see *Patton: Lust of Glory*, and at the weekend I fetched Ruth from Toddington. During the following week I saw *Gimme Shelter* on Tuesday and went to see Ruth on Thursday. In the third week, I attended college only three days, taking a long weekend from Thursday through Monday to be with Ruth on her birthday and to spend the weekend at home in Chippenham. Ruth had a live-in job with a family and it was neither discreet nor enjoyable for us to stay there on her breaks, so that meant I had to drive hundreds of miles at all hours of the day and night to sustain our relationship. This I gladly did.

I found digs off the Cowley Road at 28 Alma Place, St. Clements, propitiously positioned in the no-man's land between Town and Gown at the bottom of Headington Hill. At a chance meeting, my school friend Mike Tristram told me his brother lived in the house and had a room to spare. I meet the landlord on the day that I moved in to the squalid little property. He was an enterprising Pakistani who rented out the property and lived with his wife, children and another family somewhere else in town. This was my first encounter with the changing fabric of society in parts of England. In Chippenham, foreigners were seen only in the restaurants they owned, and the town hosted one Indian and one Chinese restaurant, plus Cavaciuti's, an Italian café next to the bridge. That was it. I had grown up in a racially homogeneous world, a world in which only Protestants and Catholics existed, and what was the difference anyway?

In the coming months, I was to meet and become firm friends with Jews, Africans, Indians and even English people with strange accents. But there was no thought of discriminating on the grounds of race, religion, social background or northern accent. I was not the kind of person who needed to cling to any group identity, and I genuinely enjoyed the cosmopolitan circumstances of this new habitat. It was more of an education than a threat. I spent much time with Atul Deshmuk, an Indian on my course, going out drinking, or going to the cinema. Then there was the suave and softly spoken Philip Goodwin from Pangbourne, northern lass Becky from Leeds, and the very Jewish Robert Kleiman from Highgate in North London.

However, there was not to be a clear separation from my previous life. I flitted between and even mixed the three worlds of Ruth, Chippenham and Oxford. I saw Ruth most weekends and made occasional trips home to Chippenham. When the end of term came on 8th December, I remained in Oxford and worked ten days at the postal sorting office in Becket Street during the Christmas rush, sitting on a tall stool in front of a battery of pigeonholes, and sorting bagfuls of cards by hand at high speed. I netted a very handy £20 for working three full days and seven afternoon shifts. Outside work, I saw friends in Oxford, played Battleships and drank. Christmas proper began on Friday 23rd when I returned home. I got pissed on Saturday, and on Sunday fetched Ruth from Toddington, and got pissed in the evening during a pub crawl.

Money was always tight. I was dependent on the generosity of my parents, a situation I found awkward. My parents were funding me through college, because the political bureaucracy had pronounced that they were rich enough to support me. Still, I did have the luxury of the £50 minimum grant from the local council! The money I lived on was not enough, but I was lucky to have an expensed car and I felt unable to ask for more. I supplemented my income by taking occasional jobs, and my ever-caring mother would slip me a few quid whenever I was at home. After Christmas, I put in several shifts at Praesidium Products, feeling more out of place there now that I was a student, and former inmate turned legitimate escapee.

As the year drew to a close, I wrote that I loved Ruth more than ever, but believed that she didn't need me. Our relationship had lasted three years, but would it survive until the fourth anniversary, I wondered. She had written to me in November:

I ought to tell you that, definitely next year I'm going abroad, so I suppose it's only fair to tell you now so you can decide what you want to do with our relationship. I love you! You love me! But we're not engaged, so? I must see more of the world and life before I get settled down. I think you understand the way I feel. Please don't feel too upset about what I say, even though I know you will. Think about it for a time, it won't feel so painful. I look forward to seeing you on Saturday.

It was agonising to be unsure about our relationship and I was so unsettled that I made a special mid-week trip to see Ruth in Toddington. I pressed her to reach a clear decision, and she finished with me. But we did meet again at the weekend, spending most of our time in bed together. It was that sort of partnership; it was precious, treasured and so full of sentiment that breaking up to move on was hard to do – for both of us. She said that she loved me more than I loved her. I understood what she meant. Ruth said she would do anything for me, yet I felt that our relationship could only be a backdrop to my desire to learn, to develop, to prove myself. I felt lucky to have such a wonderful girlfriend, but partnership was not my primary aspiration in life. I loved her and needed her as much as I could possibly love or need anyone at that time, so why couldn't that be enough for her? Why should I have to choose? I wasn't ready to make a commitment to marriage or an engagement; it would be like asking Christopher Columbus to drop anchor in mid-Atlantic on his way to discover America.

TWILIGHT AND DARKNESS

On New Year's day 1973 I got home at 3 o'clock in the morning, after spending the evening at the Rose and Crown, and then at Bernie's house with a group of other friends. Britain was joining the European Community on January 1st and we talked a lot about the pros and cons. Contrary to the vapid pronouncements of various self-interest groups, it seemed to me that the economic case for joining was weak. Rather, it should be understood as a strategic imperative to be on the inside and aligned with former enemies. After more drinking, the situation became a bit hazy and we gave up caring about the issue.

I got up late and went into the market place to sit in my favourite coffee bar for a few hours. The Galleon had been renamed The Farmer Giles, but you could still buy one drink and sit in there all day. However, I felt tired and ill and at 2 o'clock went home to sleep before going to work at eight to start a night shift. I worked nights at the factory all week, then spent the weekend with Ruth, packing on Sunday night for my return to Oxford the next day, January 8th.

Our relationship was in a twilight period, at a time when my love life became more complicated. I wrote in my diary that we were officially finished. Despite carrying on a busy social life, I became very lonely and mentioned Ruth in my diary every day. I missed her so much that when she phoned it made my day. I would write RUTH PHONED, underlining the capital letters written large across the page.

Adina and Denise were two of the complications. I had met Adina five months before, on my first visit to Oxford when I went there to buy books for the course. She was in Mike Tristram's crowd of friends, and we had all gone punting one day and to the speedway the next. Adina was of Italian stock. She had boyishly short fair hair and a sculptured face featuring a Roman nose and a broad smile. I was attracted to her outgoing personality, and although I liked to see her, I was not thinking of starting a romantic relationship. That is, until it seemed that Ruth and I were finished. Adina phoned more and more often, and I started to go around to the digs she shared with Denise and another girl. The three of them lived in the basement flat at 88 James Street, which was a conveniently short trip along the Iffley Road from my room in Alma Place. They cooked for me, we chatted, we played music, and we played Scrabble, Fish-Fruit-Flower, Consequences and the memory game 'My Aunt Went to Paris'.

One Sunday night, Adina came to see me, we watched a film, we talked and I told her that I was falling for her. But I wondered whether I could handle another romance so soon after breaking up with Ruth, and the thought troubled me so much that I had to get away to spend time clearing my mind. I left Oxford at 2 o'clock in the morning and drove the 200-mile journey to Plymouth, arriving at six in the morning. I cruised around looking for Bernie, who was living there and studying at the Polytechnic. But I couldn't find Bernie and so decided to drive to Chard to find Nick. Nick took the rest of the day off work and we talked, smoked and drank until the early hours of the next morning. I drove home to Chippenham, ate a meal, and went to bed at 4am. On getting up, I returned to Oxford feeling that I had sorted myself out.

Whatever this whirlwind trip of 500 miles in 33 hours had achieved was short-lived, because my life became more complicated during the ensuing weeks. I was spending several evenings a week at the basement flat. I could not seem to get time alone with Adina and I was becoming more and more interested in Denise, a cheeky, sexy northern girl with the most kissable mouth, a terrific sense of humour and stunning legs that were always on full display in shiny tights.

While all this was going on, Sally had also been the subject of my attentions, ever since mid-January when I took her out for a drink at the Perch Inn, a beautiful old pub by the Thames at Binsey village, on the northern fringe of Oxford. After a few dates, of the skirmishing kind, we decided it would be good fun to go on a long weekend to Paris, and I booked the outward journey for February 9th. Sally, a friend from the Social Studies course, was a lovely girl, a straw blonde with cropped hair and a striking angular face. But she was too innocent for me, and evidently saving herself up for the right man. To my chagrin, I discovered this fatal handicap after booking the trip. It proved futile to achieve seduction. Though she would lie on the bed and let me kiss her, this was the final frontier, and she lay there protecting herself with incredible dexterity and determination. Take her breasts, for example. If I strayed in their direction, Sally would cross her arms so tightly around her chest that not even a ray of sunlight could pass through. I prodded and jammed my fingers into any hopeful space to gain leverage, but to no avail. As for Paris, it was a whirlwind trip, starting at 4 o'clock on the Friday morning and ending at 9 o'clock on the Monday night. The Champs Élysée, Tour d'Eiffel, Basilique du Sacré-Coeur at Montmartre, and all the famed culture of Paris was not enough to effect a romantic trip. Perhaps fittingly, the weekend finished with the two of us being violently sick with just about all the other passengers on the ferry back to Ramsgate, the hovercraft 'flight' having been cancelled due to rough weather in the channel! To top it all, the trip had cost me a precious £20, including petrol, the sea crossing with Hoverlloyd, the coach fare to Paris, the cost of the hostel in Paris, travel on the Metro, a one-year British Passport, food, souvenirs and a ticket to see Steve McQueen and Ali MacGraw in Sam Peckinpah's *The Getaway* at Le Balzac cinema.

Despite these various romantic distractions, or perhaps because of them, I could not get Ruth out of my mind. '*Missing, missing,*

missing Ruth so very much', I wrote. And then, one day in February she phoned and we arranged to meet. I fetched her from Toddington and we drove to London for the day, and went shopping in Oxford Street and Kensington before she returned for her babysitting duties that evening. Then she stayed the following weekend with me, spending Friday night in Oxford and then driving to Chippenham on Saturday to be with my grandmother. On Sunday we spent a pleasant day at Longleat stately home with Ruth's mother, and Monday was Gran's birthday so we drove to her cosy little home in Seend and had lunch. Ruth returned to Toddington the next day, but not before we made love again. I had a wonderful time and felt we were OK once more. My loneliness and sadness withered.

During the Easter break in April, I worked several shifts at the factory, lazing about in between. A letter arrived from Ruth explaining:

I've finished with Harry (thank God). Hope you are okay. Can't wait to see you again.

She had an eleven-day holiday, and we spent it together, travelling around sightseeing, sometimes with her mother, to Warwick, Salisbury, Bristol, the Wye Valley, and Weston-Super-Mare.

Back at college, life returned to the normal mix of seeing Ruth, trips to Chippenham, and a social scene with friends in Oxford. I was spending more time now with Nicolas, Vanessa and Becky from the course. We went to see John Osborne's play *Look Back in Anger*. And, to show solidarity with my fellow students, I joined 3,000 others in a demonstration for higher grants, not that it would make the slightest difference to me financially. British students were protesting about money for themselves, while in America, students were protesting about war, with Nixon finally pulling the last troops out of Vietnam at the end of that month.

The protest in Oxford was part of a mood of revolt festering in the country, aimed at the Government's prices and pay policies, but in some cases with an ulterior agenda of bringing down the Conservatives. 1.6 million 'workers' joined a strike called by the

TUC on May Day. My friends and I decided to avoid the chaos of demonstrations that were taking place in London and other major cities, and we left Oxford the night before and drove down to Cornwall for the May Day Holiday. Nicolas had a souped-up Austin 1300 in an unfortunate orange hue, but with lowered suspension and a 'go-faster' steering wheel. Nicolas drove like the wind through the twisty and narrow roads so that we could arrive early in the morning and make the most of the day. We watched with amusement the ancient ritual of the 'Obby Orse' parading through Padstow before setting off back to Oxford.

Lectures, seminars and tutorials continued, and though most were interesting, they were merely a backdrop to my social and romantic life and its twists and turns. I did not enjoy the quantitative methods component, which was a mix of mathematics, statistics and computing. My Term Project was to write and run a computer programme. Patience was the key skill needed to achieve this objective, closely allied to determination. First, it was necessary to write the code in Fortran IV, which takes the following form:

```
DIMENSION A(11)
FUN(T) = SQRT(ABS(T)) + 5.)*T**3
READ (5,1) A
FORMAT(5F10.2)
DO 10 J = 1, 11
          I = 11 - J
          Y = FUN(A(I+1))
          IF (400.0-Y) 4, 8, 8
                  WRITE (6,5) I
                  FORMAT(I10, 10H TOO LARGE)
          GO TO 10
                  WRITE(6,9) I,Y
                  FORMAT(I10, F12.6)
CONTINUE
STOP
END
```

...but that was the easy part. The set of instructions had to be typed into a machine that translated the keystrokes into holes punched through a stack of oblong cards so that the computer could 'read' it, and that was the difficult part, for a single mistake led to disaster. A comma out of place, an extra space here or there, or nested brackets inadvertently not paired, were misdemeanours treated with utter contempt by the animated machine, which made its pronouncement by regurgitating the entire stack of cards into the output bin without so much as an explanation. How rude!

Fuck it, where is the mistake, I pondered as I sifted through every one of about 50 cards. My 'job' had been in the 'batch queue' waiting to be sacrificed and had taken three days before it was fed into the machine. The result was failure and having to re-run the programme after 'de-bugging' the written and punched code. Perhaps there were several mistakes, not one. Maybe I would have to wait a few more days before those computer people would schedule re-submission of my job. Judging by the luxurious environment provided by its organic cohorts, the computer was a God of some sort. Strange indeed, since the poly's ICL mainframe computer had less computing power than a microbe. How had it managed to brainwash these humans into voluntary servitude? It required so many cabinets and spinning tapes that it occupied a gigantic room, temperature-controlled to prevent its circuits overheating. If this was the best that Artificial Intelligence could offer, then we could sleep without fear that machines would be taking over soon.

PROBLEMS

During the last weekend in May, I drove to Toddington to fetch Ruth. I arrived at 2 o'clock on Sunday morning and turned around to drive to Chippenham. On the return journey on the Monday, I determined to sever my connexion with Ruth. It was premeditated to the extent that I had given the matter so much thought over the months, but not in the sense that I had planned exactly when to carry out my decision. It was now time to let go, time to end the procrastination and perpetual uncertainty and be released to concentrate on the future instead of trying to keep the past alive.

"Ruth, I think we should split up for good", I said.

I had never seen her so distraught. I stopped several times on the journey so that we could concentrate on talking things through. It was such bad timing to do it in the car, especially after we had been getting closer in recent weeks. The depth of her feelings took me aback. I had misread the situation by sensing that she had broader interests and weaker ties to me than before, and this had been in the mix of thoughts and emotions that tipped the balance. As much as it hurt, I kept telling myself 'Be strong, be strong, and don't change your mind.' My head ruled my heart at this time, forsaking love. It was so painful yet so necessary.

What happened next was predictable, perhaps, but not inevitable: I began dating Adina. We had been meeting every day at college, sometimes going to the cinema, sometimes just in a crowd of friends. But one Friday night we went to bed together. She stayed with me on Tuesday the following week, and we skipped college the next day, staying in bed until three in the afternoon.

Lectures had finished and the first year qualifying exams were just two weeks away. I continued to see Adina, but did not feel passionate about her. In fact, I was having difficulty staying aroused, and knew in my heart that it was time to move on. We went on a three-day trip to Dorset with Mike Tristram and his girlfriend, then to Swansea, returning the day before the first exam on 11th June. Days later, and I finished with Adina. She wrote to me saying:

Don't fight your love for Ruth, give in – love is something you should help to blossom not stifle. Accept Ruth for what she is and love her as you really do; deep down inside you there is a passion – a longing for her.

It was true, so true, but it was now too late to save the relationship with Ruth unless I was prepared to make an irrevocable commitment that would compromise my career aspirations, which in my way of thinking demanded complete dedication. Indeed, I had not given up on the thought of pursuing geology. Geology was taught at the polytechnic and I had been to see the Head of Department, Dr Alan Childs, already, and pleaded to be accepted onto the course. Dr Childs was unable to offer any assurance, but promised to discuss the matter with the college administrators. In the event, they offered me a place on the course, but entry was on the condition that I passed the impending First Year qualifying examinations of the BA course. Oh dear! Passing exams was not my speciality.

During the summer break I started working at a building site at Swindon railway station for a firm named Chivers. I didn't like the work at all and missed the third day, was late on the fourth day, and packed it in on the fifth day at the end of the week only £16.50 better off. I spent much of my time split between home and Oxford. Bernie came to Oxford and we went punting with Mike Tristram and a crowd of friends. I spent several evenings at the Three Crowns in Chippenham with my best friends from school Iain, Nick, Bernie and Greg, and felt that the good times had never gone away. On Christmas Eve we stood up and drank to absent mate Rob Noyes, who was in India with Willy Mann on the hippy trail to Nepal.

My attention turned to Denise. Her flat mate Adina was working in London during the vacation, and so there could be no embarrassing moments for Denise, who was not a student and lived and worked in Oxford. I saw her several times, but dating Denise never amounted to an 'official' relationship. One reason for this was that I sensed that Denise wasn't serious about me, perhaps because of complications with her good friend Adina. But also, I couldn't get an erection with her, despite finding her incredibly sensuous and desirable. It was strange, because I knew that the system was fully functional, as I tested it almost every day! It was the 'Ruth Factor,' and it would take me another eighteen months before I found a girl I could respond to without holding back.

I failed my exams, or to be accurate, the requirement was to pass in all five subjects to get through, but I failed quantitative methods and economics. It was no coincidence that some of my closest friends on the course also failed, including Robert and Becky, who both failed in the same subjects that I had. Because of my aversion to maths and statistics, I had no chance with Question 7 concerning differentiation, or Question 2, that required calculating the Poisson distribution of monthly suicides in Town X. There was only one thing for it: I would have to re-take the exams in September because my place on both courses depended on it.

August was a strange month. My future was in limbo until I knew the outcome of the resit exams. Ruth was in Chippenham for a week. We met several times, going shopping in Bath with her mother, and going out in the evening, but it wasn't the same anymore. I drove her back to Toddington, and saw her again later in the month, though it was evident she was seeing someone else.

ON TRACK

During the quantitative methods re-sit, I tackled daunting questions on 'regression analysis' and 'finding the coefficient of correlation between high protein diets and birth rates in ten selected countries'. Miraculously, I fared much better than before, because the letter that arrived from the poly on September 6th advised that they would be glad to see me next term for Year II of the course. It was a last-minute reprieve from the guillotine.

With a good deal of luck, I had qualified to go into the second year at college and drop two subjects. I genuinely did enjoy studying politics, law and sociology, especially to learn about the wider world, how societies functioned, and how civilisation had developed over the centuries. Reading, debate, and the chance to develop an informed individual viewpoint were important to me. Miraculously, I had qualified, and there was now a clear run to the end of the course and achieving a degree. I contemplated the idea of being a professional person, perhaps a barrister, duelling eloquently in some musty courtroom, or maybe a politician giving the Prime Minister a roasting from the backbenches.

It was an ambitious vision, but it competed with another, because I now had the option to pursue my passion for geology. Yes, it would mean starting at the beginning; yes, it would involve tackling difficult science subjects that I had not studied at school; and yes, I would have to qualify all over again to get into the second year of a course. But I knew the answer without having to analyse and weigh the pro's and cons: I could not forego the opportunity I had been dreaming of for the previous five years.

In the final week of September, I was busy preparing for my new start in life. On Monday, I drove to Oxford and went to be with Denise overnight. I began the search for digs on Tuesday, before returning to Chippenham late that night. On Wednesday, I mozzied around the town. Come Thursday, I was back in Oxford, meeting Denise and going with her to see *Lost Horizon* at the cinema. She was such a desirable girl and yet, sadly, friendship was all I could muster. On Friday, I drove back to Chippenham after meeting friends from my now former course and making a continued but unsuccessful search for suitable digs. My last chance to find digs before college began came on Saturday, when I drove to Aston Tirrold, a delightful village twenty miles and half an hour south of Oxford. It was no more than a few cottages and houses strung out along a narrow country lane. This sleepy little place had acquired temporary fame in the late sixties when that great band Traffic chilled out in a cottage during their 'Getting Back to the Country Days' period.

I had come to view some accommodation that I saw advertised at the poly. It was a charming, centuries-old cottage with a thatched roof, timber-framed exterior, and door so low that I had to stoop to enter. Inside were wood-beamed ceilings and a narrow helical staircase, accessed through a little door beside the enormous log fire in the sitting room. A well-spoken middle-aged man named Alan was renting the property and he seemed to be a decent bloke, so I accepted the offer when it came, and moved in the next day. Rent £5 a week, plus share of electricity.

Physics was the first lecture, maths the second, biology the third. Learning science had begun! The B.Sc. was modular in structure, meaning that there would be exams every term, for nine consecutive terms over the three years. I would have to pass no less than ten of the twelve subjects in Year I to qualify for Year II. Viking Hell, work had begun! It was a daunting prospect indeed, given my dismal lack of success in passing exams, and the challenge of studying physics and chemistry.

LOST AND FOUND

'Missing Ruth so much', *'Want Ruth's love desperately'*, and *'How can I prove myself to Ruth'* were some of the comments that appeared in my diary at the end of each week. Sometimes I talked to her on the phone, and I did see her in Chippenham on a few occasions. But there were no trips to Toddington and no weekends together in Oxford: we were ex-lovers but friends, perhaps in a residual way still clinging to the cosy notion that our romance would flare up again spontaneously.

Come November, and my life was still full of activities, still split between groups of friends and between college and home. It was becoming more and more costly to get around, as the price of petrol kept rising, and for a while it looked as though petrol rationing would have to be introduced. I received my allocation of petrol coupons in a Motor Fuel Ration Book for a motor car not exceeding 1,100cc. There was a six-month supply, but they were not needed. Demand for oil had increased when the markets got nervous about the Yom Kippur War in October, and Saudi Arabia and the Gulf States were pushing up the price. To make matters worse, in Britain, nationwide voltage reductions took effect in November, and after the situation deteriorated, the Prime Minister announced there would be a three-day working week from January 1974.

Ruth was still there, on my mind, sometimes on the phone and sometimes we dated as friends. Touchingly, in December we celebrated our Fourth Anniversary that wasn't, by going for an Italian meal at the Trattoria in Bath. After working three nights at the factory in the Christmas break, I got pissed at the annual works party. I celebrated Christmas Eve with friends, at the Rose and Crown and the King Alfred in Chippenham but, tellingly, I spent much of the time leading up to New Years Eve at home, alone and bored, with little to record in my diary except a deep sense of loss.

Missing Ruth SO much. My whole life is affected.

January 1974 started with three night shifts at the factory, several meetings with Ruth, and a date with ex-girlfriend Angela from Corsham. On Friday of that week, I stayed up all night at home, playing Risk and Mine a Million with Brian Sweet and Bernie.

Brian had been a year below me at school but we had become friends through rugby and, more recently, we had worked shifts at Praesidium Products. Brian had a thatch of thick, black hair and a unique gait that enabled him to walk without moving his hips. His quirky sense of humour and infectious laugh guaranteed a good time. He had an amusing way of inserting a sprinkling of nonsense words into his sentences, such as 'perryerson' for person, and he would utter 'wigwam' when there was nothing much else to say. Then there was the use of 'ish', added after the briefest of pauses if Brian was unsure of his facts or sensed that his ideas were not being accepted, for example: "she's a pretty girl...ish." A year or two back, we'd had some fun with Brian on the road from Biddestone into Corsham, when he had lain on the roof of my car as I drove along swerving from side-to-side to try and shake him off (without success, I admit). Like me and most of my other friends, Brian had not yet established himself or his true potential. He was working in the factory and getting pissed at night, and on his own admission too pissed to pick up girls.

"I find myself so caught up in my work, and there are two side effects – sleeping and drinking."

Over the weekend, I drove back to the cottage to settle in, and then on Sunday I went into Oxford to be with Becky, Robert, Vanessa and Nicolas, friends from the 'old' course. What a mixed-up existence. I saw my social studies friends frequently in the Spring Term, and my circle widened with the addition of friends from the Hotel Catering and Management Course, Hannah in particular. Hannah had a lovely character, so warm and so much fun. She had curly hair, dark brown and shoulder-length, and a slightly full figure that I found very desirable. The night I met her I wrote: *'Mmm! Yes Please.'* Hannah became a firm friend, but, as she had a boyfriend in London, I put my admiration for her to one side. She gave me the nickname Early Burly, and she liked giving hugs and extended cuddles, which I did nothing to discourage. My admiration grew.

I went to pubs with different friends and to several parties, including Nicolas's 21st up in Warwick. Oh, and I spent a night with Becky, but the romance was not consummated. I liked Becky and she was not unattractive, so where had my drive gone? A normal man would have ravaged her for pure sexual enjoyment and fulfilment, but the thought of sex was not sufficient to turn me on, it was so one-sided and shallow. In May I had a fleeting romance with Jemima, who was a friend of Alan, he of the cottage. She was a gorgeous, petite, raven-haired woman in her mid-thirties – or so she said. After a couple of meetings we ended up in bed together, and it was only then that the reality of what I was about to do revealed itself in the age of her face close-up under the harsh light overhead; and that was the last I saw of Jemima. With these exceptions, this period of my life was barren of social activity and interests. I stayed at home in the cottage in the evenings and during weekends, studying, watching TV, feeling lonely.

In the country at large, the Government had been unable to prevent the spread of the malaise, and Prime Minster Heath resigned in March. Harold Wilson formed a government, and an election was set for October. It didn't take long for the Labour Government to act, and the top rate of income tax was raised to 83 per cent.

Summer Term passed uneventfully. Romance was entirely off the scene and I was working much harder now. My friends from the BA course were fading into the distance, and although there were several students I especially liked in the group of seventy-six students in my year, I tried to keep contact to a minimum. In doing so, I sacrificed the need for close friendships. Awkward moments arose whenever there was talk of going for a drink or to a party, which happened frequently, because I had to make the same excuse time after time, or would fade into the background and hope not to be asked. Over time, they did stop asking.

During the first week of July, I sat the last batch of four exams and went back to Chippenham for the summer break. When the results came through, I found I had passed in ten subjects over the year, as required! For once in my life, I made the grade on the first attempt – no resits, no deciding interview. I was particularly proud of my achievement in the two biology exams, scoring the top mark of 80 per cent (distinction) in one and 66 per cent in another, outperforming students who had biology A level. And I got distinctions in both geology exams. The way was now clear for me to enter the second year of the course, and reach for the prize I had been dreaming of for so long.

TRAVELLING AGAIN

Brian Sweet and I had become closer friends in recent times. He and I corresponded frequently, and I was pleased to hear that an interest he had developed in photography was turning into a vocation and a worthwhile career. We had taken a week's holiday in Torquay back in March, and were now planning a holiday in the summer with Hannah and one of her childhood friends. He wrote to me from his digs in Torquay, querying *'when will we get to see their naughty parts?'*

In some respects the trip was déjà vu. My father was providing the transport, a maroon MkIII 1.6 Cortina saloon, and the trip involved a grand tour of Norway, Sweden and Finland, where I had been with Bernie, Rob and Greg three years previously.

To earn money for the trip, in the summer break I worked at the factory for a month, right up to the departure date of August 12th. I picked up Brian from his parents house in Corsham at 6am and drove to Oxford to collect Hannah and friend, before driving to Harwich to board the overnight ferry to Kristiansand. Brian and I found three bars on board the M/S Blenheim, and drank at each before retiring to the cabin. We reached Oslo on the second night in Norway and looked around the city for two days, visiting Andy's Bar, The Scotsman and other drinking establishments.

A succession of pretty towns and quaint cities flew by during the succeeding three weeks: Bergen, Voss, Trondheim, Helsinki, Stockholm and Goteborg. But the real treasure discovered on the holiday was the magnificent countryside. On my previous visit, I had driven across the southern tip of Norway and the southern parts of Sweden and Finland. This time, the trip would take me northward, firstly through Norway and Sweden across the mountainous backbone of Scandinavia, then around the head of the Baltic Sea, and finally north to the Arctic Circle in Finland to see the midnight sun. The journey back involved driving south through Finland, a country awash with lakes and odd-sounding place names, such as Leppavirta, Asillala and Mikkeli.

Wherever we travelled, the people we met spoke English well and were friendly and hospitable. It was embarrassing to compare this with the treatment they would have received in Britain, where there was no allowance for other languages and little acceptance of foreigners. On the way to Bergen we stopped in a lay-by to eat lunch. A man appeared out of the forest and gave us some fresh fish he had just caught in a lake. Touchingly, he said he was grateful for what the British had done in the war.

We had driven on some distance after lunch before Hannah realised she had left her sunglasses in the lay-by. I turned the car around, and on the way back we were bewildered to see a smart leather coat in the middle of the road, then further on a pair of black trousers, then pieces of underwear. Someone had not properly fastened her suitcase on the roof rack!

It rained in Bergen and was a miserable day with nothing interesting for us to do. Bergen is situated on the Atlantic coast and takes the full brunt of some appalling weather and rain all year round, a handicap not compensated for by the stunning backdrop of mountains, lush vegetation and quaint narrow streets with weatherboard-clad houses. Disappointed, we drove out of the town to the pretty ski resort of Voss, and then across the Jotunheimen mountain chain, the home of the gods of Norse mythology and host to the highest mountains in Scandinavia. There is almost no vegetation above 2,000 metres, and the heavily ice-sculpted mountains have a raw, foreboding beauty that seems to pose a constant threat. We played Frisbee on the largest glacier before continuing north to Trondheim. And on from Trondheim to send myself a postcard from Hell, the front of the card featuring a picture of the *Gods Expedition* or cargo-handling warehouse at the train station in the village.

The nights were cold, whether in the tent or in the car. In fact, the car was intrinsically uncomfortable, even just for two people, but the four of us slept inside when it was too cold or damp outside, or when there were so many ants or mosquitoes that settling down for the night was just not possible.

Travelling further north on our journey, we left the mountains behind and the weather improved, making the journey into Finland pleasant indeed. We stopped in Rovaniemi to sample the experience of a traditional sauna, then drove to a sign proclaiming 'Arctic Circle' and took photographs to prove we had been there, done that!

Our journey now took us south and into Sweden. When we camped in a wood west of Stockholm, by chance Hannah and I were left alone to put up the tent. Job done, we had a bit of an extended cuddle, which led to a serious embrace, then kissing – and then to petting. It had to happen. But to my disappointment and embarrassment, I could not get aroused, and that was where the romance with Hannah was launched and sunk. For some reason I could not abandon myself, could not become immersed in the moment. I sensed that my alter ego was behind me, observing, judging and silently promoting conscious thought. Hannah was

Bernie, Greg and Robert enjoying the fresh air in Denmark

Author, cleaning cars at Earle of Chippenham

Graduation: my first achievement

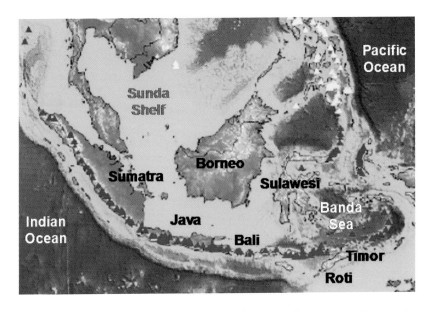

The Indonesian archipelago. Active volcanoes shown as red symbol

On the train to Bandung, Java

Fred and Dolly Hehuwat and family at home, Bandung

View eastward along the volcanic arc, Java

Life on Jalan Siliwangi, Kupang, Timor

With Mr Ing in the Karang Mas, Kupang

Stuck on the road to Soe

Losman Emban, Kapan

Peter Oematan, Prince of Molo

Market day in Nefukoko village

Talking into the night, Nefukoko

Finally, going into the field. Noil Metan, Molo. Yanto at left

Elias, Musa and Obet at base camp, Molo summit

View westward along Molo ridge

The dry land, seen from Molo summit

Protector of the herd, Molo

Typical Atoni dwelling, Manubait village

Author and guide

Weaving in the shade, Manubait

Yanto boiling an egg on the radiator

The people of Talimaman village, Molo

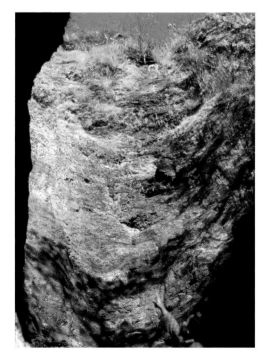

Dry waterfall, Molo

Burning the forest to grow crops, Molo

Going up country from Kupang

Author's work, living and eating area, Ajaobonat village, Boi

Author's bed, Ajaobonat

Cutting through Lantana thornbush on 'river' N6, Boi

Leaving Boi with porters

my friend. How could I adjust in an instant and be intimate with her, and would it spoil our friendship? Would I regret it afterwards? Maybe it was the 'Ruth Factor,' or maybe not? Did I fear that I would not be a good lover, perhaps physically inadequate, unable to satisfy such a confident and experienced girl? I will never know. Thinking about the issues killed any possibility that the hormones would take control.

Three weeks of the summer break remained when I returned home on 7th September. To my great delight, the next day my father replaced my trusty Anglia with a bright yellow Mk I Ford Escort with a nippy 1100cc engine. Built in 1968, the Escort was altogether a more modern car, and it saw me through the next two and a half years and 27,000 miles of travelling. My first improvement to the car was to add an 8-track cartridge player. According to magazine reviews, the quality of sound from a cartridge player was much better than from an ordinary cassette player. And so it proved to be, except that the combined noise from road, wind and engine overwhelmed the music at speeds in excess of 50mph, coincidently the minimum speed that I travelled. Still, it was a talking point, and Brian Sweet thought it was '*fantaba-roony*' when we played the *Yes Album* at full volume while driving around at high speed.

I worked two weeks at the factory to top up my depleted cash reserves. Being on night shifts restricted my social life to weekends, but there was one special occasion in my social calendar. Max Hoare was back in the country. I went to his stag night at the Hare and Hounds in Corsham, and a week afterwards was best man at his wedding in Cheltenham. A green and blue striped tie and brown suede shoes did not complement my blue suit, and my brief speech suffered from lack of inspiration. I felt guilty that I had let down my friend when entrusted with such a responsible role, and was too ashamed to bring up the subject.

Friday and Saturday night of the next week, I drank in various pubs in Chippenham before returning to the cottage in Aston

Tirrold on Sunday. Ruth phoned and then came to see me at the cottage, arriving at 1 o'clock on Monday. We went shopping in Oxford and enjoyed a fine evening together; but when she went home in the morning it left me feeling thoroughly depressed because the spark had gone.

DOUBLE REALISATION

Sarah was also studying geology at the poly. I began to take an interest in her during a week's field trip to Torquay during the Easter Break in March. I determined to get to know Sarah and manufactured situations so that I could talk to her. It took me a while to make a move because I was still a little shy, and her quiet and restrained demeanour also held me back. Our first date was on October 29th, when we had a candlelit dinner in the college courtesy of FADS, the Food and Drink Society run by the Hotel & Catering students. And so began my second long-term partnership.

Sarah was an attractive girl of nineteen, with shoulder length brown hair set in a pageboy style that emphasised her sweet, girlish nature. She was well-spoken, well-educated and enjoyed theatre. And so, it was time to take in some culture, and where better than in Oxford? For a ticket price of 75p, productions at the Oxford Playhouse represented good value. Oxford University owned The Playhouse and hosted productions staged by a variety of repertoire companies. Sarah and I saw *Much Ado About Nothing* played by the Oxford and Cambridge Shakespeare Company, as well as Shakespeare's *Coriolanus*, a production by the Experimental Theatre Club at the University.

Gastronomic experiences continued. We dined at La Dolce Vita, then another FADS dinner, and ate assorted other meals round and about; she cooked for me in Cheney, the main hall of residence at the poly, and we went to her parents' house in Marlow for lunch. We spent weekends at the cottage in Aston Tirrold. My impotence vanished. I had found release from an emotional handicap. Sarah was so gentle and encouraging and I was well and truly infatuated with her. Sarah slept with me because she believed she was in love and therefore ready to give herself. At last, I'd found a girl whose emotions and motivation were pure, like Ruth's had been in the beginning.

I was sad at the end of term because Sarah went home to her parents and it meant not seeing her for a while. On the last day of college we exchanged 'crissie pressies' and I drove home. As usual, I saw my schoolfriends and worked in the factory, but there was something different about me because I returned to Oxford before the New Year, instead of staying in Chippenham for the traditional piss-up.

FOCUS

Living in the cottage was a peaceful and delightful experience. However, the trip to and from college wasted an hour a day, not to mention the cost of six gallons of petrol a week out of a student's income. In January 1975, I found new digs before term started, a room at 48 Chilswell Road in Oxford town itself. Sarah visited the day I moved in, and we were now so near to each other that she cycled around from her lodgings in the halls of residence at the poly.

Regarding romantic and social activities, the term began as if nothing had changed. Sarah and I went to student parties, including several 21st parties, saw a highly enjoyable Roy Harper concert at the poly, and went to see *Airport 1975* at a cinema in town. But I soon became completely focussed on my studies and had little time for Sarah. The mid-point of the course was approaching and the goal I was pursuing seemed tantalisingly close. I felt pressured because the work was becoming more demanding, and it seemed as though I was on a conveyor belt, running against the movement of the belt: to stand still would be to go backwards. The course was now focussed on geology with some modules on the environment. Physics and chemistry were superseded by geophysics and geochemistry. And I chose not to take the soft options that were allowed on the modular degree, such as photography or psychology, since I felt this would dilute the purity and achievement of my science degree and reduce its value.

And so, beyond the end of January, I reduced my daily existence to a mix of lectures, coursework and relevant reading, punctuated very occasionally with a social event or a date with Sarah. I preferred to combine both, taking work to her room in Cheney Hall, or letting her sit in my room while I wrote an essay or read a textbook. All non-essential systems were shut down. It was unfortunate timing to have fallen in love at the point when I was gearing up for what I saw as the most important challenge of my life, but I knew that I was up to the challenge.

For the final two years I chose twenty-one courses, the minimum number required to obtain a degree, in a calculated gamble that I would pass them all. In addition, I planned to put less effort into the three courses that were peripheral to my interest, since only the best eighteen results would be assessed to give the class of degree.

I passed all eleven exams during Year II, taking me slightly more than half way towards the goal of twenty-one. I achieved five B+ and three A grades or distinctions in the important subjects, and got a B grade and two C grades in the three peripheral subjects that I hoped would not be counted towards the average mark: oceanography, Pleistocene ice age, and organisms and environment. My risky strategy seemed to be working.

Self-motivation allied to sacrifice was driving me in the right direction at a good speed, yet some of the lecturers were able to add favourable chemistry to the crucible in which my performance was being forged. Chief among them were Chris Topley, who taught mineralogy and igneous petrology, and Mike

Brown, who specialised in metamorphism and structural geology. They stood head and shoulders above the other staff in the department in the mastery of their respective subjects, their professional approach to preparing and delivering courses, and their ability to make lectures interesting. They were also bloody good blokes. As one of the keenest students on the course, I benefited from their camaraderie and tutelage, which in the case of Mike Brown was usually delivered as a humorous putdown to emphasise the pecking order and encourage me to improve.

FIELDWORK

The Institute of Geological Sciences (IGS), which in 1984 was re-named the British Geological Survey, accepted me as a voluntary worker to undertake three weeks of summer vacation work in North Wales with the Applied Geophysics Unit. In lieu of wages, a subsistence allowance of £7.35 a night was payable in arrears, but money wasn't the motivation. I felt sure that the practical experience gained would be an advantage later on when applying for jobs.

Courtesy of a Pits Grandstand ticket from my father, I watched Emerson Fitipaldi drive his McLaren to victory in the John Player F1 Grand Prix race at Silverstone on 19th July, before I drove to the Cemlyn Guest House in Harlech to rendezvous with Jenny Allsop, the Geophysics Officer in charge of the team. Together with three other students, we carried out a gravity survey over the Harlech Dome before moving location to Tegla Cottage Guest House in Llandegla to carry out a gravity traverse[1]. It was exacting work using a theodolite and La Coste-Romberg Gravimeter. We recorded the value of gravity at stations spaced 50 metres apart,

---

1. A traverse is set out as a single line across country, and a survey is set out as a grid of lines.

surveyed using a theodolite, an instrument that measures horizontal and vertical angles so that the absolute elevation and location of stations can be ascertained. A Gravimeter is an instrument designed to measure changes in the local gravitational field. In essence, it consists of a weight on a spring and is housed in a metal cylinder about the size of a tea urn. The point of measuring variations in gravity is to search in the subsurface for dense or light rocks that might contain minerals and metals with commercial value.

After the IGS survey was completed I drove to Anglesey to start my mapping project, a project that was a double module. It would be a contradiction to be a geologist if you were not competent at examining, describing and mapping rocks and geological structures in the field, and therefore the regulations required that all students pass this module to be awarded any degree at all.

A short field trip to Anglesey the previous year had sparked my interest in the local geology. A rich gentleman geologist named Edward Greenly had mapped Anglesey back in 1919, and there was much scope for reinterpretation and new discoveries. A further consideration was that Anglesey is a classic area of 'hard rock' geology, which was my particular field of interest, rather than the 'soft rock' geology of sediments and fossils. Hard rock geology comprises metamorphic and igneous rocks, many of which are associated with structurally complex areas and mountain chains that represent sites of continent–continent collision, that have experienced intense tectonic and volcanic activity. Anglesey is such a place, where the geological drama played itself out between the late Precambrian and Ordovician periods some 450-650 million years ago.

In Anglesey, I met up with Dave West, a fellow student who had become a firm friend. Dave was a Lancashire lad from Thornton Cleveleys, north of Blackpool. He was a tall youth with an unruly mop of ginger hair, plenty of freckles to match, and a sarcastic sense of humour that I appreciated highly. His preferred greeting to strangers was 'How's your bum for spots?' and he talked a lot about Boddingtons, or Boddies, his local ale. We shared an interest in hard rock geology and shared a caravan in Cemaes Bay for the duration of the fieldwork.

I mapped an area of eight square kilometres, roughly four-by-two, between Carmel Head on the northwest tip of the island, to Cemlyn Bay in the east. In this part of Anglesey, the coastline is dominated by cliffs that afford excellent sections of the geology, and many parts are accessible at low tide. I stayed for forty days and nights, going out into the field almost every day, come rain or shine.

Our supervisor Mike Brown kept Dave and I on our toes for a couple of days when he drew up in his ancient VW Beetle, and stayed a night in the caravan. It was not enough time to help me unravel the structural and tectonic complications of the area, but my meticulous mapping, detailed observations and well-written report earned me a double distinction in my project. However, it was so dissatisfying not to be able to return to the field to investigate problems and fill gaps in my understanding, a predicament that I was to encounter more than once again.

GOAL

To reduce outgoings I had given up my rented accommodation during the Summer Break. Returning to Oxford a few days before the start of term, I found new digs at 39 Chalfont Road, just off Woodstock Road, renting the attic bedroom in a house owned by a professor at Oxford University.

I continued the intense effort in the autumn term of Year III and gained superior grades in the three examination subjects. With my goal now clearly in sight, my entire focus was studying to pass the degree. My romantic life and social activities ceased completely and I did not even bother to keep a diary, breaking a habit of more than ten years.

In the final two terms, I still had six subjects to study and six exams to pass. And it was now a matter of priority to aim for the highest class of degree I could achieve. I was on course for a 2.1. But it would not be plain sailing and there were definite challenges ahead. In particular, how would I cope with all the maths required for the engineering geology module, the applied geophysics module and the laboratory-based applied geochemistry module?

In fact, I coped very well indeed, passing all six exams and achieving distinctions in three subjects, taking my tally to nine distinctions over the final two years of the course. I had my degree, and it was now only a question of what class. At the presentation of degree certificates on September 17th 1976, First Class Honours were awarded to only four of the fifty-seven students who passed the modular science degree that year – and I was one of them. I was the only geology student to get a First, and I had every reason to be proud. I knew that constant dedication and the sacrifices I had made were the factors that distinguished me from students who had more brainpower. Indeed, the two geology students I admired most had managed to lead balanced lives and still achieve a 2.1.

For once in my life I had come first. It felt so good. When I thought about my performance at school and the handicap I began with – even begging to get on the geology course – I felt elated at my achievement against all the odds. It was the realisation of a dream dimly perceived eight years ago when I started taking geology at school. And it was particularly important to get a First, since the outside world would discount the value of a degree from a polytechnic, even though it had been assessed externally by a national examining board.

Some months before the end of the course, it had seemed certain that I would get a degree. But when I began to think about my future, it brought awareness, even enlightenment that I would need to strive for a higher achievement. Entering the mundane world of employment was not the answer, especially in view of the state of the country. Harold Wilson had not solved any problems, and cynically but astutely he resigned to leave the hapless Jim Callaghan to deal with IRA terrorists, the unions, and a sick economy. I felt I should go further with my academic career. I had excelled in a formally taught course at a polytechnic, but now I wanted to progress to a respected university, carry out original work, and prove my ability to succeed in the self-structured and self-managed environment of academic research. A factor in my consideration was that only two per cent of school-leavers went on to take a PhD, and it certainly would be a high achievement if I succeeded.

I selected some interesting titles on the list of research topics for which government funding had been approved through NERC, a government organisation named the Natural Environment Research Council. In December the previous year I had visited Cambridge, Manchester and Newcastle universities for discussions with the particular professors, but was either rejected or decided that the subject matter or scope of the research was not sufficiently interesting. The research at Manchester, for example, was entirely laboratory-based, carrying out experiments to investigate a narrow and obscure issue to do with the chemistry of deep magma. I needed an opportunity that had wider implications, preferably that would involve fieldwork, such as the project chosen by my friend Mike McMurtry, who was going to St. Andrews University to do research on volcanic rocks in Wales.

Then, reviewing the NERC list at the end of the course, I noticed a late entry on the list of approved research topics. It was a hard rock project being offered by Chelsea College, one of the constituent colleges of the University of London. I wrote to the supervisor Dr Tony Barber on 15th June and received an application form and leaflet giving an outline of the research topic. In response to my application, a letter arrived from Dr Barber ten days later, stating that he had received 'extremely favourable references' from the referees, and would I please call him to arrange a visit to Chelsea. It went well, I was offered the post, and I accepted without hesitation.

REACHING HIGHER

Timor was a place that I had not heard of when I read the name on the list of research topics funded by NERC. Discovering that it was a small island situated in the Indonesian archipelago north of Australia had impelled me to apply, especially as the subject of the research combined my favourite specialisations, namely metamorphism and structural geology.

On my first day at Chelsea, I sat with my supervisor Tony and he outlined the immediate issues.

"The rocks on Timor are poorly exposed", he said. "I want you to go up to Scotland and study the well-exposed succession of metamorphic rocks along the Banffshire Coast. The geological history and types of rocks are analogous to those on Timor, and the experience will help you to recognise and unravel the complexities of Timor when you go there."

"And when will I go to Timor?" I asked.

"I have talked the matter over with Derek Blundell, our Head of Department, and the college will pay for one trip to Timor. You should plan to go towards the end of the dry season next year, sometime in August. This will give you about four months until the rainy season sets in around November and makes mapping impossible."

"But what about all the unanswered questions raised by the results of the first field season" I said, knowing from experience in Anglesey that there would be many loose ends and new ideas to follow up. "It can't be that expensive to fly to Indonesia."

"It's not just a question of the air fare, it's also the limitation that the grant is only for three years. If you have two field seasons, you won't have time to finish the work," he explained.

"So why can't I go there now, instead of Scotland?"

"It's already too late", Tony said. "We need to get you sponsored by the Indonesian authorities and then apply for a visa, and that could take weeks, if not months."

Tony was anxious for the work to start as soon as possible, and I had no time to find digs in London before going to Scotland on 11th August to begin fieldwork. It took me five weeks to complete my examination of the ten-mile stretch of wild coastline in northeast Scotland between Macduff and Cullen. I stayed in small hotels in the little coastal towns of Banff and Portsoy and, while in the bar of the Banff Springs Hotel, I got talking to a journalist working for the Aberdeen Press and Journal, the local daily newspaper in the Grampian region. He sensed a story and we spent a while talking about my background and why I was in the area. To my delight, a photograph and long article on me appeared in the paper on 20th August. Twelve column inches on Page 3 in the 'P&J' was quite a claim to fame!

Geological fieldwork was enjoyable and immensely interesting. I especially liked the freedom to decide my own priorities and pursue them, having only to deal with the physical constraints of tides, darkness and tiredness. Few people visited this part of Scotland and a whole day could pass without seeing another soul. Having solitude meant there were no distractions from the weighty issues that I had to contemplate. My thoughts were devoted to the challenge of deciphering the history of events that took place 400 to 500 million years ago, unseen at great depth beneath the surface. It was a jigsaw puzzle with many pieces missing, the task being to find a few and assemble them into larger fragments in order to identify the overall picture and fill in as much detail as possible using deductive and inductive reasoning with a variable sprinkling of inference and imagination. Indeed, imagination is an essential tool of the geologist, and a more important tool than the customary and iconic hammer, compass and hand lens. Visualising mountains forming, or hot rocks behaving like plasticine and being folded under immense pressure, or crystals forming in a cooling magma as it ascends from the bowels of the earth, were some of the many flights of fancy required in my profession.

And why study mountains and mountain building processes? A Dutch geologist named Rein van Bemmelen, that great authority on the geology of Indonesia, answered his own question:

"Mountain building provides the very basis of our existence on earth."[2]

He pointed out that the land under our feet would be eroded by sun and water and disappear under the waves were it not for the internal forces that created mountains. All life on the planet would be marine and man could not have evolved, let alone taken advantage of rocks and their minerals and metals to build cities, civilisations and machines.

Returning from Scotland, I found digs in Shepherds Bush at 61 Stanlake Road and moved in on 21st September. Chelsea College is situated in the trendy Kings Road, but the Geology Department was in an annexe along King Street in downbeat Hammersmith, near Ravenscourt Park tube station, and Shepherds Bush is just a short distance away by car or underground.

The first priority was the task of detailed microscope work to describe the minerals and textures in my rock samples and interpret the observations I had made in Scotland. There were no world-shattering revelations to report as a consequence of my five weeks fieldwork and subsequent cogitation. This was an unlikely prospect, as some of the most distinguished British geologists had spent years working the area, including professors H.H. Read, John Sutton and Janet Watson. It was the experience I gained that was the point of the trip, and the principal benefit. I had made a

---

2. R.W. van Bemmelen, 1954. *Mountain Building.* Martinus Nijhoff, The Hague, pp 177.

traverse across an ancient plate boundary and the site where early concepts about metamorphism had been hatched and then verified across the world.

I had been mapping The Dalradian, a series of metamorphic rocks named in 1891 by Sir Archibald Geikie after the old Celtic region of Dál Riata. The term Dalradian was applied as a convenient designation to the complicated group of rocks in Scotland to which it was difficult to assign a definite position in the stratigraphical sequence, meaning that it was difficult to ascertain the relative age of the different components and thus establish a chronology of events. The Dalradian was deformed and metamorphosed during the Caledonian Orogeny in a wide belt of crust that extends from the coast of Aberdeenshire northwards through Norway and the east coast of Greenland, and westwards across Scotland to Canada, all of which were parts of a continuous landmass before the opening of the North Atlantic in Jurassic times.

In 1893, Scottish geologist George Barrow established that there were systematic changes in the mineralogy and texture of the Dalradian rocks that recorded a sequence of increasing metamorphic intensity in zones or belts. The progression from lowest to highest metamorphism is characterised by the successive appearance of index minerals in the sequence chlorite > biotite > garnet > staurolite > kyanite > sillimanite at the highest temperature, and is termed Barrovian metamorphism. With variations that depend on the composition of the rocks, Barrovian metamorphism has been documented across the world and is normally associated with the collision of two continents. I walked across the Barrovian sequence from the chlorite zone to the sillimanite zone, where the contemporaneous intrusion of hot granites and partial melting of the host rock had complicated the picture. Because it was controversial and relevant to my work on Timor, I paid particular attention to the debate surrounding the late crystallisation of the mineral sillimanite, and collected samples for observation under the microscope.

At more than sixty pages of text in length, my project report was quite substantial, and generously supported by hand-drawn figures, photographs taken in the field, and photomicrographs taken of minerals and rock textures under the microscope. It took me ages to type the report on a golfball typewriter that luckily had a cunning mechanical overtyping facility that enabled me to erase the frequent mistakes with a white correcting ribbon. The report was completed in the first week of January, and attention now turned to planning and preparing for the trip to Timor.

Timor is underdeveloped. It has a subsistence economy based on simple agrarian technologies and techniques, and a social system that has impeded progress and modernisation. Soil erosion, low yields and malnutrition are particular problems, exacerbated by unfavourable physical conditions, particularly the unpredictable monsoons. Chinese merchants visited the island at least two hundred years before the arrival of European trading powers in the early 16th century. Chinese traders came for the fragrant sandalwood that used to be abundant on the island. Timor was renowned for growing *Santalum album*, the high quality species of sandalwood much prized by the Chinese, who used the oil in religious ceremonies and the wood to make items of furniture and ornamental boxes. The neighbouring island of Sumba was known as Sandalwood Island, and it was sandalwood that attracted the Portuguese to the region and the Dutch a hundred years later. Portuguese merchants established trading arrangements with China through their colony of Macau near Hong Kong, whereby Sandalwood was traded for silk and other items much valued in Europe.

Exploitation and control of trade in the region was not an easy affair for the colonial powers. In the 1840s, an English explorer named George Windsor Earl, perhaps a distant relative of mine, travelled to the region on HMS Alligator and helped to found a colonial base named Port Essington on the coast of northern Australia. In correspondence archived at the Royal Geographical Society in Kensington, Earl mentions that the Dutch governor in

Kupang on Timor had attacked Sandalwood Island with 300 natives from Roti Island, and intended making Sumba a Dutch colony. He further records that the Dutch were frequently attacked by groups of natives on horseback, and were attacked by tribes on the nearby island of Flores when they landed there to cut sandalwood.

I was heading for the western portion of Timor island. Until the Dutch instigated active pacification in 1915, their control over West Timor had been restricted to a narrow coastal strip around Fort Concordia on the western extreme of the island. It had been a land divided into a dozen small princedoms, often at war over boundary disputes, and occasionally united as the Sonba'i Kingdom. During the pacification, the Dutch established garrisons at several locations, and Dutch control ended the tribal wars. Headhunting raids, however, persisted up to the Second World War and the Japanese occupation. In 1949, the Dutch ceded control and West Timor became incorporated into the Republic of Indonesia.

By way of contrast, the eastern portion of Timor remained a backwater after the Portuguese reclaimed it from the Japanese. Then, in 1974, a coup d'état in Portugal ended the dictatorial regime, and the incoming socialist government vowed to dismantle the country's colonial empire. East Timor was set adrift and three political parties emerged from the vacuum, causing alarm in Indonesia because the two most popular parties favoured independence. Tension built up, to the point when Indonesian troops invaded the capital Dili in December 1975, a month after Fretilin forces had seized the town and declared independence. Indonesia established a provisional government in Dili, and began fighting for control of what became the 27th state. In 1977, at the time I was planning to visit the island, the conflict was raging, the border was closed, and the situation was a highly sensitive issue for the Indonesian government, despite covert approval by governments in the USA, Britain and Australia.

GEARING UP

Back from Scotland, my life returned to its normal mix of romance, socialising and studying. In my rejuvenated state, I also returned to my habit of going to the cinema, and especially enjoyed seeing the romantic Streisand-Kristofferson movie *A Star is Born*, the hilarious Mel Brooks comedy *Blazing Saddles*, and a great Jack Nicholson movie *The Last Detail*. The Pompeii AD79 exhibition was on at the Royal Academy. It was so fascinating that I went twice, once in February by myself and then in March with my mother, afterwards taking tea with her in the Café Royal in Piccadilly. April, May and June were especially busy months, including a nine-day field trip to Anglesey with the undergraduate students, for which I was the teaching assistant and driver of the Ford Transit minibus.

Unusually for me, I went to an assortment of football matches, including with my father to an exciting 3-3 draw between Fulham and Swindon Town in the FA Cup. Amazingly, Swindon won 5-0 in the replay, despite Fulham fielding George Best, the country's best footballer, as well as Bobby Moore and Geoff Hurst, two heroes from England's 1966 World Cup winning team! Rob Noyes and I went to White Hart Lane to watch QPR thrash Manchester United 4-0. Having spent a few years in the wilderness, including a period driving articulated trucks, Rob was now working as a laboratory technician in the Geology Department at St Marks College in London. I saw him occasionally, but unfortunately not often enough, because he commuted by train every weekday from Chippenham.

Despite the apparent normality, my situation had changed since being an undergraduate. In effect, I now had a job and was in receipt of a grant of £2,000 a year to complete a three-year project. There were no academic terms and no long breaks to spend back in Chippenham or travel around Europe. I was manager of my time and priorities, and thankfully not part of an imposing corporate structure with many levels of control. However, postgraduates were considered by the college to belong to the establishment, and I was required to participate to the extent of giving occasional lectures to the undergraduates, which I did. And to earn extra money, I worked as a Demonstrator in the practical geology classes, where 'demonstrator' meant teaching assistant to Tony. I was on hand to answer students' questions and help them identify minerals under the microscope. In practice, I took most of the sessions alone, as Tony always seemed to have other interests to pursue.

Regarding work preparation, Tony and I visited Cornwall for six days to examine the Lizard Complex, an assemblage of igneous and metamorphic rock types that also occur in the mountains of Timor. I also examined the archive of metamorphic rocks that Tony had collected on two previous fieldtrips to Timor and other islands in Eastern Indonesia. And I read the few English language publications that had been written about the metamorphic rocks of Timor and their complex tectonic history.

I needed maps. A geological map is prepared on an accurate topographic base annotated with geographical and cultural information such as contours, rivers, roads, towns and villages. I would need a set of base maps to orientate and navigate on the ground and to record information accurately. The problem was that the 1:100,000 Dutch maps of 1920s vintage were hopelessly inaccurate and incomplete. What was available was a set of 1:50,000 drainage maps constructed from aerial photographs taken in 1968 by an oil exploration company. Unfortunately, there were no contours and the scale of the photographs was too small to be of use to me for detailed navigation and mapping in the field. Molo mountain, for example, was nine kilometres long but only twelve centimetres in length on the photograph.

Tony told me that Professor Mike Audley-Charles of University College London had maps and aerial photographs of the entire island. Mike A-C had carried out fieldwork in East

Timor for his own PhD in the late 1960s, and he was acknowledged as the leading authority on the geology of Timor. He was also the central figure in an academic group carrying out research in Eastern Indonesia through three colleges at the University of London. I called him and he invited me to his house in Sussex. We sat in his study, a treasure-trove of mementos collected from Timor, Ceram, Buton and other islands in the region.

"Your research will be very important", he said. "I have seen some of the metamorphic complexes in Timor, but mapping them is not my area of expertise and it is more than twenty years since anyone has studied any of them in detail."

In West Timor, metamorphic rocks outcrop in thirteen individual mountains of different sizes, rising up to 2500 metres above sea level, and scattered along the length of the island north of a central belt of lowland. A Dutch expedition under Brouwer had examined and sampled six massifs in 1937, but not carried out systematic mapping or division into different rock units. In the 1950s, Dutch geologist Waard made a detailed study of two other massifs, Mosu and Lalan Asu, but no further research had been undertaken since then. It made more sense to extend the knowledge base and make my own discoveries, and therefore I intended to avoid the areas described in some detail by Waard and concentrate on Boi and Molo, two massifs examined briefly by German geologist Dietrich Tappenbeck during the 1937 Expedition.

"I plan to map Molo and Boi, as the brief written account by Tappenbeck indicates they harbour key pieces of information about the geology of the island", I said.

"Mike, you're more than welcome to take the photographs you need and have copies made, but please treat the originals with care, and return them as soon as possible, because I don't know of anyone else who has a set."

Tony was a member of the 'London School'. He specialised in

tectonics and metamorphic rocks, and had taken part in fieldtrips to Timor, Seram and other islands in the region. Tony had worked his way up from undergraduate, to part-time lecturer studying for his PhD, to full-time member of staff at Chelsea. A sprightly man now in his forties, Tony looked distinguished with a hawk-like nose and streaks of greying hair on his temples. He had extensive field experience in different areas of the world and particular knowledge of the regions of Britain that had complex geology, such as Cornwall, Anglesey and Scotland.

I shared an office with Laurie Richards, a fellow research student, also studying metamorphic rocks with Tony as supervisor, but in Brittany. Laurie and I became friends, sometimes dining at his flat in Tooting Beck with Sarah and Laurie's wife, and sometimes relieving the pressure of research by going to local pubs in Hammersmith. Laurie and I shared an interest in F1 motor racing, and on July 16th we set off for Silverstone to attend the British Grand Prix, armed with tickets procured by my father through a connection with Castrol. Two long-haired, bearded and scruffy students enjoyed the corporate hospitality in the Marquee at the rear of the Main Pits Grandstand, including a bar, luncheon and tea. During the race, I took a set of photographs featuring the back of spectators' heads and blurred images of tiny racing cars that appeared in the background between ears and on top of heads. But never mind, I didn't need the pictures to remember the occasion because the crowd atmosphere, the engine noise and the smell of petrol and scorched rubber were intoxicating and addictive. And it was a good time to be a British fan. James Hunt was current World Champion, and he won the race at Silverstone that day, crossing the line in a McLaren M26 ahead of Nikki Lauda in a Ferrari.

And what of Sarah? Since graduating with me from the poly the year before, she had started an M.Sc. in Geophysics at Imperial College, one of the top British colleges, especially for engineering and science. Sarah had a good brain for mathematics and liked mathematics-orientated subjects such as geophysics. Taking the

M.Sc. at Imperial almost guaranteed her a well-paid job in the oil industry. She was living in a charming mews cottage in Notting Hill, not far from me in Shepherds Bush. In the first few months of the year, Sarah and I split up and got back together again twice, but a stable period followed in May, after I went to have a meal at the mews. On that weekend, we spent a sunny day at Hampton Court. She looked so gorgeous. The sun had bleached her long brown hair and a few strands blew provocatively across her eyes; her trim body was clothed in a white Calico dress, see-through in a certain light. Simply enchanting!

We spent the following Sunday in Regents Park and at London Zoo, before going to see Gilbert O'Sullivan in concert at the Drury Lane Theatre. Animals were clearly a favourite choice that summer, because we also visited Windsor Safari Park and, later, Bristol Zoo with my parents and elder sister Diana, her husband and young daughter. I persuaded Sarah to go to a Saloon Car Racing Festival at Brands Hatch, which was the venue for British Grand Prix in alternate years with Silverstone. This was our last date before Sarah began a work experience assignment with the Institute of Geological Sciences in July. And when she returned, there was precious little time to spend together before I departed for Timor.

FINAL PREPARATIONS

'Selamat Pagi, aka kabar?' ('Good morning, how are you?')
'Saya baik sekali, terimah kasih.' ('I am very well, thank you')

Tony had arranged for me to learn Bahasa Indonesia, the language of the country. More correctly it is the lingua franca of Indonesia, a country with hundreds of indigenous languages among the many different ethnic peoples who inhabit only a few of the 12,000 islands in the archipelago; Timor alone has twenty languages. Indonesian was being spread across the country through thousands of schools set up by the government as a central component in their plan to unify the disparate nation, and it was important that I was able to understand the basics.

My teacher was Frans Hardy, an Indonesian who worked for BBC Radio at Bush House in Aldwych. I started lessons in the BBC canteen at the end of April, seeing Frans one afternoon a week for the next six weeks. He introduced me to the street or market form of the language, which would enable me to make basic conversation. It seemed to be easy to learn, though I knew it would not sink in properly until I had to use the language in earnest.

In April, I was inoculated against smallpox, cholera, typhoid and paratyphoid, and in May I began a course of anti-malaria tablets. My visa application was submitted to the Indonesian Embassy at the start of June, with the expectation that it would take a week or two to obtain and that I would be able to leave in early July. In Timor, the wet monsoon would arrive in November, turning rivers into dangerous torrents and effectively putting an end to fieldwork, and therefore I planned to have approximately four months of mapping to make the endeavour worthwhile.

But it was now July 31st and I had no idea when my visa would be granted. The waiting seemed interminable. I debated with myself whether I should go to Indonesia, or return to Scotland and continue the study I had begun the previous year. My research along the Banffshire coast had given me plenty of ideas, and there was much to follow up. If the visa didn't arrive soon, it would be too late to go to Timor, and my PhD about Timor would be stillborn. I had weighed the pros and cons on many occasions in preceding weeks, but after so much agonising deliberation, I finally made a decision to go to Scotland.

I packed that night and set out for Scotland the following day, stopping in Nottingham to stay overnight with my sister Tricia and her family. I wrote, 'PhD one year – and nothing to show for it!'

While all this was going on, Tony received some important

news. He tracked me down by telephoning my parents to find out where I was, and rang my sister the day I arrived at her house, to say that authorisation for my visa had been granted.

"It's too late to change my mind", I told Tony when I returned his call.

However, I agonised over the changed circumstances for the rest of the day, and could not sleep after I went to bed that night. At two in the morning, I got up, packed, dressed and drove back to London. I slept a little at home before taking a tube train to the Indonesian Embassy to submit my passport, then travelled to the British Airways office in Regent Street to book an open-ended flight to Jakarta. It was better, I decided, to take the exciting option that would definitely turn out to be a unique experience. Only a handful of geologists had been to Timor, and few, if any, would go in the future to study the metamorphic rocks, which had no intrinsic commercial value. Moreover, there was real adventure, even kudos, in experiencing that which few others could or would. Many more explorers had conquered Everest than had been to the mountains of Timor.

Next day, I returned to the embassy to collect my passport, replete with that elusive Visa, and afterwards went shopping to buy a rucksack and other items for the trip. There was time the following week for a visit to Chippenham to see my parents, and on Sunday August 14th my father drove me to Heathrow and I boarded BA888 bound for Singapore.

QUEST

Planet earth is covered by a mosaic of interlocking rigid pieces termed 'tectonic plates'. Tectonic plates are up to 300 kilometres thick and composed of a thick lower layer termed the mantle, and a relatively thin upper layer known as the earth's crust. In places, the crust is composed of crystalline metamorphic and granitic rocks that form the continents and is typically 35 kilometres thick; under the oceans, however, the crust is made of dense, basaltic rocks and is typically 7 kilometres thick, much thinner than under the continents. Immense forces inside the earth act on the base of the tectonic plates and cause them to move horizontally at imperceptible but measurable rates of up to 10 centimetres a year. This seems, and is, a small separation over our human timescale, but amounts to a 'gap' of 100 kilometres in a million years, and the plates have been moving around for hundreds of millions, if not billions of years. This decoupling of the plates from the deeper interior of the earth occurs where the dense, magnesium and iron-rich rocks of the mantle are hot enough to melt, which is at a temperature close to 1300°C.

Where two plates move apart, molten matter rises from within the earth and cools to form a new oceanic crust, and in places it creates spectacular volcanic islands rising thousands of metres above the ocean floor, such as Iceland. Conversely, where two plates move together, one plate is pushed down to great depths, a process that is termed 'subduction'. In this way, matter is recycled and the size of the planet stays the same. Subduction happens to the basaltic crust of the oceans and underlying mantle, and the plate commonly descends at angles between 30° and 60°.

Sediments that are deposited on the oceanic crust are scraped off the downgoing, lower plate, and become attached to the underside of the upper plate. In this way, the seafloor sediments accumulate to form a thick wedge or prism that is deformed and metamorphosed in the belt of convergence.

Although the old crust is cold and brittle as it enters the site of subduction it becomes hot and malleable as it descends to great depths. Minerals become unstable as pressure and temperatures change, and they begin to break down and transform or metamorphose into new assemblages of minerals by diffusion of the chemical elements such as silica, magnesium, calcium, iron and aluminium. At depths exceeding 100 kilometres, a fraction of the crust melts and generates a low density liquid that rises and cools at shallow levels as giant bodies of granite, and also erupts at the surface as lava. Consequently, sites of subduction are marked by a chain of volcanoes that function as vents or chimneys for the columns of magma. A good example is the Indonesian archipelago, that extends more than 3,000 kilometres from Sumatra in the Indian Ocean, to Sulawesi in the western Pacific. It has 100 active and 300 inactive but recent volcanoes. A narrow trough develops at the site of convergence where the lower plate descends beneath the upper plate, resulting in stupendous depths of water up to 11 kilometres as in the Marianas Trough east of Japan.

Continents are a special case. They consist of a crust that has a high concentration of light elements such as silica. Continental crust is therefore buoyant relative to the heavier crust that lies beneath oceans, and which has higher concentrations of iron and magnesium, and it does not get recycled in the bowels of the earth. Instead, when the leading edge of a continent reaches a site of subduction it remains near the surface, and the immense forces pushing the plates together cause the crust to bend, buckle and break, creating mountains comprised of stacked sheets or slices of crustal material and mantle. Before the widespread acceptance of the theory of plate tectonics in the 1970s some geoscientists thought that continents moved across the face of the earth as independent entities, a concept termed continental drift. However, it became known that continents form an upper but partial layer 'welded' to the tectonic plates, and therefore their horizontal motion across the face of the earth is controlled by the thick plate on which they sit.

The Indonesian archipelago is the site of a boundary between two plates that have been moving together for at least 120 million years. For most of this long period, the plate moving northwards was subducting beneath the plate carrying the continent of Asia. However, the northward-moving plate carries the continent of Australia–New Guinea, and about ten million years ago, the leading edge of this continent reached the site of subduction and began to buckle and fold. This deformation of the rocks was so intense that the crust was sliced into gigantic blocks by low-angle ruptures termed 'thrust faults'. The detached blocks were then pushed as sheets of rock over one another and the leading edge of the continental crust of the Australia–New Guinea plate. Loosely compacted sediment sitting on the ocean floor between the plates was unstable, and mobilised and flowed over, under and around the sheets of hard rock, creating a messy, chaotically arranged mixture (mélange) of ingredients. Horizontal compression and vertical uplift took place as convergence of the plates continued unabated for millions of years, and the mélange rose with the thrust sheets above the sea bed. This explains the formation of Timor and other islands that form a chain between the subduction zone and an inner arc of volcanic islands in Eastern Indonesia. So, in fact, there are two parallel chains of islands on the upper plate, and in the Indonesian region they curve around in an anticlockwise swirl centred on the Banda Sea, and for this reason are known to earth scientists as the Banda Arc.

During the 1970s, a number of universities from the UK, USA, Australia and Japan were carrying out geological, geophysical and geochemical research programmes in the Banda Arc region. A key topic of many programmes was to investigate, analyse, discuss and debate the tectonic development and structure of the collision zone in Eastern Indonesia, which from the early days of exploration had been recognised as highly complex and controversial. There were currently three different and mutually incompatible concepts regarding the geological evolution and structure of Timor and the adjacent islands in the outer, non-volcanic chain of islands in Eastern Indonesia.

Dr Alex Grady and his PhD research student Ron Berry at Flinders University in Adelaide had studied in detail the metamorphic rocks that outcrop along the north coast of the island, and had developed the *autochthon model.* They asserted that, apart from some superficial deposits, the rocks exposed on Timor are Australian continental crust and sediments that have been pushed up to the surface on a set of steep faults consequent to the collision ten million years ago, and aided by a vertical rebound of the relatively light continental mass. In contrast, a group from London University, led by Professor Mike Audley Charles, were proponents of the *overthrust model,* in which the margin of the Australian continent was pushed down under the weight of a set or stack of thrust sheets comprised of rocks derived from Indonesia, again followed by a rapid buoyant rebound of the thickened pile of rocks. A German geologist named Wanner first aired the idea of overthrust sheets in 1913, after a visit to the island during an early Dutch expedition. Then there was the *imbricate model* of Dr Warren Hamilton of the United States Geological Survey, who postulated that the structure of Timor is a chaotic mix or mélange of rocks from both plates, a model that had some support from the field investigations carried out in the 1950s by Dutchman Dirk de Waard, a specialist in metamorphic geology. Waard re-assessed the structure of Timor and proposed that the metamorphic and igneous rocks, plus their sedimentary cover, existed as dispersed, lenticular bodies in a mélange that was emplaced onto the Australian continental margin, and then collapsed under the weight of gravity, causing further disruption and chaos in the pile of rocks.

You could be forgiven for asking what the fuss is about, and who cares anyway, and the answer still might not impress you.

There was the egoistic-cum-altruistic need to make a discovery that contributes to the body of knowledge about the planet. With the advent of the theory of plate tectonics, geology transformed itself from a largely descriptive science, to a *predictive* one. (Indeed, it is debatable whether it was a science at all before the 20th Century). It came of age with plate tectonics, principally through the emergence and acceptance of geophysical techniques applied to the concept of continental drift pioneered in 1915 by visionary German geologist Alfred Wegner. Plate tectonics became a coherent theory in 1968, just at the moment I started to study geology in the Sixth Form at school, and it was becoming widely accepted during the period I was at university in the 1970s. All prevailing concepts and data had to be scrutinised and reinterpreted, and new fields of research emerged in the science. The new paradigm stimulated frenetic activity among earth scientists of all disciplines, and I, too, became entrained in the exciting wave of research and discovery that developed.

Another consideration was that Eastern Indonesia provides earth scientists with a rare opportunity to investigate and even observe processes, events and consequences at a collisional boundary that involves continental crust, and which is in the early stages of a major mountain-building episode. *Sensu lata*, the Indonesian region belongs to the Alpine-Carpathian-Zagros-Himalayan mountain belt, but the collision at Timor occurred more than 20 million years later than in Europe or the Indian Sub-Continent. The importance of studying Timor is that in some or many respects it might be a valuable aid to unravelling complexities where evidence has been destroyed by later events.

Finally, in a narrow sense, there was the practical issue of testing which of the three models of the Timor region provided the 'best fit' to the evidence, or whether a hybrid was more appropriate. Invariably in earth science, no single theory is entirely right or wrong, but the precise point of research, reflection and debate is to test arguments and stimulate the search for evidence that leads ever closer to the truth, and to a comprehensive understanding that receives widespread support.

Now *I* was attached to the research programme of the 'London School', and at the threshold of going into the unknown in search of evidence and truth.

IN JAVA

Nothing could have prepared me for the new experiences that would excite my senses and test my resilience during the coming months. No amount of listening to those who knew, no photographs, no documentary could be a substitute for the impact of direct encounters.

My adventure began while I listened to Pink Floyd as the aeroplane took off and climbed steeply into the night sky over London, piercing the envelope of comfort in which I lived, and hurtling me into the unknown and an uncharted future. I fidgeted with excitement, I stared out of the window, but the darkness only heightened my sense of going into a void, and the familiarity of the inside of an aircraft seemed out of place with my thoughts.

A surreal scene was waiting for me at Bahrain airport at 5 o'clock in the morning and under 30°C heat. Bland concrete buildings rose in the air and were barely distinguishable from their sand-coloured surroundings. It was as though the structures were audacious offspring of the desert that would one day crumble and disappear into the landscape when there was no more water. Then, only the rusting hulks of giant American automobiles would remain as evidence that man had been here.

Captain Newman replaced Captain Bunyon for the leg to Singapore. I ate a 'horrifically gruesome' continental breakfast, and then watched another B movie. In Singapore I changed to a Singapore Airlines flight for the short hop to Jakarta. It was short, but sweet, since free champagne was on offer before take-off, and various other freebies were available for the taking, including airmail letters, playing cards, postcards, free postage and wine with the meal. Not bad for Cattle Class travel.

A geologist named Michael Bunter met me at Jakarta airport, and his driver Maman drove us home to the expatriate refuge of the Kemang district. Arriving at the house, I was introduced to the national Indonesian beer, a pilsner that started as Heineken but was now named Bintang, which meant 'star'. I shared several with my host while we chatted. Mike worked for American oil company Conoco, but was a graduate of the University of London and I supposed that Tony Barber had used a Mike A-C connection to set up this arrangement for me.

I would need to visit several different government organisations and find a way through a bureaucratic obstacle course. In the morning, after a breakfast of boiled eggs, toast and milk, I was driven to the British Embassy to register being in the country, to the Police Headquarters and then to LIPI, which is the National Academy of Geology and Mining, the organisation that was sponsoring my trip to Timor. They said that I required a Semi-Permanent Residents Visa, or VBS, that would be valid for six months, but the next day was a National Holiday celebrating the 32nd Anniversary of Independence from Dutch occupation, and therefore no-one would bother to process my application today; I would have to return in two days time.

Jakarta made a good impression on me. There were tree-lined streets, colonial-style bungalows set in large grounds, huge clusters of brightly coloured tropical flowers, and beautiful mosques. Nevertheless, this definitely was the third world. Behind both sides of Jalan Thamrin, the main road through the business district, there were gigantic open sewers, in places fringed by shantytowns. Across the city, millions of people were milling about. On the pavement, I was accosted by the enticing smell of noodles and sticks of chicken satay emanating from food prepared on wooden barrows and makeshift stalls, and the roads were alive with the movement and noise of bicycles, mopeds and cars, as well as donkeys pulling rickety carts. 'Bustling' was hardly the word: more like 'boiling' with activity. After the enforced holiday, I went to the police again, then the office of the Director of Immigration, then LIPI, then back to immigration, then back to LIPI. It now transpired that the VBS was not what I needed, but a Residence Permit known as a KIM card, and for this, I would need to travel inland to the city of Bandung.

Mike's driver Maman took me to Gambir railway station. Going to Bandung by train was a fascinating experience. In Jakarta, the train rumbled slowly through squalid shanties, where people lived beside the track in precarious shelters assembled from cardboard boxes, plastic sheeting and any other scrap material that afforded some privacy and protection from sun and rain. Java was a highly crowded island, the home of 100 million people living a predominantly rural existence. The city acted like a powerful magnet, constantly attracting migrants from the countryside, the fate of extreme poverty and unsanitary conditions surely being worse than the impoverished rural conditions they had left behind; but in the city, they at least had a small if improbable chance of succeeding in the urban lottery for a better life.

Once outside the sprawling metropolis, the train snaked across the coastal lowlands and followed a swathe cut through the carpet of iridescent green padi fields, shimmering in the blazing sunlight, and gradually but surely approached the hazy, purple, volcanic mountains where Bandung lay. Enchanting! Inside the cool, clean and modern train, hot, sweet tea was served in a tall glass with a metal lid that kept out little flying beasts. Outside, shouting and laughing children emerged from behind trees and lined the tracks at every kampung (village) on the way, forming a noisy, bubbling eruption of brown faces and flashing white teeth. For them, a passing train was an event, an opportunity to relieve the monotony of playing without the luxury of toys.

Four hours out of Jakarta and one hour late, the journey ended at Bandung station. A crowd waited in anticipation of earning some money, shouting to the passengers for attention. They were the army of boys and young men who could transport you to wherever you wanted to go in town, either by taxi or becak ('baychak'), the three-wheeled rickshaw; or they were 'agents' who merely escorted you to a taxi or becak and expected a tip. I decided to walk to find a hotel. I didn't yet trust myself to negotiate a fair price and would be really cross with myself if I later discovered I'd been ripped off.

I strode out towards the centre of the sprawling city of 1.5 million inhabitants, astonished that a place unknown at home had a population greater than any city in Britain except London. Stately public buildings were testaments to former colonial days, standing like the pyramids of Egypt as glorious remnants of a former advanced civilisation in the dreary chaos of the backward present one. Bandung had been the centre of Dutch power in Indonesia because it was situated at altitude some distance from the coast, rendering the climate more tolerable for the white administrators, and lowering the risk of dying from a range of horrible diseases that had no cure, then as now in the example of malaria. Dutch planters had introduced coffee, tea and a variety of fruits and vegetables, and many shops, cafes and hotels had sprouted up in Bandung to serve them.

The Grand Hotel Preanger on Jalan (street) Asia-Afrika caught my attention. In return for a room with breakfast, I handed over 6,000 Rupiah, which cost $15 at the prevailing exchange rate of about 400 Rupiah to the dollar. My bedroom had a private bathroom and a separate lounge, as well as a friendly yellow gecko behind the curtain. I dispatched the large cockroach skulking in the wardrobe, leaving the squashed remains in situ as a warning to its friends and relatives, or as a meal for the little reptile.

Back out on the street, I absorbed the wonderful atmosphere of the city, the crowds, the noise and the smells. Bandung was alive with a throng of people walking, talking, watching, loitering, cycling, cooking, selling, hustling, begging. Right in the centre of town, a prostitute called me from the other side of the street. I walked on, but felt curious and stopped to talk to the next one. She held my hand and started a conversation.

"Saya tidak tahu", I said, meaning no, though the literal translation was 'I don't know.'

Back at the hotel, an attendant lurking outside my room offered the services of a masseuse: 2,000 Rupiah. or $5 for an hour, and 10,000 Rupiah for the night. I got my satisfaction by saying "besok", meaning tomorrow, because I had already learnt that this was a polite Indonesian way of declining a difficult or otherwise unpalatable request. It avoided disappointing the other person when turning them down, because it kept open the possibility that their wish could be granted at some unspecified point in the future!

Friday's breakfast comprised of runny boiled eggs and tea without milk, set on a filthy tablecloth adorned with dirty tableware. I walked miles to the *Departemen Imigrasi*, only to purchase some forms I later found out I would not need. I began to tire of all the bureaucracy, and left to go to the Geological Survey of Indonesia (GSI) for help. This was a sensible move. Dr Hartono, the Director, offered to assist and delegated the task to Soebardjo, a senior officer, who delegated it to junior officer named Suwiyanto, or Yanto for short, to begin helping the next day.

My feet are killing me, perhaps I have walked ten kilometres today. Back at the hotel, I peeled off my socks and relaxed. I have been so focussed on getting the admin done, and so busy bouncing back and forth between government departments in this game of bureaucratic ping-pong that, except for the light breakfast I suffered this morning, I have not eaten for two days.

From the hotel, I walked west along Jalan Asia-Africa, then north on Jalan Braga, finding a Korean restaurant where I enjoyed a splendid meal, choosing the dishes from a set of photographs and washing the whole lot down with a cold Bintang.

Saturday's eggs were identical to Friday's, despite my admonition that they should be cooked for five minutes. I walked to the Geological Survey and borrowed a driver to go to LIPI, meeting Yanto, who helped with the forms. My next port of call was immigration, where I parted with 1,000 Rupiah and had every fingerprint and thumbprint taken twice, and in triplicate, presumably for three different departments or as a pragmatic precaution against inevitable loss of up to two sets. Britain could certainly learn from the Indonesians about job creation schemes. Formalities completed, I was assured that the KIM Card would be ready in a few days, and Yanto volunteered to collect it and bring it to Jakarta for me. Progress!

Not only had Hartono assigned Yanto to assist in Bandung, but he had also decided that Yanto needed some experience in the field, and therefore that he would accompany me to Timor. While in Bandung, I heard that Dr Alex Grady from Flinders University in Australia had been denied permission to go to East or West Timor that year, despite the fact that his university was sponsoring an active geological research programme in the region. Dr Grady had been in East Timor at the time of the Indonesian invasion, and been evacuated to Atauro Island in a boat hired by Australian media magnate Kerry Packer. I concluded that Dr Grady was *persona non grata*, despite the Australian government's tacit support for the invasion. However, as I later found out, no foreign geologists were being allowed into East Timor, and I believe that my visit to West Timor had passed through a loophole in the bureaucratic procedures.

I returned to Jakarta on the train that evening, taking a taxi to Mike's house. He told me that a major earthquake of magnitude 8.3 on the Richter Scale had struck Eastern Indonesia three days earlier, and caused a Tsunami on the islands of Bali, Sumba and Lombok, close to Timor. Tragically, about a hundred and fifty people had died. Some had wanted to catch fish that became stranded on the foreshore when the sea pulled back in advance of the incoming wave, and those people paid the price with their lives. Anxious to let my parents know that I was safe, the following morning I walked to the main Post Office situated in Pasar Baru and sent them a telegram.

QUAKE FAR AWAY OK HERE BON VOYAGE LOVE MIKE

Terse, it's true, but words cost money and I was confident that the message would be appreciated and understood. I also had some letters and postcards to send, but was not sure how this was done. I studied the activities of the customers before making a move. In the middle of the expansive floor of the imposing public building was a long table with large plastic bowls of glue atop. Three principal techniques were in use that day. Either the stamp was dabbed into the bowl to get sticky, or glue was spread on the table and the stamp rubbed over the sticky patch, or a finger was inserted into the bowl and glue spread with some accuracy over the back of the stamp. After gluing was complete, letters were being carried to one of two men sitting unassailably high on stools on either side of the entrance. Their job was to frank stamps with a wooden gavel. I opted for the glue on the table approach, and then handed over my postcards as I left, making sure that they were franked first, just in case someone decided to re-use the stamps and throw away my precious correspondence.

That evening, I wanted to take my host out for a meal, to show appreciation for his hospitality. Mike drove the two of us to a Korean restaurant in Block M district and ordered frogs' legs, spicy crabs' claws, nasi goreng (fried rice) and Bintang. Perhaps it was predictable that the result was a night spent on the toilet, but the positive aspect of the enforced nocturnal vigil was that I enjoyed reading *One Flew over the Cuckoos Nest* that I borrowed from Mike's bookcase.

This delay in Java, on top of the previous wait in England, cut the time available for field research by at least a third. I was so disconsolate, that the situation was constantly on my mind tormenting me. However, there was nothing more that I could do in Jakarta to speed up the bureaucracy, so I returned to Bandung to spend more time at the Geological Survey; at least there, by talking to the geologists, I could add to my knowledge of Indonesia and perhaps Timor.

By coincidence or providence, while queuing for a ticket at Gambir Station I was recognised and approached by Dr Fred Hehuwat, the Director of LIPI, who invited me to stay at his house in Bandung. Fred was a Dutch-educated Indonesian with a good command of English, and had travelled widely in the course of pursuing geology. His Dutch wife Dolly was welcoming and friendly, and she served a delicious dinner that night. Yanto came to the house, and we three men chatted all evening. We talked about my KIM Card. Reading between the lines, I surmised that the man dealing with my application had been caught taking unauthorised levies (bribes), and then dispatched to Jakarta. This, apparently, explained the delay in issuing the card. I wasn't sure whether the delay had occurred because the next man hadn't been bribed to complete the task, or because the first man had gone and no-one had bothered to go through his in-tray, but I felt that further questioning would not be polite or fruitful.

Breakfast next morning was delicious, consisting of porridge eaten with a heap of tasty, raw palm sugar, followed by toast with slices of water buffalo tongue. Yanto and I went to Immigration, but the card was not ready. Then from Fred's house, I took a short walk to the River Cikapundung, where women were washing clothes on stones and joyous children were bathing nude, a timeless sight. It was here that the remains of *Homo erectus* or 'Java Man' had been discovered, and it was humbling to think that distant cousins had inhabited the area at least 800,000 years ago.

Back at Fred's house, I took an Indonesian-style bath. In the corner of the bathroom was a walled enclosure that contained water. I picked up the long-handled pot from the top of the wall, dunked it in the water and tipped the cold contents over my body. It was a chilling but invigorating experience! Cunningly, the water fell on the sloping tiled floor and disappeared down a hole in the corner of the room. The toilet was a hole in the ground, only suitable for a crouched position, and no tissues, just clean up with water and the left hand. This presented no particular problem to me, since I had been to France several times!

After a couple of days, I sensed that my presence made the house crowded and was causing some tension among the family, so I arranged to go to a larger residence in the same street, a house occupied by an elderly couple from New Zealand. Friday's breakfast at the Ritchie's consisted of papaya followed by a main course of toast topped with Marmite and cheddar cheese; I could have been at home in England!

Another day of enforced leisure. Fred and Suparka picked me up in a Toyota Land Cruiser and they took me to a volcano about an hour's drive away. Java is an island of volcanoes, and Tangkuban Prahu or 'upturned boat' is the nearest active volcano to Bandung, only 30km north of the city. We walked some of the way down inside the crater to a solfatara that was spewing out white sulphurous smoke that smelt of rotten eggs.

On Saturday, I walked to Immigration to see if there was any progress in the application, and waited around until my KIM card finally materialised at 2 o'clock. It was difficult to believe that the day to go had arrived. I felt no jubilation or great relief, just a renewed narrowing of focus to proceed with all haste now that I was back in control of the travel schedule.

I said a genuinely fond farewell to Fred and Dolly, and went to the station with Yanto. In Jakarta, we booked into a *'minus 29 star hotel'*, sharing a dingy room with dirty blue walls and a smelly toilet. We searched outside and found a Padang restaurant near the hotel, Padang being the cuisine of South Sumatra. Our food was served in a selection of small dishes, and we tucked into a delicious assortment of fish, chicken, boiled egg and fried rice, which we doused in a spicy chilli sauce called sambal, a condiment that is ready to consume after it begins to smell putrid.

Unlike Bandung, Jakarta was very humid. I lay lifelessly on my bed in shorts and nothing else, sweat rolling down my face, even without any deliberate expenditure of energy on my part. Any faint possibility of sleep was reduced further by the perpetual noise from other inhabitants, including a person who insisted on playing a simple flute of some kind. I learned that the other guests were in transit, being shipped out of Java and 'transmigrated' to less-densely populated parts of the archipelago. Migrant Muslims from one ethnic group would be transplanted and expected to live harmoniously side-by-side with Christians from a different ethnic group. I wondered whether this expedient remedy wasn't shoring up problems for the future. When there were 10,000 uninhabited islands in the archipelago, I also wondered if the policy was being driven by an ulterior motive that was more sinister and connected with creating a homogenous population and single religion.

In the morning, Yanto and I took a taxi to the airport and boarded a Douglas DC-9 bound for Jogjakarta in eastern Java, and then Den Pasar on the island of Bali. On the way, there were stunning views of the chain of active volcanoes that form the backbone of Java island, and they protruded threateningly through a light cover of cloud. It was a low altitude flight and at times it seemed that the craters were toothless mouths of giant creatures lying in wait to ensnare unsuspecting aircraft passing overhead.

From Den Pasar we continued in a Fokker F28, a short-haul jet aeroplane with eighty seats and two Rolls-Royce engines, a useful aircraft for short runways and island-hopping journeys. Within a short time, we flew past Sumba and then it was a while before the western tip of Timor came into view. Only 470 kilometres long and no more than 110 kilometres wide, Timor is a small island that seemed adrift in a vast blue ocean. In 1699, the great 17th Century English explorer William Dampier visited Timor, and in *A Continuation of a Voyage to New Holland* he made the following observations about the island.

...and a little before sunset we saw, to our great joy, the tops of the high mountains of Timor, peeping out of the clouds which had before covered them as they did still the lower parts...The whole of the island Timor is a very uneven rough country, full of hills and small valleys. In the middle of it there runs a chain of high mountains, almost from one end to the other.

I became animated as the detail of the island became clear and I could see the outlines of Kupang, and make out individual features in the landscape. The aeroplane circled once and landed a little after 1 o'clock. It was August 30th, and I had been waiting for this moment for more than a year. At last, I had arrived.

IN JEOPARDY

I had arrived in Timor, but it would take another six days before I reached the field and commenced my work. Frustration was heaped on frustration. Indonesian governments had established layer on layer of bureaucratic formalities and controls right down to village level, a system that simultaneously served three important ends. It enabled central government to gather political intelligence from the far-flung reaches of the diverse country; it helped to create national sentiment and identity; and it helped the government understand local needs in respect of economic and social development. But the roots of the system were traditional, and again socio-political, in that settlements and tribes were suspicious of their neighbours and required travellers to be introduced to the local prince or headman as a courtesy when crossing tribal borders.

It would be necessary for me to visit the authorities in each administrative area and be granted permission to reside there or travel through. So, for the next two days, there were formalities to complete in the capital Kupang before I would be allowed to go up country: multiple visits to the police, the governor's office and the local *Departemen Imigrasi*. It was fortunate indeed that Yanto was present because he could speak good Indonesian to the officials, he would carry some authority as a representative of a government organisation, and as a Javanese, he was a member of the ruling caste in the country.

Yanto and I stayed two nights in a losman (guest house) and ate at the Karang Mas, a restaurant on Jalan Siliwangi with a delightful sea view and resident prostitutes. Karang Mas translates as 'Golden Reef', a reference to the coral reef that lay exposed beneath a balcony overhanging the sea at the back of the restaurant. Other, higher reefs occurred inland, a testament to the phenomenal uplift that had taken place in recent times due to the tectonic collision. Before I left England, Tony told me to seek out the owner of the Karang Mas, an ethnic Chinese man named Chiang Liang Ing, as Mr Ing was an influential person who could help with arrangements and logistics and act as a *poste restante* for correspondence. I had no idea whether or not money changed hands, but I knew that it was important to maintain the relationship with Mr Ing for the benefit of myself, Tony and others in our research group, and I determined to meet him. We sat together for a while and chatted in a mixture of English and Indonesian, and, because there was nothing specific to ask for at this point, at the end of the conversation, he had agreed to provide assistance whenever requested.

There was nothing much of interest in the town itself, so I walked along the shore to a fishing village, which had makeshift houses and a rudely constructed fence on the beach side. It looked more like a shantytown. Fishermen wearing sarong and fez-like hats were repairing nets on the beach. They were not Timorese, but Rotinese from Roti Island. There were hardly any ethnic Timorese in Kupang or its immediate hinterland, and I would have to wait until I reached the interior, and especially the mountainous areas, before meeting the indigenous people.

For the next leg of the journey, Yanto and I would be travelling by bemo (microbus) along the main road that led inland. In fact, it was the only road through Timor, and traversed the province from west to east parallel to the long axis of the island. Our destination was Soe, a market town 110 kilometres east of Kupang, from where we would strike north to Kapan and then 18 kilometres west to an isolated and prominent mountain named Molo to begin fieldwork.

As we journeyed inland, I found the landscape surprising. Clearance of trees for agricultural purposes and centuries of uncontrolled trade in sandalwood had contributed to the development of open savannah landscapes, in contrast to the primary rain forest that dominated the large islands in the region, such as Java, Sumatra and Borneo. Typically, the vegetation cover here consists of tall grass and scattered trees, with occasional stands of white-barked Eucalyptus clinging to the higher slopes.

Soe is 900 metres above sea level and the terrain became hilly as we approached the town. At a bend in the road, the Bemo ran wide on the unmetalled road and put its nearside wheels into a pothole as our overfull vehicle tried to ascend a hill, and we came to an abrupt halt on the gravel surface. I got out to assist the driver and co-driver, but Yanto and all the other passengers remained in their seats. I motioned to the group inside the bemo to try to get them out and therefore lighten the load, but to no avail. Yanto got out and explained that the passengers had paid to sit during the trip, and not to be inconvenienced by doing the work of the driver! A jack retrieved from inside the vehicle by the co-driver was used to lift the offending wheel, and stones were put underneath to give grip. Clouds of grit-laden dust spat into the air when the wheels span, but eventually our vehicle lurched out of the hole and our journey continued.

Dinner, bed and breakfast at the Losman Bahagia in Soe cost 2,000 Rupiah and our room was clean and reasonably presentable. Afterwards, we walked into town. It was a cloudless, starry night, and the intense heat of the day had dissipated skyward, leaving the local inhabitants feeling cold. Men wearing traditional Timorese clothing were milling about aimlessly. They wore brightly coloured lengths of cloth that they wrapped around their bodies, and many had bare feet or wore plastic flip-flops. A Selimut wraps around the lower body and is worn down to the knees, much like a kilt, whereas a Selendang is slung like a shawl around the upper body. Arms and lower legs remain bare.

The native Timorese had emerged from the Stone Age without learning new technologies, merely adopting instead of copying.

Incredibly, they still relied on trading to acquire metal objects and jewellery. Weaving was the chief craft at which they excelled, using a wooden spindle because the spinning wheel was unknown. They made their garments from cotton and dyed them in bands and stripes of bright indigo, red and yellow extracted from particular leaves and bark, this custom being replaced by the use of man-made dyes purchased in local markets.

Central government in Jakarta had recently divided Timor into new administrative regions headed by Bupati (Governors), and Soe was the capital of the region that now included the former princedom of Molo. So the following day, Yanto and I went to the Bupati's office, the police station, then back to the Bupati's office. Formalities complete, we boarded a Bemo to Kapan at 3 o'clock. It was bursting at the seams, with about twenty people crammed inside the microbus, travelling along a potholed stone road that surely would be impassable in the rainy season. Our journey was hot and incredibly uncomfortable, and it was a huge relief to alight some hours later.

Kapan was a small place, bigger than a tribal village yet hardly qualifying as a town. In the main street there was a guest house and two shops, where shop meant permanent wooden stall offering a disparate assortment of minor goods, such as matches, packets of dried noodles and bars of soap. We went to see the Camat ('chamat'), the officer from the Department of the Interior appointed by the Indonesians to uphold his family's traditional position as the local rulers. In other words, the Camat was a Prince.

"Father, I come to ask permission to travel through your district on a mission to discover scientific facts for the benefit of your country and its people", I began, pausing for Yanto to translate.

"I come with the approval of the Director of the National Institute of Mining, and I travel with his chosen representative Mr Suwiyanto. I carry letters of approval", I said, retrieving a bundle of papers from my shoulder bag, "including one from the Bupati in Soe."

I gave a long presentation about the purpose of the visit to the area; I showed my maps, coffee was brought out by a servant, and we were later invited to dinner. Our host's name was Peter Oematan and his family name meant 'Blackwater'. In appearance, he was a shorter and darker version of Omar Sharif. He had a relaxed and inquisitive disposition that I warmed to, even more so because he could well have taken exception to my long hair, beard and relative youth. Clearly, though, he liked me, or at least he was enjoying the enhanced notoriety of having a foreigner travelling half-way around the world to his fiefdom to carry out research for a university.

It was a town without electricity. The more fortunate, like the Camat, had a diesel generator, the less fortunate used butane gas lamps, and the least fortunate relied on lamps fuelled by palm oil. Or were there also families too poor to afford lighting at all? Yanto and I checked in to the losman, a building without a full compliment of glass in the windows and with a corrugated tin roof, like so many others in Kapan. There was no kitchen or restaurant, so it was indeed fortunate that we had a dinner invitation.

"Pak ('Father') Camat, when do you expect the rainy season to start", I queried at the dinner table, "I have been told November." He replied that the rains would start in October, and there had indeed been dark clouds in the sky that afternoon as Yanto and I approached the town.

Well, I'm afraid I'm going to have to say 'I told you so'. This refers to my thoughts in England that it wasn't worth coming to Timor for the geology. If the rains begin in October – well it's already September and there's so little time left. Depending on circumstances, I might decide to outlast this year's rainy season, find a temporary job in Indonesia and renew my visa so that I can return to the field. More likely, I will return home having failed to obtain enough information for a thesis.

ATONI AH METO

The Camat proposed to come with us to Nefukoko, a village on the north side of Molo mountain, where he would introduce Yanto and me to the people. He had a VW jeep, which arrived with a driver early the next morning.

We went for breakfast in the town before setting off on a twenty-kilometre journey that would take us two hours. Ours was the only vehicle in the district and we arrived at Nefukoko in the manner of royalty – which of course the Camat was anyway. A gong rang, summoning tribal and family elders from the neighbouring settlements. They assembled and squatted in a circle around the Camat, under the shade of the large tree in the centre of the village, the Camat clearly showing his authority by lying casually on his side, propped up by an elbow. At a signal, everyone migrated to a large hut for lunch and a procession of five women brought food down from a house up on the hill. Back under the tree, three topped coconuts were brought onto the scene, and I was given one to drink from. It is traditional in Timor to drink from young coconuts before the milk hardens into meat, and the nut is full of a cool and most refreshing liquid. I was to discover that in the field, coconut milk is a lifesaver because there is no fresh water to drink in the dry season.

An intermittent stream of elders arrived all morning and afternoon, and it seemed that the Prince would enjoy his court all day. As a gesture of respect, when elders arrived it was their custom to offer the Camat gifts of *Areca* palm nut, Betel plant leaves, and powdered limestone, which Timorese chew to produce a concoction that induces mild euphoria and imparts a blood-red stain on teeth, tongue and gums.

After dark, the Camat invited me to sit next to him, and a selendang was brought for me to wrap around myself for the cool evening. Women brought beds down for me, Yanto and the Camat, but there were no mattresses, only planks of wood to rest on. He talked through the night, and some participants dozed off for a while. I felt very privileged indeed. It was a great honour to be accorded such status at a gathering of the local people, with the

Camat talking to them under a moonlit sky about how to improve their agriculture, and what crops to grow.

Their way of life might seem traditional in the sense of unchanged over the centuries, but this was far from the truth. Their daily lives and the structure of their society had been revolutionised by the introduction of many crops and domesticated animals. Between them, Chinese, Portuguese, Javanese and Dutch traders introduced water buffalo, horses, cows, corn, cassava, rice, sweet potatoes, coffee, tobacco and various kinds of vegetables and fruit, such as potatoes, onions, cabbages, tomatoes and apples. Prior to these contacts, the Timorese were hunter-gatherers. Nowadays, when crops failed, they would return to their original dependency and forage for leaves, shoots, berries, seeds, roots, tubers, bark and fruit. As a result, their lives remained intimately tied to the plant life, and they possessed an incredible knowledge of each species, not in a biological sense but from need in their daily lives. They knew which plants were best for making a range of medicines, dyes for clothing, furniture, firewood, and building materials for the construction of houses and fences.

It was a tragedy that the adopted practice of cultivating subsistence crops had altered the delicate balance of nature on Timor. Cutting down the forest to make fields led to erosion of the soil on the mountain slopes. Soils were thin and susceptible to removal by wind in the dry seasons and by landslides in the rainy season. There was over-reliance on crops that needed plenty of water in the growing season, yet the timing and amount of rain on Timor was highly unpredictable and people went hungry when crops failed. Indeed, famine was becoming an annual event, something that would never have happened in their pre-agricultural existence. Essential nutrients required by the crops could not be replaced quickly by natural processes, and their fields were left fallow for many years while the people moved on to cut down more forest. I pitied the impoverished Timorese, who were now bound to this precarious existence. It required an enormous investment of their time, especially fencing the fields in order to protect the crops from grazing and damage by water buffalo, cattle and pigs – animals that had been introduced onto the island.

Our party left in the morning, after a breakfast of fried rice, potato cubes, boiled eggs, pieces of chicken and a green, leafy vegetable. Five carriers and guides accompanied Yanto and me into the field. Two of them carried my rucksack, but I was not comfortable with the idea of paying someone to make my life easy, and soon insisted that I carry it myself. We walked past Manubait kampung to the Noil Metan, the 'Black River', where I was so desperate to get started that I decided to make some geological observations. I traversed upstream and downstream with Lias, leaving the others to climb to the top of Molo and establish a camp on the summit.

I had come to make the mountain share its ancient secrets and shed its mysteries for my personal benefit. I could not accomplish the task alone, since I would be reliant on help from the local people to act as guides, carriers, cooks and assistants in so many other ways. I would need to show due respect: it was their mountain, perhaps home to spirits and gods.

Molo is an elongate mountain about nine kilometres or five miles long, with a central ridge that attains a height of 1,636 metres or approximately 5,400 feet on the eastern end. More than 1,000 metres above me and far beyond my view was the summit. As I found out, the gradient to the top was steep, and my poor physical condition took its toll very quickly as I ascended.

What a climb. I soon tired. My legs began to feel like lead, and for a long time I had to keep repeating, "Must go on, legs must walk" in rhythm with my steps, otherwise I would have stopped. And the climb seemed endless because the peak could not be seen. But later, I had no choice but to rest, and my stops became more frequent and longer. Eventually, I was grabbing the trunks of Eucalyptus trees to help pull me up the slope, and clutching at long straws of dry grass to retain balance, otherwise in my weakened state I would have tumbled backwards. Once or twice when I stopped I felt I just couldn't continue. I lay down and went to sleep for a few minutes, but managed to pull myself together and carry on. I was stopping after a dozen or so small steps. I just wanted to lie down and sleep. I was constantly and acutely aware that I had the symptoms of exhaustion, and so I had to keep my presence of mind and carry on. I put some gum in my mouth, but no amount of chewing could release enough saliva to wet the back of my parched throat. It was getting dark now, and beginning to rain. On and on I had to go, my paces reduced to one-foot stumbles. I took off my boots and socks because they seemed to weigh a ton, and I gave my camera and shoulder bag to Lias to carry. I completely lost track of time and had no way to assess how much longer the climb would take.

Then Yanto appeared and gave me a Kretek. Never before had a cigarette tasted so good and been so satisfying. The sweet taste and smell of the cloves was so refreshing. I was at the top and the walk was now slightly downhill to the camp. My muscles were so tired they were reacting involuntarily, and my walk was very jerky, somewhat like a mechanical man. One of the men brought me sweet, black coffee and I stopped in the rain for a while before I was able to continue the last 100 metres to the camp. When I reached camp, I downed a pint or more of coffee, ate dinner and fell asleep, exhausted.

My guides had made a small shelter among the trees, using leafy branches to make a roof of sorts. A welcoming fire burned in the open entrance of the shelter and was kept alight all night after the meal. The temperature had dropped to 10°C or lower, and I felt quite cold. Everyone slept in full clothing, my guides wrapping their bodies in selimut, and me donning a beige cord jacket over my shirt and T-shirt to try to keep warm.

It had been a difficult matter deciding what clothes to take to Timor, not least because I was restricted to one rucksack for all my gear, which included maps, notebooks, a compass, hammer, camera equipment, and plastic bags for rock samples. In the field, I wore stout boots, long-sleeved shirts and green army surplus trousers with plenty of pockets. Sandals, T-shirt and shorts would have been more appropriate in the heat, but covering up was necessary to protect my soft feet and white body from an assortment of natural hazards, including reptiles, insects and the sun.

Monday September 5th was the first full day of mapping, two months later than I had planned. I hired three men at 400 Rupiah a day per man, a rate recommended by the Camat. This would cost me a grand total of £11.50 a week plus food for their support. I walked along the summit ridge and marvelled at the enchanting view across miles of brown and straw-coloured hummocky terrain with its scattered stands of trees, and the dry riverbeds standing out like the bleached bones of a skeleton picked over by vultures.

Seasonal changes in air pressure above Australia and Asia cause the movement of hot air masses back and forth across the equator, and this governs the gross distribution of rainfall in Timor. The island has a climate that features a dry monsoon that is particularly harsh relative to the rest of Indonesia, because Timor is the Indonesian island furthest from the equator and it lies in close proximity to the dry continent of Australia, a mere 500 kilometres to the south. Consequently, the climate of Timor is capricious, and the island frequently experiences early rain, or worse, prolonged dry seasons that cause drought and lead to famine in the affected areas. Timor's landscape is parched and brown in the dry season. Most rivers become dry, the soil cracks and trees shed their leaves.

A jagged ridge snakes its way along the summit of Molo mountain, and there are three separate peaks, from east to west: Toli, Naijabi and Sesnub. On both sides of the ridge the slopes are steep and dangerous, some too dangerous to visit. But in pursuing my goal, I at times risked life and limb by venturing to places where even my guides refused to go. Climbing up and down sheer faces of rock, or jumping across gaps in narrow ledges was beyond their level of commitment, but I enjoyed taking the risk and felt I was doing my utmost to scour the mountain for clues. It also gave me a wonderful sensation that I was the first *Homo Sapien* to set foot in those places. I tried to understand the guide's point of view, since I doubted that they were scared of the physical challenge, and I supposed they saw no point in expending effort in going nowhere of importance, just to come back!

They asked if I was looking for gold, which had been one object of several Dutch expeditions until the 1920s, and non-commercial amounts of gold can be panned from rivers in Timor. Perhaps my guides retained their suspicion even after I denied it, after all, what other reason could there be for staring at rocks, making notes about them, and taking samples away?

Trees and dry grass covered the mountain and there was almost no exposure of rock for me to study. And because of the tropical climate, exposed rocks had been weathered into a friable, rust-red lateritic soil. Useful exposures formed only one per cent of the area, I estimated, and the large gaps in-between concealed nearly all boundaries between different rock types and the specific interrelationships between them; yet it was of fundamental importance to observe these contacts. I soon became disillusioned with my mission.

On the other hand, I quickly came to admire my guides for their agility on the mountain, their hardy nature in adversity, and the simplicity of their lives and thoughts. Their balance, leg muscles and stamina were supreme, since it was normal for them to walk everywhere barefooted. Despite the intense heat, the men would go all day without drinking. Entangled in this admiration for the people was a profound sadness that more and more external influences would further erode their traditional culture, and that a modern way of life had the potential to assimilate or destroy their communities. I was now intimately involved with their condition; I lived it, I felt it, I became immersed, attached and painfully aware of their plight. At times, I seriously considered staying in Timor so that I could live with the people, learn their language and customs, and write a definitive social and anthropological study. What is the human cost of development; is development always progress; and should primitive people be left alone? Those were important issues, but these people were not in the spotlight and they had no local, national or international champion to highlight their cause. Perhaps they didn't want a champion; perhaps they were not aware there was a cause?

They refer to themselves as Atoni Pah Meto, which translates as People of the Dry Land, and they speak Uab Meto, also named Bahasa Dawan, one of the family of Austronesian languages spoken on the island. They are the aboriginal people of Timor and racially distinct from the East Asian races that predominate in Indonesia. Melanesian (Papuan), Negrito and even Pygmy features are discernable among the Atoni, who characteristically have dark brown skin, frizzy hair and round eyes. They are thought to be descendents of the first wave of modern humans who migrated out of Africa about 80,000 years ago, and who travelled as far as Papua New Guinea and Australia. Conversely, the dominant peoples of the archipelago are lighter-skinned, straight-haired Asians with oval eyes and a Mongoloid appearance, who arrived later from mainland Southeast Asia. And unlike many other parts of Indonesia, Christianity had touched the people of Timor, both east and west. My guides had biblical or other Christian names, suitably altered for local pronunciation: Obet for Robert, Lias for Elias, Musa for Moses, and Sala for Shelah.

My guides called me Pak Mike. An ingrained sense of deference led them to wait until I had eaten my fill before they finished the leftovers, and they would even retreat to a different area of the camp to eat their meal. A Timorese handshake does not include any shaking, but is gentle and executed by touching finger-to-finger without involving the palm. Often, the left hand is clasped around the right forearm, to convey that the handshake is given with 'all respect'.

At irregular but frequent intervals throughout the day, they would yell words and short sentences across the mountain, and receive return yells from somewhere else. It kept them in touch at a great distance, and yells could be heard coming from the kampung far below. Yelling was also used to guide travellers to the camp, in daylight or darkness. Though I came to learn about two hundred common words in their language, I could never make sense of their yelling, and wondered if it was in some way coded, perhaps to throw a screen around their activities, or was a remnant of an older language still used for communicating on the mountain.

On the evening of the second day in the field, there was much more yelling than usual, because replacement guides were coming up from the village. In the morning, Yanto left on his own mission, and Musa and Lias were changed out. I was sad to see Lias go; I had come to like and trust him, and the two who remained looked as though they did not want the job.

I left camp at 8am and continued mapping towards the highest point on the western end of the central ridge. Obet complained of feeling ill from the sun and asked to go back to the camp. I suspected that Obet was lying, but sent him back anyway. At the risk of being taken for a ride, I had to be sympathetic because all sorts of horrible illnesses could befall them out here, including life-threatening diseases such as malaria. I returned to the camp just before 3 o'clock and found Obet pretending to doze and making muted noises as if he was in pain. I allowed him to retain face by giving him two aspirins so that he could pretend to recover. Et voila, Obet regained his health and dignity in minutes. Never had aspirin been so efficacious. It was clear from this behaviour that Obet did not want to accompany me into the field, and so I made him Camp Boss.

Four coconuts and a live chicken had arrived at the camp. Not by themselves, of course, but brought by one of the guides to supplement food rations and to earn the man some extra money. Obet and Sala grasped the chicken, and while one man held the legs and wings, the other held the head and cut its throat with the knife in his spare hand. They held on while the chicken performed a few spasms and the blood dripped out of its gullet. More spasms while the feathers were being plucked, then over the fire to singe off the last hairs. Deftly, they split the body down the middle, removed the innards, and finally laid the scrawny carcass on a griddle of small sticks to cook over the fire. I was given half the body and the wings, and the guides devoured what remained. Half an hour ago one live chicken, now all chewed up inside three hungry bodies.

We have no matches, so I hope they keep the fire going all night. Foolishly, I gave away my store of matches in Nefukoko to the old men who were delighted to be able to make fire by striking a match on a stone. I instructed Sala to put more leaves on the roof of our shelter, since the sky was clouding over. He didn't make a big effort. It rained afterwards, but nothing too serious yet. They asked me if they could go home if it rained during the night. Are they afraid to be on the mountain at night, or is it that the journey is just like a routine commute for them? Well, it's OK if they go as long as they return to cook breakfast at 6am. It's a two-hour walk down the mountain for me, so I'd prefer to stay here and get wet, thank you very much. Communications are OK for simple matters. Last night we played poker with my deck of cards; tonight again, I hope. It becomes dark at 6 o'clock and there is very little to do when you can't make fluent conversation and the lamplight is too dim for reading (not that I have a book to read!).

Many Atoni in the remote areas have only a rudimentary understanding of Indonesian and I had started to learn their language, to try to converse effectively using a mixture of the two. In practice, I learnt the vocabulary by pointing at objects and asking for names in Dawan, then used a dictionary to translate the English into Indonesian so that I could increase my vocabulary.

Breakfast was ready at 6 o'clock, as asked for, consisting of a small amount of tinned fish (yet again) suffocating beneath a mountain of boiled rice. Obet spent the day improving the camp, including putting more leaves on the roof and sides of the shelter. During the day, I encountered a wild boar that ran away squealing at the top of its voice, twice met black scorpions under loose stones, and had a six inch stick insect advance up my trouser leg, presumably in search of something to chew. I also saw a herd of small wild horses. They took fright and hurriedly retreated over a ridge, except for the white stallion who showed he was leader and reassured himself that the danger had passed by pausing for a moment on the crest of the ridge to look back at me, before rearing up, swivelling on his hind legs and disappearing over the crest.

I sent Sala to Kapan for provisions and passed the evening chatting to Obet. He told me that his mother and father were dead; his father had died in June and Obet left school to manage the garden, which is the patch of land where a family grows vegetables and root crops. I was beginning to trust and like Obet. Obet said he didn't want to leave me on the mountain, and, in any case, the Camat would be angry if he did! Seemingly, they were under obligation and could not back out. I felt reassured that I was not entirely at their mercy.

Despite the arrival of two men bearing two live chickens and four coconuts, provisions were running low by the sixth day. I decided to go down the mountain and stay in the village of Manubait. My rucksack was heavy with rock samples, and our descent was slow. Obet offered to carry it and I agreed, despite feeling doubtful about the ability of the diminutive boy. But I was quite taken aback when he put the pack on one shoulder and set off at a pace approaching a run, leaving me far behind and in complete admiration.

Manubait kampung was rather enchanting, with thatched huts scattered among the trees at different levels on the hilly ground. The people lived in clusters of family-centred hamlets that collectively formed a settlement or village. A typical house is round in plan elevation, with bamboo walls and a conical roof covered with a palm leaf thatch that reaches almost to the ground. Houses rest directly on the ground without flooring, and have a single, low entrance and no internal partitions.

Although it was not the primary growing season, there were many fruits in the village to supplement my diet: banana, coconut, mango, papaya and terong Belanda (cherry eggplant). Tobacco was grown there, and I tried a cigarette made from locally-grown leaves, hand-rolled in a strip of soft bark from a Lontar palm tree and tied with a thin string of bark; it was hot, but tasted sweet and would be acceptable if nothing else was available when a craving came along.

With some relief, I found a site where I could wash, a public place with water fed by a system of hollow bamboo trunks, and prepared for the first wash since I arrived in the field a week ago. The several women who were beating clothes when I arrived didn't stay long, I assume out of respect for their guest, and so I took off all my clothes and went berserk under the glorious waterfall.

In the Molo area there was no electricity, no running water or sanitation, and no civil infrastructure. Almost nothing was wasted in their society, as evidenced by the paucity of litter and the recycling of bottles and tins for personal and domestic use. Children of school age either worked alongside their parents, or walked up to four hours to get to the nearest school, which was in Soe. Their diet was clearly inadequate, and I saw children with swollen stomachs and quite a few adults with goitre, their necks horribly swollen from lack of iodine in their diet. There was no western medical treatment unless the sick could walk or their relatives could buy basic supplies in Soe. And in the drought they were experiencing that year, there was simply not enough spare food to feed all the domesticated animals. Donkeys were an important beast of burden, a valuable asset owned by few, yet near the village I saw a donkey that had died of starvation. Pigs and dogs foraged and were in noisy competition with each other. I had the experience of crouching down to defecate in the bush, with the raucous sounds of snorting pigs and growling dogs right behind me vying to be first to eat my hot turds.

Husbandry of domesticated animals occupies a central role in the lives of the community, particularly water buffalo, pigs, chickens and dogs. Buffalo have the highest value. Ownership represents wealth, in several respects, since buffaloes constitute the essential component of the bridewealth, and are sacrificed as payment in return for help with sowing and harvesting, or they are traded for treasured items such as silver coins, jewellery and coral beads. The pig is a common animal, since it has a lower value, and like buffaloes, it is sacrificed for a variety of rituals. Of all the animals, dogs had been domesticated first and were used for hunting deer, but could be eaten by humans to supplement the supply of meat in the diet when times were hard.

Villagers had surrounded me ever since my arrival in Manubait. An unoccupied house was prepared for me, but within minutes, it had filled with an assortment of men and children, curious to observe every movement, every detail. I would be sleeping on a wooden bed with no mattress, which didn't bother me as much as the likelihood that the heat at night would make sleeping a fitful affair.

Sala arrived early in the morning with provisions. I was displeased when I checked the inventory against the written list I had given to him: no coffee; four boxes of matches, not six; one packet of cigarettes, not two; twenty-four eggs, not twenty; and 1/2kg of sugar, not 2kg, and with four of the five bags broken. Displeasure turned to anger when he asked to be paid for the full day and, perhaps harshly, I paid for three days not four. Two days later, a new helper named Mateus arrived from Kapan with all the goods I had ordered. I was pleased with him, and I looked forward to an evening meal of fried chicken, fried onions and fried eggs. The next day, Mateus said he felt ill and I let him stay in the village.

This evening I discovered that two packets of coffee are missing. Yanto discovered that some biscuits mysteriously disappeared today. Furthermore, while he was having a wash, one of his cigarettes disappeared. We suspect

Mateus, particularly since only yesterday we were discussing how we thought he was lazy. He has a habit of just taking cigarettes or picking up our possessions and looking at them. So, the two men who Pak Camat has assigned to me for the rest of the month are people I can't trust – and the third man hasn't yet turned up.

I heard that the Camat had ordered most of the able-bodied men, women and children in the area to improve the road from Nefukoko to Kapan. A group of five hundred people had worked day and night for a week to repair a 500-metre stretch of road. My wonderment and respect increased enormously when I saw the result a week later. I guessed that the people were willing but unpaid participants in the scheme, and that their obedience to the Prince would be repaid when it was possible for pickup trucks to bring goods in by road. This would save many hours spent walking great distances to obtain goods that were a luxury to them, but quite everyday items to westerners, such as rice, tinned food, salt, soap, cooking utensils, and matches.

Although the weather was at times overcast, most days were very hot indeed. I saw an indication of how much rain fell in the wet monsoon when I walked to the River Noni. It had looked like a narrow white vein when I saw it from the top of the mountain, but the riverbed was about 300 metres wide, completely dry and strewn with tree trunks and millions of large boulders.

NO TURNING BACK

Tony arrived in the camp on September 15th. I had been expecting him for the past few days, and he arrived with a couple of helpers and with post from my parents, sisters, grandmother, Sarah, Bernie, and Barclays Bank, a most useful statement showing there was £3.92p in my account.

We climbed the mountain on the second day of Tony's visit. I was becoming supremely fit and my legs took me up in only two hours, despite going at a slow pace. I had believed that Tony was visiting to supervise and help me with my fieldwork, but he had his own agenda, and the next day the two of us left the area for a ten-day jaunt to an assortment of localities.

Today, I really felt like chucking it all in. I have been frustrated with the lack of decent geology, but even so, I have wanted to complete the mapping. I've only been here two weeks and now I will be spending a couple of weeks with Tony, just swanning around looking at nothing in particular. When I return to Molo, the rainy season could have started and I'll be even more against staying here. If I leave Timor having completed very little worthwhile research, then my PhD is in jeopardy. What can I do about it? I had a dream of doing a first-rate job here and enjoying the work so much, yet I'm depressed.

Tony had hired an ancient Land Rover for the duration of his trip. It had no air or oil filters and a leaky radiator; it overheated at regular intervals, requiring consumption of water, our most precious commodity. Our party drove out of Manubait and were in Nefukoko in less than two hours for an overnight stop with the Kepala Desa. Late in the evening, some soldiers arrived and came in for tea. They were on a mission to catch a gang that was cutting sandalwood trees for the oil, an illegal act. Coincidentally, earlier in the day we had seen a dozen or so men carrying sandalwood near the village. The army contingent left in a Land Cruiser with the Kepala Desa and returned at 1 o'clock in the morning with five men who they had arrested. I have no idea of their fate.

The following morning we drove to Kapan, at which point I lost interest in where on the map we were going. However fascinating the journey, however beautiful the scenery, I could not put aside an inner conflict.

There are long periods when I have a dual personality, like schizophrenia but with both characters being on the stage at the same time. One second I am exceedingly angry inside, the next moment I am telling the angry persona that I should enjoy everything while I can. An internal debate is raging. There are two sides to this particular coin, but the maxim is the same on both: life is too short. Yes, on one hand it's too short so enjoy what is happening, and, yes, on the other hand it's too short so don't waste your time on peripheral activities. So I've got to make an effort as never before. Resolve is what is needed here.

Timor's roads were absolute hell to travel over in a vehicle, and we averaged less than 10kph in the Land Rover, shaking violently in our seats in the cramped and superheated interior of the brave vehicle as it jerked in and out of potholes and over large cobbles. Frankly, it would have been easier to walk, and much less stressful on mind and body.

We were heading for Mutis, at 2,427 metres the highest mountain in West Timor and like Molo, composed of metamorphic and igneous rocks. On the way, we stopped at Oenun, a settlement with two huts. We stayed in a hut that was not a house, but a store containing a thousand dried cobs of corn in the eaves. It had no holes for windows, and the entrance was the height of a child. A densely thatched roof reached the ground, and was a haven for wildlife. I estimated that each cob had ten cockroaches crawling and feeding on it, making a total of ten thousand cockroaches, not including countless others promenading all over the thatched roof. Periodically, the roaches dropped onto the floor, my bed, my head. Adding to the domestic menagerie were a hundred or so tiny silver moths flitting about playing kamikaze pilots in my coffee.

The next day's excursion involved a long and boring walk, and this pushed me to the point when I decided what I would do.

I'll dispense with the geology of Timor and leave as soon as practicable. I will take a detour on the journey home and spend some time on Bali, but I'll get home for Christmas, that's for sure. I plan to spend the winter sorting out the geochemistry equipment at Chelsea to make it work. Then in the spring I'm off to Scotland for about four or five months, and my thesis will be on Scotland, to hell with Timor. I plan to tell Tony this evening.

I let Tony go into the field alone the next day, and I went

straight on to Aplal, a village near the border with East Timor. A small aeroplane flew overhead, low in the sky, travelling towards the border, and I could see smoke in that direction. I wondered whether it was a spotter plan investigating a fresh skirmish or battle between Indonesian forces and the Fretilin movement.

After a good chat with the Kepala Desa (Village Head) of Aplal, he arranged lodgings that were relatively luxurious. My bed had a mattress, and I was able to have a decent bathe in the river. In the village, I bought some real cigarettes, having survived on some ghastly local tobacco for a few days.

I explained to Tony before he went into the field that morning that I wanted to be able to hold my head high and know in my heart that what I did was worthwhile. Whether it was a PhD on Scotland or Timor or Outer Mongolia was a secondary issue now; the important point was that I wanted it to be a good piece of work that would stand the test of time.

When he returned that afternoon, his comments were most emphatic.

"Mike, too much time, effort and money is already involved for you to give up in Timor. Our research programme and group are working on Southeast Asia and not on Scotland, so it's Timor or nothing."

Reluctantly, I joined Tony in the field the next day. Staying put in the village was an alternative that gave me nothing useful to do, and staying would have been worse because I would have to deal with an endless stream of people coming to peer at me. We walked for three hours and climbed a steep hill, just so that Tony could see the view from the top and get an overview of the geology.

Another day that I could have been working on my mapping area. I had another conversation with Tony about my dilemma. He's determined that I complete as much work here as possible and he thinks that there is plenty of information for a thesis. Also, he said that it doesn't matter whether I am satisfied with the work, but more that I have done something which will be of value for my future prospects.

I didn't see it that way. Tony and I had such different characters. Tony was not a man for detail. He constructed grand interpretations and went in search of scraps of confirmation, or *vice versa* would make a quick observation and extrapolate wildly, whereas I needed to look at everything so that vital evidence would not be missed in the construction of the big picture. Tony had the advantage of being vastly more experienced and knowledgeable than me, but, as much as possible, I wanted to start with a clean sheet of paper. Tony possibly genuinely believed that I would benefit from the two-week tour, but it was his own agenda and he never asked me what help I needed. I only wanted to be back in my mapping area.

We set off for Kupang the following day because Tony was returning to London and Yanto to Bandung. We talked more about the problem with which I was struggling, after which I felt much brighter, happier and now determined to persist until the rivers became flooded. Airing the problem, sharing the problem, and a chance to reflect had tipped the delicate balance the other way. Uppermost in my mind was the threat from Tony that I would not get a PhD unless it was about Timor. It was ironic that Tony was not only my mentor but the focus of my resentment and doubt.

FAITH, HOPE AND CHARITY

After a break of two days, I returned inland on Saturday October 1st. Mr Ing, the owner of the Karang Mas, hailed a passing truck to give me a lift up country. An ethnic Chinese man was at the wheel, leading me to suspect that there was a prior arrangement with Mr Ing. A dozen or more large sacks of rice and nine barrels of diesel lay in the back of the pickup. And in true Indonesian style, the back was crammed full of people sitting on top of the goods: nothing useful was wasted, not even space, and no opportunity was lost. The driver invited me to sit with him in the cab, and we enjoyed pleasant conversation on the way. He was a hospitable man, paying for our soft drinks in Takari, and refusing to accept payment from me when I got out in Soe.

As the Bahagia was full, I walked to the Cahayu losman. I asked if there were any westerners in town, and found out that a German preacher lived in Soe and ran a Protestant church up the road. I decided to pay a visit. The church was packed and the congregation was so large that it spilled outside the entrance to listen to the service. An English-speaking couple singled me out and invited me to dinner at a house close-by. It turned out that Ester and her husband were connected with the church, and the preacher and his wife were present at the meal.

Built in western colonial style, the house had electricity, a ceiling, decent furniture and was by far the most luxurious home I had seen while in Timor. An electric organ was on prominent display, there were pictures and ornaments all about the room, and a sumptuous buffet awaited us on a long table. At this point, my subconscious mind sprayed a stream of thoughts into my consciousness, and I felt a rising sense of hostility towards my hosts. It was an insult to Christianity, and a scandal for the church to act this way. These hypocrites were living like royalty on the proceeds of donations they shamelessly collected on a plate from impoverished and undernourished Timorese who came into their church, barefooted – I had seen it with my own eyes that very day. Now that there was a coherent summation in my mind, I became incensed and poised to convert the emotion into a jet of invective.

At exactly that moment, Ester asked me "What is your religion?" meaning 'which denomination of Christianity are you, Catholic or Protestant?'

I follow no religion; in fact, I despise it. It was a deterministic decision that I had reached in my youth. It is not an indifference, indecision or vagueness of mind – it is a conviction that organised religion is a political system, a ruse to concentrate power in the hands of a few dictators. Religious leaders establish systems that sustain power by brainwashing the masses and denying them the initiative to find simple, liberating truths about existence. Religions implant the questionable notion that an all-seeing, all-knowing, all-powerful entity will look after any human animal if it follows a set of man-made rules, that include what can't be eaten, when rest should be taken, and what should be worn. They have hijacked culture! All this on the pretext that a higher being is required to explain what exceeds the feeble capabilities of human beings. How anthropocentric. If the 'logic' is that a god is required to create suns, planets and life, then surely an even smarter and more wondrous celestial entity is required to create that god? It seems to be a puzzle that has no rational solution.

Tony had already advised me that, to an Indonesian, a person without a religion is assumed to be a communist, and that it was better to lie and say you were a Christian. On October 1st, 1965 – twelve years previously, to the day – the communist party of Indonesia was blamed for staging the coup that led to the downfall of President Sukarno, Indonesia's founding father. In the aftermath, soldier and citizen alike summarily executed 300,000 people in Sumatra, Java and Bali. But I was never one to conceal the truth in the face of direct questioning, never one to feel ashamed of my principles, or hide them, and I wasn't going to start now.

"I have no religion", I said, in conversation-stopping style.

Ester told me that Russian people have no religion and are communists, and that communists are jailed in Indonesia. The preacher went further, quoting from some gospel or other.

"Only a mad man does not believe in God", he said.

So that's it, I'm mad; it's official, because a pompous nobody claiming to be one of God's official representatives on earth has decreed it. His mind could not recognise or acknowledge the distinction between following a religion and having a belief in a god: to me, one was preposterous, the other tolerable, if misguided. Perhaps God did exist, though God only knew why, but organised religion was so abhorrent to me – in part for reasons that were right in front of me that evening. The preacher's wife was rather more sensible or polite about the matter, and chatted to me in a friendly way at dinner. She had been in England for five months in 1955, training in some sort of theological institute in Glasgow; loved Derbyshire. He had been in England during the Coronation year, had travelled to Bath and Bristol, and spent a week in Weston-Super-Mare, poor thing.

Despite the controversy, I was invited to attend the evening service, perhaps for my salvation! A succession of hymns started the proceedings, sung in a distinctly melodic Polynesian-style lilt that I found enchanting. Four members of the congregation gave separate testimonies about some salvation or other in their personal lives, before a long bout of praying set in. Ester lent me an English language bible, which I thumbed through during the sermons in the three and a half hour long service. On reading the bible, I noticed that it was full of glaring contradictions. But the passages referred to in the various sermons ignored the contradictions and bad points. It was flagrant brainwashing.

Many of the congregation would have walked out of the bush to be at church, and most would have received minimal formal education, if any. They had no conception of the wide world beyond their little island, if they knew that they were *on* an island. The Timorese lived precariously tied to the vagaries of the natural world, and were animists by tradition. How could they begin to comprehend what was in the bible: the concept of a Roman Empire; of Pyramids, Pharaohs and slaves; of building a floating home for elephants, camels and other animals they had not seen – let alone be convinced that any of it was relevant to them? In conversation with my guides on the mountain, they asked me if aeroplanes had big lights on the front to be able to fly at night. They didn't even understand the present world, never mind the situation in the Levant 2000 years ago.

I could tell that the preacher had re-written his sermon in order to use the encounter at dinner with me to make a point. He said there were many atheists in Europe, and equated this with a darkness that was increasing, and he foretold that an Anti-Christ would arise in Europe. I appreciated being equated with an Anti-Christ, since I was definitely anti the idea that Christ was a being ordained from outer space. In this regard, Judaism was so much more sensible.

A Land Cruiser picked me up in the morning and took me to breakfast at Ester's sister's house, from where I walked to the church to attend the morning service. I was determined to stay the whole two hours to demonstrate my broadness of mind and tolerance of others, and therefore to have the last 'word'. I certainly appreciated the irony that the preacher had the embodiment of an Anti-Christ sitting attentively in his congregation.

RETURN TO MOLO

After the service, I packed at the losman and caught a Bemo

heading for Kapan, the town at the end of the gravel road leading towards Molo. The driver cruised around for almost an hour to find passengers because, like a fairground ride, there was no timetable and the trip did not start until the vehicle was full.

I alighted in Kapan and was so pleased to be invited to stay with the Camat in his modest, yet superior house, with a tin roof and electricity. We had become firm friends.

"Pak Mike, are you remembering your girlfriend", he queried, with his head tilted and a playful smile on his face.

"Yes, every day", I replied, lying somewhat. He then took me completely by surprise by retrieving a beautiful selendang from behind a cushion and giving it to me as a present for Sarah. What an honour!

I had shown an interest in his native language, and the two of us passed the rest of the evening exploring vocabulary in a 'point, name and translate' game.

I was without transport and asked the Camat to find me a horse for the onward journey the next day.

Plodded off into the distance on a rather small horse – or was it a pony? Great fun. No saddle, and plenty of bones sticking in my getting-more-tender parts. What with a roll-up in my mouth, and riding this slow mule, I felt like Clint Eastwood and could hear the music from 'For a Few Dollars More' ringing in my ears as I passed along the dusty track, and I whistled the tune as best I could.

After a while, the point came when I just couldn't take any more pain, or attempts by the horse to bite me, and I sent the animal home with one of the guides. My party continued, we walked to Sau village and topped a few coconuts, then proceeded onwards in the dark. On the next leg of the journey, the Paman Desa (Sub-Head Man) guided us from Sau, and he swung a torch forwards and backwards so that we could both see the way ahead; even so, I stumbled a few times. To my embarrassment, the Paman Desa managed perfectly well in a pair of flip-flops. Finally, about two hours after dark, our journey ended and we reached

Lelowatan, a village on the southeast corner of Molo and the place where I would stay for the next five days. It had been a long, tiring walk over hilly terrain. I had no maps, but from experience estimated that the ten-hour journey translated into a distance of twenty kilometres.

Now that I had explored the summit of Molo, my task was to explore the slopes. This meant staying in some of the villages that circled the base of the mountain, and making traverses up the river valleys that radiated out from the summit ridge.

I climbed to the top of the mountain with four guides the next day. I really only needed one, so there was a series of exchanges with them. I explained that I would pay 400 Rupiah a day for one man, and the men could take it in turns to work, but after a brief huddle, their spokesman said they preferred to work together and take 100 Rupiah each. I was grateful that they were not being greedy, and later paid them 200 Rupiah each. These men were willing and considerate helpers, especially in cutting down vegetation that was in the way of progress, or lending a stabilising hand across difficult jumps, or offering themselves as ladders to help me climb up or down the face of dry waterfalls. Since I first arrived on the mountain, I had been amazed at just how stable and agile the men were. I noticed that they walked with feet splayed, putting all their weight on the front part of the foot for maximum down force per unit area. It was simple physics! I tried this technique, and it worked, even though some effectiveness of the downward force was translated into slippage between foot and sock, and sock and boot.

In the village that night, I attended a ceremony connected with a recently orphaned child. There were plenty of prayers, two songs and a sermon or tribute. I guessed that the whole village was there, chatting away merrily, and the meal was organised into two sittings, the men first, and with me at the head of the table as honoured guest. Roast pig, boiled rice and maize were served, and the men packed in four or five platefuls each. They ate with only a metal spoon, following a custom from earlier times when they had fashioned spoons from buffalo horns. Optionally, at the end of the meal, it was an acceptable practice to swill the mouth with water and spit the contents in a single high-speed jet onto the dirt floor.

I went into the field alone the next day, and managed with ease to walk up the mountain and down the other side, knowing where I was at all times. My level of fitness was excellent, which together with the restricted diet had done wonders for my physique. On the other hand, I had been drinking unboiled water during the last couple of days, and though I did not feel unwell, some bumps on my legs began to itch again. They had given me no trouble at all while I had rested in Kupang and drunk boiled water.

Back in the village, I sat talking to the village Bapak (father) all evening. Spirits resided in the mountains, Bapak told me, and then looked at me earnestly and confided that spirits had taken away the memory of a woman who got lost on the mountain and did not return before nightfall. The next day a search party found her alive but "She couldn't even recognise her children", I was told. And Bapak had just heard that a white man had been on Naijabi peak trying to capture the Devil.

"It was me", I said in Bahasa, "but I was just trying to capture some rocks!"

THE DARK SIDE

Early in the morning of October 9th I left Lelowatan and walked southwest around the base of the mountain to Talimaman, a relatively large village about four kilometres distant and two hours travel on foot. Out of respect for their customs and hospitality, it was my policy to accept every invitation and offer I received, and to fulfil every request asked of me. I had to leave a good impression among the community to show that my English tribe was civilised and respectful. However, sometimes this was at the expense of my sanity, and the invitation to attend 'church' in Talimaman was just such an occasion. It was a long and dull service in the hut. Sitting about fitting in was highly frustrating when there was work to be done, and the problem became acute when I found myself walking out of the hut to go to someone's house to sit about, just because I had been invited. It was 4 o'clock by the time I escaped. Too late to go into the field, I went to the river to wash, but wasn't left alone for a second. Back in the hut, the claustrophobic situation persisted, so I walked out on the pretext of stretching my legs – but was followed again.

The evening soon passed, and no sign of food. I decided to go to sleep. I feigned tiredness for such a long time that I wondered what day it was. Eventually, I reclined on the bed and pretended to nod off – no good, because they didn't bat an eyelid. There's no scope for privacy of any sort. What a f——-g drag. Food arrived, and I asked to have it tomorrow, then said I wanted sleep and began to undress. No-one budged, and I continued down to my underpants, revealing my scabby white torso, and hopped into the sleeping bag. Again, no-one budged, and their conversation continued. I couldn't get to sleep for being annoyed, and tossing, turning and moaning didn't get me anywhere. I got up to go outside for some peace and quiet, and the woman of the house asked me if my bed wasn't good. I muttered, probably very impolitely, that I couldn't sleep for the light and the talking. It produced the desired effect and they left me in peace, but I didn't half feel like a spoilt child.

After breakfast of rice and strips of papaya, I set off in a good mood, accompanied by a penunjuk jalan (guide). On the way through Beskin village an old woman emerged from her hut to examine me. She took a long look at my face, and then touched me on the arms, I think to reassure herself that I was not an apparition. She looked about 100 years old, but was only 70. Her son was a guide to Tappenbeck when Tappenbeck passed though here doing research on the 1937 Brouwer Expedition. The old man told the touching story that Tappenbeck had promised to send him a photograph of them together, and he was still waiting.

While walking up the dry bed of the River Palelo I discovered an important locality, but when I continued upstream there were no more outcrops and I was '*pissed off*' for the rest of the day. The rocks were red, reddish-brown and green-coloured cherts belonging to the Palelo Group, of Cretaceous age. Cherts are chemically precipitated deposits of silica laid down in deep water far away from contamination by sands and muds eroded from continents and brought into the sea by rivers; but here they were interlayered with fine-grained rocks named tuffs, which are deposits of volcanic ash. This was a key piece of evidence that the Palelo Group originated on an active plate margin, active in the sense that there must have been volcanoes and therefore subduction in the vicinity. In turn, this meant that the Palelo Group belonged to the Asian plate, not the Australian plate prior to the arrival of Australia at the subduction (collision) zone in the Miocene. It was strong evidence in support of the London School of Audley-Charles, Barber, Carter and Milsom.

I was often asked what I was looking for. My simplified explanation was that I intended collecting about one hundred samples of rock. Every day when I returned to Talimaman village, someone or several people would ask 'Dapat?' (able to?), meaning 'were you able to collect some rock samples today?' In fact, the old man of the house I stayed in was counting how many samples I had collected, and every day would subtract the total number collected to date from one hundred, reckoning that the job would be complete when the answer was zero.

It was my normal practice in the evening to review my field observations and annotate my geological map. That night, the frustration of the day resurfaced, triggered by the added stress of being watched intently by three people as I tried to work in the dingy light of the solitary oil lamp. The little flame was barely able to keep itself alive and flickered pathetically in the neck of the bottle.

Tried to do my maps, but I've made such a mess of the whole operation that I might as well go home. I wonder what will happen about my crappy

Ph.D? Shit, no smokes – the only luxury there is – and none for tomorrow either, What a f——-g drag. How will I feel about Sarah, about geology when I get home? Shit, I wish I was home now, I'm so pissed off.

Now, I don't mind going without 90% of the pleasures and comforts of the world I normally inhabit, such as electricity, television, radio, music, books and newspapers, theatre and cinema, pubs and alcohol, decent tobacco, cold drinks, fresh milk, proper meat and vegetables, a comfortable bed, privacy when desired, or the ability to travel in comfort without effort. Nor do I mind missing my parents, family, Sarah and friends (at least for a while), and living here sweating my guts out working, without anyone to talk to, constantly hot, tired, dirty and thirsty, 9000 miles from home – well this I can tolerate. The only thing I ask for is interesting geology – and so far there has been none. Why the hell should I go through all this if I don't have to? I am not enjoying it, and it would only be worth it if I were dedicated to some cause beyond the calling of ordinary mortals: a kamikaze geologist, perhaps.

When I woke up, I sensed a fading grasp on a dream, the first dream I remembered having while in Timor. I was back in college and then at home, talking to my father and thinking that I couldn't believe I had been away six months. In fact, I did wish I was home, or preferably that the work was finished and I was relaxing in Bali.

In my unsettled state, I was prone to complain to myself about matters that would have been trivial under normal circumstances. An almost daily preoccupation was the matter of food and other provisions. I would write a list of provisions and send a guide to the nearest place that had a shop, though some of the fresh foods might have been bought from people in the neighbourhood. Quite often, there was only a passing resemblance between the order and the delivery, not only in composition but in cost. I did not want to interrogate my guides: sometimes the exact quantity or particular item might not have been available, in which case the guide would have to get what he could, or make a decision to buy a substitute. And prices might vary considerably, because bargaining and even bartering could be involved. But, there was always the suspicion that some of the goods and money were meeting the guides' needs, especially as incorrect quantities were always on the low side, never more than had been ordered. Was I now paranoid as well as schizophrenic? I could not begrudge a certain amount of pilfering when they had so little, but were they taking advantage, assuming in their naivety that I would not be suspicious. On the other hand, it was their custom to share everything, and I wondered whether the reduced quantities were an expression of the local rules of fairness.

In mid-October, a LIPI geologist named Jan Sopaheluwakan arrived unexpectedly in the village from Bandung, intending to stay a month. The fact that he knew my whereabouts was proof that the bureaucratic system of control and communication worked well. And it started a new chapter in my story.

When we went out in the morning, it was obvious that Jan was not used to fieldwork. He stumbled and fell about, felt too hot, was gasping for water all day long, and found climbing very difficult indeed. We had a pleasant stroll, but I suspected that Jan was not enjoying the experience. *'Never mind',* I wrote, *'I'm glad he's here'.* Clearly, Jan was a city boy and sent to field under instructions, but he had a good attitude to the task and the experience would stand him in good stead in his career.

Our second day together was another slow day in the field, and Jan was ill on the third day. On the fourth day, the two of us were so thirsty that we drank our way through seven coconuts, but at 25 Rupiah each, I wasn't too worried about breaking the bank.

We were now working the riverbeds to the southwest of Talimaman, and having to walk ten to fifteen kilometres a day in blistering heat. It must have been 40°C in the shade, but we didn't work in the shade. More than once, we arrived back in the dark after being out for twelve or more hours. Despite being weary, tired, hungry and sore from the day's exertion, walking at night was an uplifting experience when a bright moon cast a silvery-grey light on the countryside, and the silvery-white bark of the

Kayu Putih (white tree) added to the ghostly effect. In Timor, the air was clean, the sky cloudless and a myriad of stars would be out on show at night. It stimulated a special, magical feeling and I will always be able to recall the image in my mind.

At every village I made it known that I was looking for souvenirs, and I kept a list of people that I wanted to give presents. Each village or settlement offered something different, ranging from nothing at all to a steady stream of items brought in by the local inhabitants. I had already bought two buffalo horn spoons, two selimut and four selendang. The spoons were four to five inches long with exquisitely carved handles featuring serpents on the shaft and a bird head at the top. And in Talimaman, I finally managed to purchase a bracelet for myself. Bracelets are called gelang perak, but not all are made of silver as the name implies. My bracelet was made of melted-down Dutch coins. It was thick, wide, heavy, and featured knob-like protrusions at regular intervals around the perimeter. It was a common sight to see Atoni men wearing such bracelets, and now I could enhance my semi-native appearance by wearing one, in addition to the cummerbund-like selendang that I tied around my waist every day and the sheathed knife that hung from my belt.

Talimaman was the best place I had stayed, but after twelve days in the village it was time to move on so that I could map a new area. As we prepared to leave, one of the guides insisted that we photograph him wearing Jan's watch. Evidently, a watch was a status symbol possessed by few; in fact, except for the Camat, I could not recall seeing anyone with one.

Two families helped us in Talimaman, providing shelter and food, and the women cried as we made our farewells. I paid families at the end of my stay in the villages, and this was always a difficult moment for me — and perhaps them. The villagers were not familiar with the idea of a commercial arrangement for board and lodgings, and the Camat had not set a rate. I did not discuss an amount at the beginning of my stay because I was sure this would lead to problems, not only for me but perhaps lead to infighting among the villagers. And so the practice was to tell them they would be compensated at the end, and I would make a judgement by considering the level of support and the length of my stay, hoping that my offering met or exceeded their expectations. I made my judgment on knowledge of the price of foodstuffs and the amount I paid my guides, and of course, I discussed the situation with Yanto or Jan when they were with me in the field. The average daily rate I paid was 400 Rupiah, that is, an average of $1 a day, which I thought compared favourably with a price of approximately $3 a night for B&B in various losman in Kupang and Soe.

Jan and I had to walk about ten kilometres around the perimeter of the mountain to the next village, Kona, and to use Kona as a base to explore the very steep, northwestern slopes of Molo mountain. In Talimaman they told us that the people on the other side of the mountain were head-hunters, which I hoped was a reference to disputes of times past, when heads would be taken in retribution.

Our progress to Kona was slow because the four guides wanted to take frequent stops, and the man carrying my rucksack was unable to bear it for any length of time. To lead by example, I took the rucksack and set off at a rapid pace, which I maintained for an hour or more, eventually leaving all but one man trailing far behind. The day was extremely hot, and I sweated gallons of perspiration. Mid-afternoon, we arrived at Bes'ana and had a meal with the Kepala Desa. Muslim Jan ate eggs and sat at a small table by himself, while the animist-Christians locals and the visiting atheist Mike tucked in to a feast of fried pork and potatoes. We got going again, having replaced the guides with four others, and we walked for two and a half hours in the dark to reach Kona.

I sensed that the people were rather unwelcoming, and felt uncertain of how Jan and I would be treated. I was sore-footed and tired, and slept relatively well on the wooden bed that night.

However, in the morning I again felt uncomfortable about the people. They asked for money, but we explained we would pay the Kepala Desa when he arrived.

Jan and I bought some coconuts and set off in the heat. It was even hotter than the last place. Sweat pored off me all day, even after sunset. Though I walked miles every day, I was experiencing tiredness in my legs, and a lack of stamina, after having reached a peak of fitness more than a week ago. I guessed it was weariness, or even fatigue, caused by debilitating heat and strenuous physical activity, probably with a contribution from poor nutrition.

Another day in the field.

Set out today ready for a long journey up the river, but the going was extremely difficult and slow; eventually, we were forced back – having travelled only about 300 metres. And Jan is so slow. Tried another river, but couldn't get beyond 50 metres! There will be another large hole in the map of Molo. I wish the next man or woman better luck. Returned at 3 o'clock after only seven hours in the field.

In the village, a boy spotted a huge bird sitting high in a tree, and he was instructed to fetch the gun. It was an ancient flintlock rifle, a long-barrelled affair with brass trimmings. They said the gun came from a Portuguese man, but could not remember when, but I guessed that it would have been at least 120 years ago, because in the 1850s the Dutch and Portuguese had finally decided how to carve up the island. The boy approached the tree and climbed stealthily until he sensed he could go no higher without disturbing the bird. BANG! The gun made a loud noise and the bird flew away. Perhaps I should have brought my Webley air rifle and had a go myself!

We left late the next day as well, at about eight in the morning. I became exhausted and could not climb the last part to the top of the mountain, as intended, and we were back at four. In the village, the schoolchildren were on holiday because it was the hottest time of year. I knew it hadn't just been my imagination!

Jan and I returned early the next day. I was not strong enough to climb the mountain. That infamous Irish gremlin Di O'Rea had struck, and I was clearly at a low ebb. And I was sleeping fully clothed, because the sleeping bag made the red bumps and sores on my legs itch.

The problems in recent days have further hindered my final attempt to make sense out of the geology. There is nothing I understand, I have not made adequate observations anywhere, and the map is incomplete and very confusing. I have been a total failure. How can I justify the failure? If I tried to explain and list the reasons why, they would seem pathetic indeed. I feel that I was destined to come here, but destined to be hindered throughout. And my negative temperament only serves to exacerbate the problem. I must stop having negative thoughts. I must try to do a competent job on Boi mountain, but I really fear that the rain will prevent me from completing a map, and I anticipate that the exposure will be just as poor as in Molo. It has all been a waste of time.

Trivial happenings tested my patience to the limit at this time, when the limit was artificially low. I moaned to myself for comfort, for there was no one else to whom I could moan.

The cigarettes will run out tomorrow, which is a real nuisance. I had planned to stop smoking when I came to Timor, but it is my only pleasure in a world without people who I can talk to that will understand English, without electricity and all the benefits it bestows, without a pillow or mattress to sleep on, without transport of any form, without a selection of food, without hygienic conditions, without decent washing facilities. But should I complain when I can choose to leave this way of life behind, whereas for the people here there is no escape?

In my frustrated, tormented and exhausted state, my feelings had polarised to the negative end of the scale, yet in more positive moments I could acknowledge that progress had been made. I had divided the diverse assemblage of metamorphic rocks into three principal units, and made the surprise discovery that about forty per cent of the mountain consisted of younger sedimentary and volcanic rocks, which I had also mapped. In addition, I had taken many measurements of structural features, and managed to find ninety specimens of rock that were worth taking for further study.

It was true that the spirits of the mountain had made my quest difficult, but they hadn't had it all their own way.

Jan and I left Kona for Manubait on the morning of October 27th. We were on the brink of leaving when the Kepala Desa from Bes'ana arrived. As he approached, people scampered about doing nothing in particular. Someone had the presence of mind to drape a clean selimut over the back of a chair that had been brought outside for him to sit on. Jan and I had to stop and chat and eat more food. Then, the Kepala Desa asked to buy my camera, and asked why Jan and I needed two between us. I explained that they both belonged to the Indonesian government. White man, white lie.

I had now walked the entire circumference of the mountain and was back in Manubait where I had started six weeks previously. In the morning, Jan and I climbed to the top of the mountain. It felt so good to be on the top once more, but I had mixed feelings. Although I was glad to have completed the work to the best of my ability, I was sad to return to the spot where I had started with such high aspirations, and it brought tears of disappointment to my eyes. I saw that my task was completed and decided to leave for Kapan early the next morning.

It was now Saturday 29th October, a month since my return to Molo. A month is a long time when you have been working all day every day, and I was looking forward to a rest. I wanted to reach Kupang in a day, and so our party of six rose at 2 o'clock in the morning and we ate a hearty breakfast of rice, chicken, fried eggs and onions before departure. I gave my trusty but highly-worn plimsolls to Obet and vowed to walk to Kapan in flip-flops. We left the village at 3 o'clock in the morning under the light of a full moon, so light that I was able to write in my journal as we travelled. We were in Kapan by 9 o'clock, having walked about twenty kilometres. I said an emotional farewell to Pak Camat, and Jan and I took a Bemo to Soe, arriving at 11 o'clock, taking in lunch at the Bahagia and making closing out visits to the Bupati and the police. Our Bemo left for Kupang at 2 o'clock, and arrived just after 5 o'clock. It had taken only fourteen hours to travel about 130 kilometres, including the formalities in Soe, a great improvement on the three days of the inbound journey.

What an enormous relief it was to be back in Kupang, not least to be able to have a proper wash. Jan and I went on an eating binge at the Karang Mas, scoffing through several meals. I ate fried pig, fried eggs and rice, followed by beefsteak with chips, eggs, and salad, followed by a heaped plateful of Es Campur, which is a sweetened dessert of fruit topped with crushed, flavoured ice. I ruminated on the thought that I had just spent 2,550 Rupiah on the luxury of cigarettes and soft drinks, but earlier in the day had paid a man a mere 750 Rupiah to carry a heavy rucksack in blazing heat for many hours over arduous terrain, and it occurred to me that there were many worlds on this one planet.

BOI

After a day's rest in Kupang, we went to the Bupati's office to obtain the documentation necessary to visit Boi. Provisions were bought for the trip, including tinned mackerel, corned beef, dried milk, and margarine. I was tempted to succumb to buying some of the more expensive western goods on the shelves, such as Quaker Oats, Hero jams, Marie biscuits, Nescafé and condensed milk, but they were much too expensive, especially the 8-ounce jar of Nescafé, at $8. That evening, Mr Ing kindly took us to see a boxing competition, paying for ringside seats, though it seemed only fair because, by then, Jan and I had eaten at the Karang Mas three times that day.

On November 1st I hired a Land Cruiser and we set off after breakfasting on good food and cold drinks at the Karang Mas. At Takari, fifty kilometres inland from Kupang, we turned north off the trunk road towards Boi mountain. It was a very rough and uncomfortable ride to Taemaman at the end of the road, and a great relief to arrive and rest for the night. The weather was highly threatening, and looking west, in the direction of Boi, Jan and I reckoned we could see rain failing on the mountain.

A seven kilometre walk to Ajaobonat settlement took us to our destination the next morning. Our guide's behaviour was different to the people I had met on Molo. This man did not ask for cigarettes, but would put two fingers to his mouth and jerk them horizontally forwards and backwards a few times, pursing his lips to complete the mimed request. When we stopped to give him a rest, he asked how much I had paid for the vehicle that had brought us to Taemaman; I lied, since it was best not to reveal the sums involved, or give an indication of what cash we might have. He also showed considerable interest in the contents of our luggage, craning his neck to get the best view whenever a bag was opened. His face had a look of disgust and contempt when I paid him 1,500 Rupiah for the journey, despite this being twice the amount I'd paid in Molo for considerably longer journeys.

Ajaobonat was a settlement of four huts occupied by two families. It provided the only shelter on the west side of Boi mountain, and the choice was to stay there or make camp in the bush. A small river flowed nearby and I went there to take a look. The water was too shallow and full of slime, leaves and other flotsam to be fit for consumption or bathing. Despite this, we decided to stay in the settlement because the shelter and assistance would be better than in the bush.

Jan and I were allocated an empty hut, which was a shed or store, because there was only one room and the ceiling was so low that I could not stand upright. Men rallied around and brought a small table and some wooden benches. They also built a bed, and I was fascinated as I watched with considerable admiration as the object took shape. Four holes were dug into the earthen floor to mark the corners, and a sturdy, Y-shaped branch that would be a support was inserted in each hole. A bamboo pole was slung in the V of the supports on both long sides, and a set of bamboo struts was placed widthways down the length of the structure to form a base. Finally, a mat made of platted bamboo was laid on top as a mattress. Bingo, an instant bed!

I lay on the bed motionless, sweat dripping down my face in the stifling heat of the late afternoon, the sun still powerful despite a shield of haze and clouds. We were soon joined in the hut by six uninvited villagers and three dogs, also uninvited. There was hardly room for anyone else in a space measuring 8 feet by 16 feet! I wanted to get settled in, but I was reluctant to reveal the contents of my baggage. I became highly agitated about the tensions of the day. All we had done was to walk a few kilometres, and now another day's work had been forfeited by hanging about waiting politely for favours from the villagers. We had arrived at 11.30 and it was now late afternoon.

I paced around in front of the door for a long time, occasionally stopping to glare inside while I tapped my foot with impatience. I came in again and began stomping feet, tapping fingers, sighing, hanging my head, acting restless – all to no avail.

Perhaps the body language was foreign to them, since they made no sign that they would leave; or it must have seemed like a good show and they were waiting to see Act II. Finally, I had to prompt Jan to explain, politely, that we had headaches and wanted to rest, and the crowd departed. Privacy was not a concept the Atoni seemed to understand, and in any case, I think they were staying with me to be polite to their guest. Whatever the reason, I felt cross!

Earlier in the day, I had been cross for a quite different reason. Jan and I liked to eat fruit, especially pineapples, which were juicy, full of flavour and satisfying. We asked for them every place we went. When I asked if there were any ripe pineapples in the village, the answer was 'no, because the pigs eat all the ripe ones'. I was perplexed and irritated by their attitude. With what justification could they complain that the land cannot grow much and that they live on rice and maize – and yet let the pigs eat a valuable and nourishing source of food?

At bedtime, I kept my clothes on because of all the insects crawling over me. But the heat drove me to strip and climb into my sleeping bag, which made me hotter and itchy. I got up and dressed. Heat, itching and the sound of dogs yelping and children crying kept me awake past 2am until I lost consciousness.

In the morning, it required explanation to prevent the whole village following us into the field. We managed to cut the number down to two, but after a while, the party had increased to nine, including a dog. As I set off, I noticed that the weather was cloudy, and there were a few spots of rain.

Boi is a small elliptical mountain measuring about five kilometres long and two kilometres wide. It rises in the centre to a modest height of 680 metres. Deeply-incised valleys of the rivers Niti and Noni cut the mountain at right angles and afford relatively good exposure across the mountain. And in contrast to Molo, I experienced few problems ascending the mountain via the smaller river beds. With some relief, I concluded that the physical exertion would be less and the work more rewarding. Indeed, I would encounter interesting types of rock and be excited by some of my discoveries.

Geology not too bad along the Niti, and I must keep my fingers crossed for the future. The people here are OK, but it's very unfortunate that the living conditions are bad, especially the lack of clean water for bathing and washing clothes. Jan and I smell like the people here, a pungent mixture of stale sweat, filthy clothes, earth, wood fire and festering stagnant water. Very unpleasant.

Some relief came the following day. As we pushed further along the Niti, we happened on a pool with clear water, and were able at last to wash properly. It felt so good, even after the unpleasant task of putting dirty clothes back on afterwards. A little further on, we found a large pool and went for a swim.

I can't describe just how relaxed and pleased I was. The water was warm, the air warmer, and the water CLEAN. We loitered there for over half an hour, just splashing about. Wow! Not a care in the world remained as my situation was washed from my mind, as easily as the dirt from my body.

In fact, there were pools of water at intermittent locations on the two main rivers, probably indicating that the mountain had already seen some rain. I noticed that the wind was getting up, and presently the sky became completely overcast. Soon after, spots of rain began to fall and we heard thunder not far away. It became louder and closer, and then came the downpour. After sheltering, Jan and I continued a little further before deciding to return to camp. On the return leg it bucketed down again, the rain falling in heavy torrents that reduced visibility to a few yards. And after the rain stopped, moisture began evaporating from the hot soil and rocks and made the atmosphere incredibly humid. It was so humid that the air was fully saturated and excess moisture appeared as wisps of steam that rose into the air. It was like a sauna, and my body and clothes were dripping sweat onto the ground in constant streams.

It had started raining at 2 o'clock. Jan commented that the monsoon rain began a little earlier and lasted a little longer every day during the wet season, and I feared that my fieldwork might be coming to an end. The onset of torrential rain on the second day opened the old wound festering in my mind: had I collected enough information for a PhD, or would it all have been a waste of time? In my journal that night, I recorded many pages of anguished discussion, re-hashing all the points.

I think I need four weeks to complete the task. But if it rains and I can only work half-days, then I need up to eight weeks, to the end of December, but the rain will turn the rivers into torrents, and therefore the work would have to stop before December. It's that straightforward! At the end, the sum total of my fieldwork on Boi and Mol might only be six or seven weeks. Is this enough for a PhD I ask myself? It certainly is not the answer comes winging back. On several occasions I have aired my misgivings about coming here and staying here – yet I will continue, even though I feel that the better path would be the one home. Why don't I just give up? Am I just keeping up appearances to avoid the shame of quitting? If I leave, would I be letting down the whole college, the Indonesians – and myself? There is no-one here to discuss the matter with, and the problem lies entirely with me to solve. It is my decision, a decision debated and contested only by myself.

On November 5th, the third day in the field, we trekked across to the River Noni, a round trip of about eight kilometres. It was the hottest day so far. Indeed, it was so hot that I could not stand still on the rocks for more than a few moments, despite wearing boots, and my back felt as though it was on fire, only the shirt protecting me from being barbequed alive. Jan and I went for another bathe, and just as we were dressing, the rain came; it was 1.58pm, slightly earlier than the onset of rain the previous day. We sheltered for a while, and then set off for camp.

Boi mountain was a small area, but on it was exposed a diverse assemblage of rocks that provided key pieces for the jigsaw puzzle that I was trying to assemble. Mercifully, ascending to the top of the mountain was a relatively easy task compared with climbing Molo, and the reward much greater. To my surprise, I discovered that the summit area was formed of peridotite, a dark, dense rock primarily composed of olivine and pyroxene. Peridotites of different varieties form the mantle, the thick layer of the earth that lies beneath the crust, yet here it was sitting on top of a mountain. Underneath lay a thick body of metamorphosed gabbro and dolerite, which are intrusive igneous rocks typical of oceanic crust, and these were resting on metamorphic rocks that originated as ocean-floor basalts and marine sediments.

Peridotite-gabbro-dolerite-basalt make up the main components of an association of rocks given the term ophiolite, which is a thick slice of oceanic crust and mantle that has been obducted, that is, squeezed up to the surface when two plates push together. Obducted ophiolites are intact slices with mantle peridotite at the base and with a 200 to 300 metre thick metamorphic zone beneath them that passes downwards into unmetamorphosed rocks. This was not the situation on Boi, where the combined thickness of the metamorphic rocks beneath the peridotite was more than 1500 metres, and therefore it was more likely that the components had been assembled in a subduction zone beneath peridotite in the mantle of the overriding upper tectonic plate.

Jan was leaving the next day, and I would be alone to the end. We had developed a camaraderie that sprang out of sharing unfamiliar and arduous circumstances, and I would be sorry to see him go. Our last day in the field was *'another blaster'*, but there was no rain to ameliorate the discomfort temporarily. It was a long journey that day. I had almost no stamina to continue, and found the relatively easy journey back to camp difficult.

FINAL PUSH

Every day, I kept my determination strong by lying to myself by thinking *'Only ten more days'*. Ten days was far enough ahead to prevent me slowing down, but close enough to provoke encouragement. The simple delusion of having the desired goal defined and within sight was an effective way of motivating myself; my ambition was the stick, my self-deception was the carrot.

On Monday 7th, I managed to achieve good progress in the field and was quite pleased, if exhausted by 2 o'clock when I decided to begin the journey back to camp. My chief predicament that day was how to deal with the certainty that I would run out of sugar within a day or two. What would be my preferred drink: coffee without sugar, or milk without sugar? Would the powdered milk last? Could I afford the luxury of coffee *with* milk? On another day, I had to cope with the loss of the flannel that I took into the field to mop the sweat from my brow. I had kept the cloth damp and clean by wringing it in the pools I came across on my travels, and it had provided much-needed psychological comfort.

Each guide that came with me unwittingly provided material for my journal. One day there was a lazy man. At one point, he said we could go no further. This meant that he could not be bothered to go on. However, it certainly was possible to go further, but the going was not easy and required some cutting of the undergrowth and passage up a steep incline. Nothing else for it, I thought, and so I unsheathed my knife and managed to go another 60 metres up the river. At 2 o'clock he said "Let's go now", meaning let's go home. When I finally decided to start the return journey, there was a choice of routes. The guide chose to leave the river, and at first I didn't mind because he was taking a more direct route. But when I thought about it, I did mind, because the river led directly to the village, the way was lined with trees that gave shade, and the gentle gradient of the river was less tiring than the steep climb we had embarked on to go cross-country; he just wanted to get home with all haste.

One day there was the boy who repeatedly and frequently asked me the time. He was talkative and inquisitive, which was all right up to a point. That night as I sat in my room poring over the aerial photograph of Boi, by the light of my torch, he came over to peer and three others soon followed. I was hunched closely over the photograph, but his hand kept darting in and pointing to the rivers and mountain peaks while repeating their names. In the field that day, I had explained that I was looking at a photograph taken from the air, and shown him the rivers and peaks. Now he was showing off, which I suppose was only natural, and I didn't have the vocabulary to give a polite explanation of why I wanted him to stop, so I stopped working and left him to it while I recorded the situation in my journal.

One day there was the guide who started out on a different route in the morning, and mentioned the word photo at least twice as we left the village. It clicked that he was guiding me up the hill where I knew there was a small settlement, expecting me to take some portraits of the inhabitants – probably his relatives. Quite possibly, the people would have offered something in return, perhaps a couple of eggs as was offered to me once before, but I could not allow myself to be led wittingly into such a trap. I took the usual route. The family on the hill turned up that evening to have their photo taken!

For a day or two I was preoccupied with flies, which had multiplied a hundred-fold since it had rained. They were attracted to me by the rotting flesh smell of the festering sores on my body. Many of the fifty or so sores were on my lower arms, lower legs, ankles, and on my backside close to the waistline. They were circular lesions up to a centimetre or more in diameter and stood proud of my body like volcanoes. They formed scabs, beneath which the bacteria were eating my flesh down to the bone. Because I sweated so much in the direct sunlight, the scabs were wet, soft and they stuck to my clothes, and then were tugged or even ripped open when I moved. My forearms were exposed, as were my legs just above my ankles when my trousers lifted when I walked or climbed. The flies would gather round like pigs feeding at a trough. It was a breed particularly resilient to the danger of alighting on human beings. The little critters had a very squat elevation as they crouched on the skin, and a hard, direct hit from above would not kill them, only give me a sharp excruciating pain on the sore. And the flies were able to alight and feed without causing a sensation, and I had to keep remembering to look down and check if they were there.

And then, I invented an effective technique. I would swipe down on the beast just hard enough to trap it, then roll it sideways away from the wound, only then pressing down hard to kill it. Game on! I kept score on Wednesday 9th, killing nine and having eleven escape. I started well, racing to a 4-0 lead; however, they pulled back to 9-9 after an hour's play, and won 9-11 in extra time. Of course, I had no chance of winning in the long run, since the supply of fresh forces against me was inexhaustible and I would always tire or lose interest as the day progressed. If I was to win consistently, I had to restrict the game to no more than half an hour.

Ajaobonat was a sleepy little hamlet. This time of year, just before the monsoon broke, was the hottest period and a time when it seemed that all human activity ceased. Dry season chores were completed in the cooler part of the year, and now men and women alike were waiting for the rain so that they could tend their growing crops. The place was listless, but not lifeless. I recorded many observations concerning my interactions with the people, or happenings that I considered unusual. Among them was the dog that stayed next to his master despite taking a repeated beating with a stick; the ritual that children and adults alike threw stones at all domesticated animals; and the year-old child who was tethered to a hut by a length of rope and left to play in the dirt. Then there were the negotiations over food and souvenirs brought to me by a host of visitors, and the frequent hints or requests that I should give particular possessions to them, especially my watch and camera.

A man has just arrived in the hut with a radio cassette player blasting out music at full volume. It's the only one in the area, so is of some importance. The room is full, with six more people and two lurking in the doorway. The man wanted to see my watch, and so did everyone else, and so I gave it to him to examine. It's a digital watch with a black face, and he didn't know how to work it. I play a trick of rubbing the face on my trouser leg and at the same time cunningly depressing the button that activates the display, then I reveal the face with the time showing in red numbers. This really knocks them out around here, and I hope they think it's magic. Maybe it'll stop them asking me to give it to them.

Their values were so different to mine, and they had no external reference points that might enable them to understand a different culture, such as mine: no newspapers, no television, and virtually no contact with the world beyond a few miles of their village. I had the awareness; I had to be tolerant and accommodating, yet only to a point, since I had to keep mind, body, and essential possessions together in order to function. Arguably, I was losing the battle for my mind and body, but I retained a firm grip on my material possessions, at least the essential and treasured items. In addition to various requests for my watch and camera, one of the men kept asking for my map case. It had a shoulder strap and the man intended to use it to carry his *Areca* nut, Betel leaves and crushed limestone. A pack of cigarettes went missing from my room, and so it went on. A war of attrition was being waged, and I had to remain alert to confront the forces of entropy.

Then there was the woman who cooked my breakfast. She came into my room every morning, timed for when I was likely to be asleep, and helped herself to three mugs of rice, more than I could eat in two days, let alone one breakfast. She was feeding her family, but I suppose in her eyes it was quite natural that people shared, especially the rich visitor in receipt of her hospitality.

An intermittent flow of men arrived in the evenings to ask if I could change single 500 Rupiah notes, worth US$1. 500 Rupiah was a high denomination note in this part of Indonesia. It presented them with a difficulty, but I had taken plenty of small change from the bank in Kupang and could oblige them. Then one night, a man came to change a 5,000 Rupiah note, and I had to lie and say that I didn't have enough money, in order to conceal the whereabouts of my secret stash of more than 100,000 Rupiah. Had it been a test?

Thursday, November 10th was a day for stumbling. My guide must have been counting the number of times I fell over, because he told the story to his friends in the village that evening. He related the circumstances of each of three big falls, leaving out references to minor falls and stumbles, maybe because there were so many.

I was working the north side of the River Niti, attempting to get to the northern peak, named Bikmela, where I hoped to observe a boundary between metamorphic and sedimentary rocks of quite different ages. Though the horizontal distance was no more than 900 metres in map view, it was strenuous work because the slope was steep, and the dry, narrow river beds were densely overgrown with a tangle of vegetation. I almost reached the top on N6, one of the little rivers I had named, but was forced back by the undergrowth of *Lantana* thorn bushes, despite crawling on hands and knees and having my guide chop the bushes in front with a machete. I was dripping with sweat, my clothes were soaked, my shirt was ripped to shreds, and my arms and shoulders were bleeding from the scratches. I walked down and tried to go up an adjacent riverbed, but felt done in and returned to camp.

Another day over. I thought this at about mid-day, and each day I think "Another day over" a little earlier in the day, so that I can boost my flagging motivation. If this trend continues, the days will fly by and I'll be back in England three weeks before I leave here!

Saturday was also a hard day in the field, but I arrived back at camp in a good mood because I did not feel so tired, I had just washed, and the air had cooled down when the sky became overcast and it spotted with rain. I polished off the remains of a tin of peaches, and made myself a hot, sweet 'lemonade' from sugar and Tamarind seed pods that I had just bought from a visitor to my room. Afterwards, I walked to a place outside the settlement where I knew I could shit in private. I was puzzling why the toilet paper I left at this place got scattered in all directions, when I was disturbed by a dog nosing forward in the darkness towards me. As I left the scene, I spotted another dog nearby, and it wasn't long before the two were snarling at each other in competition for their fresh meal, and dispatching the paper willy-nilly.

The next day, I again failed to get to the top of Bikmela because of the dense vegetation, this time on river N8 on the northeast extremity of Boi mountain. It was a blistering journey back in the heat, and I felt wearier than ever. It had taken me almost three hours to go 500 metres up the riverbed towards the peak, and it took more than an hour to get back down to the main river.

On the journey back, and while I rested in the luxury of my favourite pool, I tried to form a realistic assessment of my progress. I had been mapping Boi for eleven days, which was not a long time. And yet, the key exposures were to be found along the Niti and Noni rivers, and I had completed my observations along these and several other dry riverbeds. There was almost no exposure on the summit area between the two main rivers, though I had discovered a body of serpentinite and been able to map it around the summit and take some samples of fresh rock. I had already seen and mapped the location of the principal rock types and had collected evidence of their relative ages and structural position within the metamorphic complex. And my collection of samples comprised an interesting selection of rock types, including specimens of the potentially controversial 'Granulite' that Tony had alluded to in one of his publications.

I reckoned that seven more days work might be enough.

So, then and there, I decided to continue for another week, and leave the following Sunday night to arrive in Kupang on the Monday. In all likelihood there would be a bemo to catch in Taemaman because people travelled to Takari on Monday to go to the market. Decision made. It changed my outlook, much for the better, and I stopped wishing that something terrible would happen to me so that I would have to return early. At different times, I had wished for a broken leg, snakebite, sting from a scorpion, or something else of a serious nature. But I just wasn't lucky enough, because the only injury I had sustained was a cracked nail, the result of a careless moment the day before when I gave my right thumb an almighty bang with my hammer against an immovable rock that I was examining.

In the evening, a guide brought in some more Asam (Tamarind) and two bunches of bananas, the small and sweet variety known as pisang mas, the golden banana. I mistook him for the man who last night I had asked to bring me some bananas, and

I bought the two bunches from him for the equivalent of 7 pence. However, ten minutes later the actual man I had asked arrived bearing a shoulder-full of bananas, and I felt a certain obligation to purchase from him.

I got away with buying only two bundles, and am now the owner of 56 bananas! Correction, 42, because I ate 14 straight off.

Six days to go, and counting down. It was a long, hot day in the field, and I complained to myself of sore feet, sore from the sores not from blisters, but I managed to stay out in the field for ten hours. Not unexpectedly, bananas were on the menu for snacks and lunch during the day. Tuesday was an unremarkable day of seven hours in the field. On Wednesday, I was woken at 4.30am when Ibu (mother) came in to let the chickens out of my room. Their hens and chicks slept under my bed. Because their wings were not clipped, the adult hens could fly short distances, and at any time of day would flap noisily into the trees and announce their arrival with a lot of cock-a-doodle-doodling.

It was an eight-hour day in the field. I set a cracking pace, feeling fitter than I had been since Kupang, and reached the River Niti in twenty minutes when at times it had taken me thirty. While bathing in my favourite pool, I daydreamed that I was in the Cross Keys pub in Hammersmith, sitting chatting to Laurie, and this led to my first craving for alcohol since I had been in the field. Usually, I focussed intensely on the job in hand and ruthlessly excluded all thoughts of the external world, since it was dangerous to think about what was beyond the confines of my circumscribed existence. Opening a window onto my normal world was an agonising distraction that was potentially fatal to the mission.

Back at the settlement, I had more thoughts about continuing the fieldwork, perhaps starting on another mountain. But I had no base maps, my residence permit would have to be renewed, and there wasn't enough time to make a return trip to the Geological Survey in Bandung since the full monsoon was imminent. A moment later, I projected forward to being back at college and reflecting that I had been stupid to leave the field before mapping had become impossible. I then pictured Tony saying that it would have been possible for me to have continued the fieldwork, and why hadn't I stayed.

EASIER SAID THAN DONE I'm afraid. It would be absolute hell to stay longer than I have already planned. When I am relaxing in England removed from the hardships it will be easy to say "Oh yes, I could have carried on." BUT NO WAY AM I STAYING LONGER.

Three more mugs of rice were taken on Thursday morning. Breakfast consisted of rice without meat, meaning that the family had eaten the remainder of the chicken I had purchased the night before. I had slept badly and was tired. Out in the field, I had a stomach ache and felt the weakest I had ever been. Not much was achieved that day, and even the guide had to stop a few times because of the heat. My sores were getting worse and were troublesome, especially the ones on my backside and ankles. The scabs stuck to my underpants and were tugged painfully when I walked, while the sores on my feet stuck to my socks and opened every night when I undressed.

Life is full of surprises. On Friday evening, after a blisteringly hot and tiring day in the field, I had a good chat and laugh with the people, the first time in Ajaobonat and belatedly on the brink of my departure. It started with me writing some of the local language and then reading out the words I already knew. A man to whom I had given a water bottle starting talking to me. He had made a string carrier bag for the bottle so that he could carry water on his shoulder. He offered to make one for my bottle, for which I thanked him. The conversation swung around to the subject of my knife, a conversation started by one of my guides, a young man named Tues ('Too-ess'). I say young man because he looked about seventeen, but he was twenty-three years old, had been married, and had witnessed the death of his wife.

"Saya dapat pisau" he said, meaning, literally, 'I can take knife'. Well, I had to point out that five others had already asked (or rather told) me, and that I intended to give it to the Paman Desa in Takari, a ploy I thought of to prevent them arguing among themselves. Immediately, three of the men were outraged because they didn't like the man in Takari, and said that the knife should be theirs because I was staying with them. I pointed out that the knife was no good anymore because it had a big chunk missing from the blade's cutting edge where I'd been hacking my way through the undergrowth. Tues said that it didn't matter about the gash in the blade because they could smooth this out, which I knew to be impossible. After further good banter, they did say that I could keep the knife if I wanted.

On Saturday, I made an early start, at 7am to be precise, with the good intention of getting a lot of work done because it would be my last day in the field. On the return journey, I bathed in 'my' pool for the last time, taking off all my clothes so that I could wash them out. It hit me that I was leaving the field and I yelled "Owyay" in a moment of sheer joy, just as the Atoni had done when we were on the top of Molo mountain.

I had decided not to work on Sunday, the last day, partly to prevent the possibility that items might go missing from my baggage when it would be too late for me to notice the loss or come back, and partly to get organised for leaving the following day. Sunday was spent going through all my belongings and choosing what to leave behind for the people of the village: matches, cigarette papers, ruler, pencils, shorts, trousers, underpants, pan scourer, plate, mug, plastic bags, rice sacks, film box, soap, sugar, and tea. It wasn't much but it was all I could give, and the people seemed grateful.

Monday came. I said farewells and was choked by a mixture of emotion for their plight, their stoicism in the face of enduring hardship, and relief that my arduous adventure was ending. I also felt a twinge of conscience at leaving the field when I still had the strength to carry on. My stamina had been sapped by the physical and mental toil of working three weeks without a break, but my spirit was still willing to push if there was an overriding reason to continue, which now there was not. The advent of daily rains could not be far away, and my mapping had covered every part of the mountain. I had an impressive selection of rock samples from Boi, eighty-five in all, and a good handle on the tectonic structure.

Following a batch of requests, I took photographs of different groups of people who had come in from I don't know where, dressed up in their Sunday clothes. The local radio cassette player appeared in three photographs, each time with a different man.

Just after 3 o'clock in the afternoon, I left the settlement with three guides, and I was sitting comfortably in the schoolteacher's house in Taemaman before 6 o'clock, having my first in-depth conversation for several weeks. Mr and Mrs Manoe were a kind and civilised couple who I had met on the inbound leg of the journey to Boi. That evening, they fed me a sumptuous meal of chicken cooked in coconut, accompanied by cabbage and red beans, washed down with a cold drink, my first one in three weeks. They were kind and accompanied me to the village boundary the next morning to say farewell. Damn, I thought, there is no bemo, and I'll have to walk back to Takari.

It had been a cloudy night and it was a cloudy day, and the air temperature was bearable. I stopped walking to seek lunch at Hoeknutu, about fifteen kilometres from Takari. A Nissan Patrol was parked in the village, and I learned that some Chinese men from Kupang were hunting game in the area. I approached them and scrounged a lift. I was not surprised that the men were friendly and spoke good English, since this had been my experience with all the ethnic Chinese on Timor. They had shot dozens of pigeons, a deer and a monkey. At 1.45pm, the expected happened and there was a downpour of rain, now fully fifteen minutes earlier than when I had arrived on Boi. We set off shortly afterwards, eight of us crammed in the jeep, with my baggage, their luggage, four guns and a large jumble of dead animals in various stages of rigor mortis. Discomfort did not register, I was so grateful to be given a lift and so looking forward to being in Kupang. Arriving about 6 o'clock, I thanked my benefactors and went in search of a losman, booking in at the Wisma Bachtera on Jalan Imambondjol.

Author and Max outside the Bachtera, Kupang

Catching the prahu from Kupang to Ba'a (Roti Island)

Greg's yacht in Benoa Harbour, Bali

Balinese landscape

Balinese temple

Kuta Beach sunset, Bali

Off-road scrambling with Greg (left) and Kim

Gunung Batur volcano, with recent lava flow and solfatara

Brian and Nick at the Genesis concert, Knebworth

Bernie, Nick and Clint at Lake Dallas, Texas

Author presenting at SEATAR Meeting, Bandung

Sangkuriang dance, Bandung

Lake Toba, Sumatra Island

Batak houses, Lake Toba

Author's accommodation, Lake Toba

Batak grave, Tomok

BRINGING IT
ALL BACK HOME

RECOVERY ON BALI

The ordeal was over. Realisation that the fieldwork had ended gradually permeated my consciousness. The harsh existence of the field was fresh in my mind but no longer pervasive or oppressive. A new reality was taking over. Deciding on the date of my departure from Boi had been a watershed, a point beyond which thoughts of life in England, thoughts of people dear to me, thoughts of what I was missing had entered my mind with increasing frequency, the closer the time came to leaving the field. Images would flash through my mind and stimulate transient thoughts of seeing Sarah, my grandmother, my old schoolfriends in Chippenham; or meeting my parents at Heathrow Airport on my return; or of being on a beach in Bali sipping cold drinks and munching pineapples. However, although I was on the return leg of the journey, I was still deep inside this foreign land half-way around the world, and home felt really far away.

Having now bathed and changed into clean clothes, the priority was to go to the Karang Mas, order my favourite dishes, and see if any mail had arrived from England. As I chomped through Cap Cai, Nasi Goreng and Beefsteak, I read letters from my mother and from Laurie at college. My plan was to spend Wednesday to Friday on Roti, a small island southwest of Timor, then fly to Bali on Saturday for a holiday, and finally return to England in time for Christmas, still a month away.

I assessed my finances and discovered that I could have lived a more comfortable and nutritious existence in the field, but frugality had been necessary while the length of my trip had been uncertain, and I was glad to have money left over to buy presents and to use for my trip to Bali. I had left England with £1,000 cash, which I changed for US$1,890 and which could have lasted a long time on Timor, but the balance would evaporate rapidly now I was back in the material world.

A day of leisurely activity followed. I shopped, bought cassette tapes of Timorese pop music, and a water buffalo skin wallet from the Chinese shopkeeper who had given me a lift the day before. At the Travel Bureau, I arranged and paid for the last batch of rock samples to be sent to LIPI in Bandung. I stepped on the weighing machine to find that I had lost two stone while on Timor, and weighed only 60 kilograms. Crikey, at only 9 stone 6 pounds, I was lighter than at any other time in my adult life.

That evening, a local man came into the Bachtera and offered me two beautiful selimut from Sumba. At $100 each, they were much too expensive, and I reckoned that I would find something more reasonable the next day. My patience paid off. Within 24 hours I had acquired a selimut and two selendang for a total of $30, and four Dutch Ringgits for a total of $25. 'Ringgit' is the name for the currency in Malaysia, but here they referred to Dutch coins, and I had just purchased two 2½ Guilder coins dated 1930 and 1931, and much prized by the Timorese. However, the selimut was my prize piece, a wonderful item of woven fabric from Savu, another island neighbour of Timor.

As there was no urgency to leave, I had not booked a flight to Roti and was pleased to have stayed another day in Kupang, and thereby obtained some especially good souvenirs. But what seemed to be a decision of no consequence turned out to be prescient, and provided me with a much better alternative to my dream of flying to Bali. An Australian named Greg was waiting for me in the reception of the Bachtera. Greg and three others were sailing from Sydney to Singapore and had landed at the nearby island of Roti en route. But they didn't have the right documentation, and an army officer had marched them down the main street at gunpoint and thrown them into jail. Greg and his friend Kim had been released to go to the regional army headquarters in Kupang, but neither of them spoke any Indonesian. Luckily, word had reached them that a white man who could speak Indonesian was in town, and Greg had come to me in search of help.

We found our way to army headquarters and got to see two officers. I explained that the Aussies were only tourists, on a holiday sailing to Bali, Jakarta, and Singapore. They had landed in Roti in innocence of the law, I continued, merely to take some parcels to a relative of a person in the Indonesian Embassy in Darwin. One officer thought that the Aussies should be sent back to Australia, but the more senior man chewed the matter over and then decided that they could proceed to Bali straight away, taking a letter from his office to army headquarters there. We would have to return tomorrow to collect the letter of authorisation.

I spent the rest of the day with Greg and Kim, playing pool in a pool hall, playing cards in the losman, and eating in the Karang Mas. Like me, my new friends were in their twenties. Greg had the frame of a Bulgarian weightlifter, a mop of curly fair hair, and a womanising twinkle in his eye. He was a self-made man and the yacht was a tangible benefit of profits made from his chain of jean shops in Armidale, New South Wales. Kim was a mate, a school teacher, a tall athletic man with film star looks. I was so relieved to be able to talk English freely, using vernacular, joking, and knowing that I would be understood. And to make my day I was invited to sail to Bali with them on Greg's boat.

ALL AT SEA

Late on Friday morning, with letter in hand, we walked to the seafront to catch a prahu (boat) bound for Roti Island. Because there was a reef on the shoreline, the boat was moored some way out to sea. First, we had to wade out to a large rowing boat that was rocking spiritedly in the choppy sea. Worried that the precious contents of my rucksack would get wet, I carried it on my head while trying to steady myself in the waves and swell.

An Indonesian prahu looks like a cross between a Chinese junk and an Arab dhow. This one had a diesel engine and a single mast afore-deck for auxiliary power. Our captain stood in a jerry-built cabin at the stern of the 60 foot boat, behind which, hanging out to sea, was a small, rectangular wooden enclosure that served as a toilet and carried a pole bearing the flag of Indonesia. It was an easy matter to board the prahu, since the gunwale was low in the waterline anyway and the boat was heavily laden with a cargo of passengers jam-packed together and huddled on the deck, each one clasping precious parcels like birds with wings outstretched to protect their offspring on the nest. The captain motioned to me, Greg and Kim to sit in a privileged position on the roof of his cabin. He shared with us some small delicacies of rice, fish and orange juice for lunch, and the boat departed shortly afterwards.

Keeping the coastline of Timor in view enabled the captain to navigate during the first sector of the journey. On each side of the boat, a large wooden rudder was lashed to the stern with stout rope, so that a man on either side could steer the vessel. At first, the sea was calm, but it became rougher in the late afternoon after we were clear of Timor and began crossing the twelve kilometre wide strait between Timor and Roti. To the south, there now nothing but open water to the coast of northern Australia 500 kilometres away. Threatening clouds approaching from the south presaged the advent of a storm, and fresh winds funnelled waves in two directions through the narrow strait, which so confused the little boat that we seemed to be riding a bucking bronco.

Plywood, bed frames and jerry cans were tied to the roof of the cabin, but the ropes were loose enough that we were able to find secure handholds among the paraphernalia; or we thought we were secure. A rope holding the plywood gave way and the three of us slipped off the top of the cabin into the water, plop, plop, plop! I went in with my shoulder bag, and my first thought was that the money, passport and important travel documents would be ruined. My second thought was that the boat was sure to carry on without me. I was a foreigner whose disappearance would be inconsequential, and my rucksack contained useful items, so why would the Captain bother to turn around and find me in a swirling sea under a dark grey sky?

No option but to swim, I thought, but should I go back to Timor or try to find the coast of Roti? Surely, it would be more sensible to swim towards the boat, but the boat had disappeared quickly from view in the high sea. I caught occasional glimpses of Greg, bobbing up and down a few metres away, but there was no sign of Kim. I tired within minutes from the effort of keeping afloat in my heavy, water-laden jeans, and every time I crested a wave, I went under and swallowed a dose of saltwater. It dawned on me that I had no chance at all of getting back to land. It was a stark situation. And then, it entered my head that the Timor Sea is a shark-infested stretch of water, and I was in a channel for the passage of the voracious killers.

To my amazement, the prahu appeared in front of me over the crest of a wave and was bearing down on me fast. The boat seemed enormous and threatening at close quarters. I thought that the bow would smash into my head and the flow of water would drag me underneath, so I pushed against the hull with my outstretched right arm to manoeuvre myself along the starboard side, and scrambled on board over the low gunwale. Greg and I climbed back on to the roof, secured the remaining items and held on for dear life. Kim had managed to grab the side of the boat as he fell, and had hung on desperately to rescue himself from the water, his leg bleeding from a slight injury. His good fortune in staying with the boat ensured that the captain was aware that Greg and I had fallen overboard.

Conditions worsened. Sunset was approaching and the sea became rougher, antagonised by winds generated by the fall in air temperature. Large waves towered over the boat, which seemed to be taking off over the crests and crashing back down on the sea, causing the timbers to creak and groan disconcertingly. The passengers were highly animated with anxiety and fear, some were sick, and water was washing over the bow and right along the deck to the stern every time the boat ploughed into the crest of a wave. With his knowledge of boats, Greg remarked, helpfully:

"If she breaks up, she'll break in the middle."

After what seemed like an eternity, the storm passed and the waves subsided. As the sun slipped below the horizon, a bright moon rose and lit the sky. The captain brought us some local 'brandy' or rice wine. It smelt like meths and had a ghastly taste, with a hint of vanilla. It had turned cold, my clothes were wet, and I was shivering. But I was emotionally drained from the experience, and managed to sleep a while. About 9 o'clock the boat pulled into a beautiful bay and dropped off about twenty passengers before continuing to Ba'a, the capital of Roti.

Bob and Jim were the other two travellers in our party. They arrived in a motorised dinghy and the five of us were soon safely on board the yacht. I was mightily relieved. If the prahu had gone down I would have been unable to swim with my rucksack, which contained maps, photographs and notebooks recording all my work from day one in the field, and Poseidon would have taken it all to the bottom of the sea. I could have survived if I had ditched my possessions and jeans, but I would have waved goodbye to my PhD. So I had two lucky breaks that day. The contents of my shoulder bag were soaked, and the ink had run on all the paper documents, but luckily the all-important KIM card and several other official letters were still legible.

Greg's boat was a real beauty. It was a 50 foot, 28 tonne ketch, all in white, with main and mizzenmast, six berths, a bathroom, separate toilet, a well-stocked library and storage space everywhere – mostly crammed with Aussie beer, wine and spirits. That night, the lads slept out on deck, but I opted for the master bedroom and a comfortable double bed. Luxury!

It was the morning of November 26th. We completed formalities onshore with the police and army, bought 120 litres of diesel and left harbour mid-afternoon. Under canvas and motor, the boat cruised at 5 to 6 knots, and we would be sailing 24 hours a day on three-hour shifts at the helm. Our course to Bali would take us northwest across the Savu Sea, skirting the island of Sumba before heading almost due west and within sight of Flores, Sumbawa and Lombok among the inner volcanic islands of the archipelago. I hoped that sun and salt water, combined with a better diet, would help to heal my sores, which I had found out were tropical ulcers.

Day 2 at sea and I joined Greg on the 6-9am watch, taking over at the helm for a couple of hours to get the feel of the boat. A fishing line was stationed permanently off the stern, and that afternoon a 15 pound beauty took the bait and was reeled in flapping its silvery body frantically from side to side in panic and bewilderment. Greg filleted the beast and served some tasty fish steaks that evening. Most of the day was spent in sight of the northern coast of Sumba Island, a large golden brown silhouette on the horizon. On Day 3, I took the 12-3am watch, played backgammon with Kim, read a little, talked to Greg, and did the 3-6pm watch before spending a few hours singing along to Bob's guitar music. That night we encountered a patch of phosphorescent protozoa that flashed with purple light, and enchanted us as the boat churned through the water. The next day was uneventful and the boat cruised happily along under sail; I took the 6-9am watch. Next morning, after 90 hours of sailing, the journey of 500 nautical miles was complete: we had arrived at Benoa Harbour in Bali.

PARADISE ISLAND

After we anchored, a dug-out approached, pulled alongside, and two boys introduced themselves. For a small fee, they were willing to look after the boat while the crew was ashore, and they would wash clothes, buy food, repair the boat and do any chores. Greg didn't want strangers on the boat, and he agreed only that one of them would assist in completing the administrative procedures. This involved visits to the harbourmaster, police, navy, immigration, customs, and quarantine.

Formalities could not be completed until the next day, and immigration advised us not to go into town until then. However, we were eager to explore our surroundings and we motored in the dinghy to Benoa village on the other side of the harbour. We found that the village was the centre of a trade in turtles, and hundreds were being landed from various boats. It was a pitiful sight to see the helpless creatures, still alive and lying upside down on the decks with their legs tied. A restaurant on the seafront had turtle on the menu, and I disconnected myself from the reality I had witnessed to tuck into delicious turtle soup for the equivalent of 50 pence and turtle steaks for 75 pence. Boys were selling rings made of turtle shell, and I bought two, one for myself and one for Sarah.

Even before I left England, I had hoped I would make it to Bali. It had a reputation as an enchanting island, famous for its natural beauty and the charm of its artistic people. My original intention was to stay a few days, or no more than a week, but now I was in the mood to stay several weeks. I had good travelling companions, money in my pocket, and no pressing reason to be anywhere else but this tropical paradise.

Like Java, Bali is situated on the inner volcanic arc of the subduction zone, but is a much smaller island, measuring only 90 by 130 kilometres. It is dominated by six volcanic peaks and covered with lush vegetation that thrives on the fertile volcanic soil and abundant rain brought by the wet monsoon. An ancient belief in Hinduism has survived on Bali, even in the midst of the influence of Islam, which became predominant in the region by the 16th Century. Religion is central to the lives and society of the Balinese, and finds expression in architecture, craftwork, painting, dancing and daily rituals. Temples and shrines are everywhere, in every house and even along the roadside.

Lots of people accosted us on the streets of the capital Den Pasar the next day, trying to sell paintings, wood carvings, wooden chess sets, batik, and English newspapers at twice the printed Rupiah value. They all persisted in the face of repeated protestations, and one man even followed us into a restaurant. I was tempted to buy a leather briefcase costing £20, as a present for my father, but on inspection, the quality of the workmanship was poor. Kuta Beach was the next stop. Kuta had a reputation as a place to watch the sun go down and up repeatedly under the influence of magic mushrooms. Along the main street that led directly away from the beach, there were restaurants selling magic mushrooms served up in soup, on toast and in other dishes. Marijuana was being sold openly, and prostitutes were available if so required. I had tried hash once or twice in my schooldays, but the experience had made me feel queasy or had no effect at all. I did not intend experimenting with mushrooms, because what could be stranger than reality? Regarding the prostitutes, I had been without sex for more than four months and was quite able to wait a while longer, especially given the high risk of catching a venereal disease. It was a pity though, as the girls were beautiful, slender, brown-skinned and had a most enticing demeanour.

Greg and Kim were my companions that day, since the other two travellers had a personal agenda. Greg and Kim wanted to hire motorbikes to ride around and see the island. They enquired with several hustlers on the street until they made a connection. I tried three different bikes up and down the street while Kim and Greg tried scramblers. After much bargaining there was no agreement on price, so we walked to the beach. It was a beautiful tropical beach with coral sand and fringing palm trees basking beneath a brilliant blue sky, but the sheer number of white bodies crowding the view spoilt the exotic scene. Freshly made cold tropical fruit juices were on sale at snack bars for 75 Rupiah. I tried papaya and pineapple before we left the beach and returned to the taxi, a big American car we had hired from Den Pasar. At the taxi, there was more bargaining for motorbikes with the persistent touts who were hanging about. Greg and Kim made their choice and only needed to return the next day with cash. I also managed to agree terms, but had to go to the owner's house to sign some document or other. He wanted assurance and reassurance that I possessed an international driving licence that included motorbikes, so I had to pass off my ordinary UK car licence to get the deal completed. I reunited with my friends and we headed off back to the boat.

Cockfighting is a popular sport on Bali, an activity carried out in small public arenas in villages, and in stadia in the towns. Apart from one German woman, Greg, Kim and I were the only foreigners at the contest in Den Pasar the next day. A throng of punters squashed themselves around a concrete square marked with white lines that defined the field of contest. Interesting preliminaries preceded every bout. Owners brought the two contesting animals into the ring, squatted down and then aggravated the birds into a fighting mood by rough handling and plucking a few feathers on the back of the head. Each bird was allowed to peck the other one once, to raise the level of adrenalin. All the while, the punters were shouting in order to bid for and obtain bets with someone else in the crowd, there being no bookies. Shouting, hand signals and waving of money ensued. Birds were taken to their corners, a gong was struck and the birds set free. Each animal had a long, backward-facing steel spike strapped to its left ankle. When they met, sometimes the birds bowed heads and displayed a collar of feathers around their necks, sometimes one animal commenced the fight by jumping up and toward the opponent, feet forward and poised to make a deadly strike into the gullet of the other with a vicious downward sweep of the spike. An early strike and a clean strike would end the bout in seconds. Less fortunate animals were wounded, and the fight would go to a second round. If two birds strutted around eying up the opponent, they were placed into a small wicker basket, which immediately led to fighting.

During the bouts, the audience was silent, and Greg received hostile stares and reprimands for his loud shouting. We were interested in the spectacle of the contest, whereas the locals were serious about the financial outcome. They were not spectators, they were speculators. Then, a punter asked if he could bet for us. Each of us put in a small wager of 500 Rupiah, and after several bouts were well ahead before ending with 1,000 Rupiah each. Fighting had started at 11 o'clock and was set to continue until late afternoon, but we tired of the spectacle by 1 o'clock and left to ride across the island to Sanur.

Riding my Suzuki 185 was fun. It felt a little heavy at slow speeds, but was not difficult to learn to ride and had enough power to impart a feeling of exhilaration when I opened the throttle. If only the owner knew that I had never ridden a motorbike before. What a huge feeling of freedom it was riding around wearing a T-shirt, shorts and flips-flops on almost empty roads, and being fanned by a delightfully cooling breeze. There was a more serious side, however, and I had to remain alert for unruly drivers (i.e. all of them), careless pedestrians (i.e. all of them), and brainless chickens (ditto). Too many of the young Aussie tourists flew home lying prostrate across three seats in the aircraft because they had received serious injuries on the road. In Bali it was commonplace to see vehicles travelling the wrong way along a one-way street. Some Aussies discovered the culture shift too late to understand that it was in your interests to give way, even when it was your right of way.

Sanur was on the east coast of Bali, where the up-market international hotels were situated. We stopped at the Hyatt Hotel and strode past the officials guarding the entrance, as if we were residents. I had never seen such an idyllic sight: low thatched buildings nestling among palm trees and bushes of flowering plants, the golden sand and shallow blue sea, and a gigantic swimming pool featuring a bar in the middle. After a drink and a swim we tried the Bali Beach International and two games of ten-pin bowling in a modern alley in the hotel. I had promised to treat Greg and Kim to a decent meal, as part payment of my fare for the trip on the yacht. I booked a table at the Hyatt restaurant and we returned at 9 o'clock. After a blow-out meal and three bottles of wine, we retired to the bar upstairs for a sing-along with the resident pianist and had a fart-lighting contest.

A lazy morning followed because it rained heavily, and I wanted to catch up on some sleep and write letters and postcards. In the afternoon, Bob managed to hire a motorbike, so there would now be four musketeers. We rode to Kuta Beach for fruit juices and jaffles, an Australian toasted sandwich with cheese and fruit filling. After the sun disappeared from view, the beach became more crowded, with many hundreds of tourists and an army of young Balinese selling assorted souvenirs. They were all seasoned and charming hustlers, even the beautiful little Balinese girl no more than ten years old who tried to sell me a bikini for my girlfriend.

"I don't have a girlfriend", I said. She said I could buy it for my sister. "I don't have a sister, and I'm all alone." Ah, then I should buy the bikini bottom for myself, she said.

Not much happened the following day. Greg and I had turtle soup and turtle steak in the village, returning to the boat to pack for the departure next morning.

By way of contrast, our journey northwards the next day was quite eventful. We rode through five downpours of rain, Bob's luggage fell off his bike, my luggage fell off my bike, Kim's bottle of spare fuel broke, my bike wouldn't start for a while because it was wet, and when we arrived at a losman in Ubud, Bob's fuel bottle 'exploded', spilling two litres of petrol over the floor of the bedroom. Bob exploded too, swearing profusely for five minutes or more. On the bright side, our losman was fairly clean and comfortable, and remarkable value at 50 pence a night.

We visited an outdoor restaurant in the town centre and homed in on the local delicacy of roast suckling pig. A baby pig was roasting over a spit until the skin became crispy. It looked delicious and we all placed an order. When it came, the meal consisted of rice and onions, crackling, strips of tender and juicy meat, fried and crispy blood, and sausages that were sections of intestine with the original contents included. Bile sausages, now isn't that a novelty! After eating and watching several cockfights in the town centre, we left in search of souvenirs.

Ubud is famed for its community of painters and the unique style of Balinese paintings. Scenes set in the rain forest or rice field are traditional subjects. People, monkeys, birds and an assortment of Balinese-Hindu gods adorn the canvas, sometimes illustrating a mythical scene. They are drawn or painted without the benefit of toning and shadow and therefore do not have a true 3-D perspective. But the colours are exquisite and the detail astonishing. Away from the main street we visited galleries that had been set up within the house of the artist or dealer.

A high wall surrounds a typical Balinese house and encloses a courtyard containing several open buildings and small temples situated in each cardinal direction. Dark brown volcanic rock is the only local building material, and with the abundant vegetation and steamy atmosphere this creates an earthy feel at one with the natural habitat.

Prices were in dollars in every shop, an indication of how much the local economy was geared to tourism. Bargaining is *de rigueur* on the island, as elsewhere in the country, but is a difficult art for westerners to master. Everywhere we went we expressed disbelief at the prices, but disbelief is only the start of the bargaining process. Starting and finishing prices are set according to a tiered scale in which Balinese pay least and Japanese and American tourists who arrive by coach pay the most. One gallery owner offered a multiple discount because: [a] I could speak some Indonesian; [b] I looked like a student; [c] I was not travelling on a tour, and: [d] I was not a gullible tourist who assumed that the prices were fixed, but was prepared to bargain. One shop owner offered me a painting in exchange for the denim shorts I was wearing. However, the practicalities of taking a painting in my luggage deterred me from buying anything, irrespective of whether or not money would change hands.

I ate a breakfast of duck eggs, toast, papaya and banana on the terrace of the losman the next morning. My motorbike had a flat tyre and required a new inner tube, which I finally tracked down at a repair shop. Bob still felt ill with a cold, and he left the party to return to the boat. Greg, Kim and I continued our journey northwards, passing through Pujung before the tarmac road turned into a bumpy and slippery dirt track, which my comrades fully exploited on their scramblers; I did my best to keep up and only fell off once.

We arrived at Kedisan, a village built on the rim of an enormous caldera crater created by a prehistoric volcanic explosion. A contemporary cone named Gunung Batur sat majestically in the centre of the caldera, its peak in the clouds and its flanks surrounded by a crater lake containing vivid blue water. It was a breathtaking sight. A small parasitic cone on one side of the mountain had been active in recent years, spilling enough hot lava to create a land bridge to the rim.

We had to dash into a restaurant to shelter from the rain, then booked into a losman for 300 Rupiah for the night. I woke at 5 o'clock. A heavy mist completely obscured the view, but cleared as the morning wore on and enabled us to watch brown smoke billowing from the parasitic cone. It was overcast and cold, and we donned plastic raincoats to ride down to the northern coastal plain, to the town of Singaraja. Singaraja was not an inspiring place, so we left and rode to nearby Lovina Beach and checked into a losman. Greg felt ill and did not eat that evening, and I went to bed early to keep warm. It rained all night, clearing at about ten in the morning when we set off for the journey back to the boat.

Four lazy days followed. On Friday, Greg and I rode to the Bali International Hotel in Sanur to buy my ticket to Jakarta, before we headed out to Kuta for an afternoon on the beach. We returned to the beach on Saturday, swimming in the warm sea and diving head first into the waves. It was scalding hot weather, and I caught mild sunstroke. On Sunday, I slept all day, and on Monday we rode to the airport to bid Bob farewell on his trip to England.

There was much more action on Tuesday. Kim and I returned from a swim at Kuta Beach to find Greg half cut on whisky. So we all got stuck into the reserves of alcohol on the boat and enjoyed some good conversation and jokes. Greg and Kim kept asking me to stay with them on their journey to Singapore, and return with them to Australia. It was a sorely tempting offer. I knew almost nothing about their country, but from what they said, it seemed like a great place to be. Greg was drunk and in no condition to go out, so I borrowed his bike and rode with Kim to the Bali International in search of entertainment and cocktails.

It was probably appropriate that the cabaret artiste in the nightclub was named Gloria Bang, since she looked like a goer. Her act finished about midnight, and so Kim and I moved on to the Hyatt in search of more entertainment, but there was none. As we left, Kim decided he wanted one of the giant ceremonial banners that lined the driveway to the hotel. They resembled narrow sails and were mounted on 10 foot high bamboo poles that were easily removed from the ground. Kim uprooted a pole and leant it against a hedge. His plan was to walk around the hedge and pick up the banner on the other side, near the bikes. However, the security guards who were approaching us had an altogether different plan. Kim and I calmly walked on, prepared to say nothing and leave in innocence, but the game was up. A guard snatched the keys from the ignition of my bike and accused us of stealing the banner. More security guards appeared and they were carrying the banner as Exhibit Number 1 in the case for the prosecution. A tug of war ensued with Kim and I trying to wrestle the pole from five guards – and vice versa. Indonesians are not exactly tall or muscular, and the result was a stalemate. Then the manager turned up and the miscreants were chaperoned into the hotel, where a heated discussion ensued. Finally, police arrived on the scene of the crime and Kim and I were taken to the station at Den Pasar.

It was no Black Maria, but a pickup truck fitted out with two park benches in the back. Kim and I sat on one bench, and three pistol-packing, truncheon-toting, helmet-wearing policemen sat on the other. At the station, we were able to be jocular with the captain and his cohorts, and the situation was defused. When we were released we managed to scrounge a lift back to the hotel, getting completely soaked in the pickup during a huge downpour that added to the farce. It was warm rain, and I removed my shirt to enjoy the experience. When we arrived at the boat it was 4 o'clock in the morning. Where had the last four hours gone?

The last few days before my departure were a little quieter. I bought some more souvenirs as presents, I ate my last meal at the 'Turtle Restaurant', and sat on the beach at Kuta for the last time. It was a truly magical sunset that evening, with the somewhat cloudy sky set on fire, and the sea a shimmering expanse of multiple hues of orange.

Greg and Kim accompanied me to the airport at Den Pasar on the morning of Saturday December 17th, and we sat about having a drink until I boarded a Garuda Airways DC9 at noon. It was a sad farewell after a month of close companionship. I liked Greg and Kim very much and we had shared some truly unforgettable experiences. I hoped that they regarded me as a mate. Should I have stayed with them, I thought, as the plane lifted into the air? I was sorely tempted, and had given this prospect much thought, but the PhD meant too much.

EXIT

Reaching Jakarta, I took a taxi to the Hotel Marco Polo. My room had three luxuries that I had been without for four months: air conditioning, a television and a bath with hot water on tap. And to make a welcome change from Indonesian food, I bought wholemeal bread, butter, ham and Edam cheese at a nearby supermarket and made sandwiches in my room. An apple pie that I purchased at a Danish bakery completed the meal.

I took the train to Bandung the following day and was welcomed at Fred Hehuwat's house like an old friend. I wanted to thank Fred for the undoubted help behind the scenes with the bureaucracy, and it was an important protocol to make an appearance at the government department that sponsored my visit, and to visit the people who had helped me at the Geological Survey of Indonesia. In the morning, I met Jan and Yanto at LIPI, went to the Geological Survey, and called my mother and father to tell them that I would be home for Christmas. I spent the next two days in Bandung at leisure, making last minute purchases to complete my Christmas shopping. Many of the shops in town had Merry Christmas signs and decorations, and I was getting in the mood.

Back in Jakarta, I stayed my last night in Indonesia at the Marco Polo, and once more ate homemade sandwiches in my room. The next day was Friday December 23rd, and perilously close to Christmas. As my flight to Singapore was not confirmed, I made sure that I arrived at the airport well before the check-in time. After some running around and waiting, I had to pay an extra $35 to secure a seat, but at least it was in First Class!

At this point, my plan began to go wrong. At Immigration, I was told that I did not have an exit permit and could not leave the country. I was astonished that anyone would need to have a permit to leave a country, and angry that neither the travel agent nor the airline, nor anyone I knew in Bandung had advised me of the need. It was explained to me that the exit permit was required because I was travelling on a residence permit, and the sponsoring authority would have to clear my departure. They told me I would have to go to a particular department in the city. As this could delay my departure, perhaps for more than a week until after the New Year, I decided to try to bluff my way through, and I sneaked past the desk at immigration and made my way to the baggage check-in counter.

Man 1 checked my boarding card and then my hand luggage, OK so far; then Man 2 asked to see my boarding pass, and when he turned it over he remarked that there was no stamp from the Immigration section. Damn! I returned to Immigration to a different booth, but was told for a second time – in no uncertain terms – that I could not go through without an exit permit. No amount of pleading, of pulling a long face, or of showing total disappointment and utter frustration helped. Perhaps I should bribe someone, I thought, but what if I bribe the wrong person? Quite possibly, I could have bribed several people up the long chain of officialdom and got no result, or been reported and then slung into a ghastly jail.

I took a taxi to the British Embassy and just managed to catch the Vice Consul as she was leaving for the Christmas Holiday. After some hesitation, she offered to write a letter for me to take to Immigration. My polite request to be smuggled out in the Diplomatic Bag was considered an unusual and rather impractical request that had no chance of meeting with success. I had taken a calculated risk in making a silly joke, but it paid off because she was kind enough to write the letter and drive me to LIPI's office, which was closed. A security guard gave me another address to go to, and I jumped into a taxi. More frustration: the address was Komplex LIPI, but the driver took me to Komplex *Slipi!* Well, it sounded the same and was a simple mistake. I paid the driver and took another taxi, this time to the Cathay Pacific office in Jalan Thamrin, the main drag in Jakarta. I cancelled my flight. By a stroke of good luck, the man on duty had been in the Cathay Pacific office in Bali when I had booked my flight. He was a charming man and helpful throughout. He confirmed my new flight reservation to Singapore, but I was on the waiting list from Singapore, and might not get home for Christmas. Still, nothing more could be done now, and so I checked in at the Marco Polo again. The radio in the room was playing Christmas songs, but this time I wasn't in the mood, and settled down to watch Ironsides and Baretta on the television.

Next day, the 24th, did not go smoothly. My taxi took me to LIPI, as requested, but after I entered the building I found out that it was the wrong office. So I walked about a kilometre in the rain to the correct office, arriving just before 8 o'clock and a little weary from carrying my rucksack. I had my letter by 9 o'clock, and took a taxi to the Department of Immigration, where I bought some forms and a folder, filled in the details, and eventually found where to take them. The man who accepted the documents told me that I must report to another Immigration office first, and return later. Another taxi ride, another place. Two hours later, and I was on my way back to the first place, tiring fast, having carried by rucksack everywhere with me.

All the taxis going past me were full, so I hailed a helicak (scooter with cabin for three passengers). I showed the driver the address, and a moment later he asked to see it again. He kept the card, and looked at it about six times in the space of two minutes. I doubted whether he knew where the place was, and he had some kind of speech impediment, which meant I couldn't understand what he was saying. Added to this, he was a half-wit. Luckily, I had some notion of where the place was, and we arrived without delay under my instructions.

At the office, four men took it in turns to inspect the documents and scribble or stamp approval on bits of paper. And then at 1 o'clock, at last I had my exit permit! I took a taxi to Cathay Pacific's office but the door was locked. Luckily, my friend was there and let me in. I was booked on a Qantas flight from

Singapore. Another taxi ride, but this time the final one. Everything went smoothly at Jakarta airport and Singapore airport, and at 9 o'clock that evening I boarded the Qantas flight to London.

Well, here I am on a QANTAS jumbo. Eight hours to Bahrain, and seven more to Heathrow. It's now December 25th. Merry Christmas Mike.

DISPLACED

I returned to the same spot on the planet that I had left a mere five months ago, but I returned from another era and another world where I had spent a lifetime. And I did not fit into the familiar world in England. It seemed as though I had been on a walk in space attached to a lifeline from the mother ship, and then been pulled back in to find myself on an alien spacecraft. The former, external reality of my time in Indonesia now existed only inside my head and would remain there forever, inaccessible to others. I could not prove that it had existed or still existed. My mind could not be plugged into a machine and the experience replayed with full sound, smell and emotion to an audience. Though they were tangible evidence, the notes, photographs and souvenirs, however interesting to others, were merely curious exhibits that did not have the power to recreate the environment I had lived in, or evoke in others the exact and real feelings and emotions. And the ulcers, the last of which took six months to heal, were now out of the context to which they had belonged, and were real yet inexplicable in the safe, sanitised surroundings in which I found myself. My mind was not settled. It was a weird feeling sensing that I had moved on, when no-one and nothing outside had changed.

In January 1978, I moved into new digs at 12 Ellingham Road in Shepherds Bush. It was a decent-sized bedsit at the rear of a terraced house, and afforded me the isolated and private habitat I needed in order to be effective at thinking, reflecting and developing my ideas during the long hours I liked to concentrate in order to find inspiration. I was at my most creative when I could shut the world out and maintain a constant focus on problems for hours on end, especially from late in the evening through to early in the morning. While an undergraduate, I had at times studied all night and then appeared in lectures in a semi-comatose state.

It was to be a busy year, filled with a wide variety of social events and outings that exploited my privileged position as a resident of London. And there was a greater involvement in the affairs of the college. As well as field trips with the undergraduates, every Thursday in term time I demonstrated from 11am to 1pm in Igneous Petrology and from 3pm to 5pm in Metamorphic Petrology, which earned me a grand total of £8.80 a week.

Dr Alex Grady arrived from Australia to begin a sabbatical from Flinders University in Adelaide, and spend a year at Chelsea College. He wanted to study the college's extensive collection of Timor rock specimens, and have discussions with members of the 'London School', myself included. I quickly came to like Alex very much, reinforcing my appreciation of Australians that had begun on meeting Greg and Kim in Timor. Alex was a big, affable man with a thoughtful and thorough approach to his work, traits that I respected highly. Our relationship got off to a good start, and we went for a meal at the Mata Hari restaurant in Euston with Sarah and Alex's wife Jan.

Sarah had matured from a girlish student to a young businesswoman. Her clothes were sophisticated and her glorious head of hair was loosely permed and lightened to a honey-brown colour with streaks of lighter colour. We spent much time together in the first few weeks after my homecoming, either at my digs or going out to the cinema, the theatre or for dinner. We saw Clint Eastwood in *The Gauntlet*, the hilarious *Young Frankenstein*, *Star Wars*, Ridley Scott's star-studded movie *The Duellists*, and the one and only Billy Connolly in *Big Banana Feet*, as well as *Man and Superman* at the Savoy Theatre, and a Royal Shakespeare Company production of *Wild Oats* at the Piccadilly Theatre. However, from about the second week in February I saw Sarah less often, no more than once or twice a week, until I ended the relationship on 8th March just after I returned from a three-day field trip to Cornwall with Tony and a group of geology students from Utrecht University.

A specific reason did not emerge from the fog of my dissatisfaction with the current state of my life. Because of my trip to Timor I might have changed in some way, either permanently or temporarily. I thought that the root of the problem lay in the delay in receiving my rock samples from Indonesia. It was three months since I had returned, and it was not clear whether they had left the docks in Jakarta or were somewhere on the high seas. My research could not continue without them. There could be several different explanations for my behaviour, but the fact was that at a time of major distress I felt compelled to face the situation alone.

Three more months passed without confirmation as to the whereabouts of my samples and no one seemed able to expedite their transportation. I kept myself busy by delving into published research regarding the geology of the Indonesian region, as well as everything I could find about Timor itself, the language, the people, its history and geography. And I wrote rudimentary translations of key geological papers written in German, Dutch and French by going through the texts a word at a time with an appropriate dictionary.

VARIETY AND SPICE

Then there was Tina, a girl from Putney who I dated for more than two months straight after finishing with Sarah early in March. She was a bright geology undergraduate at the college, and I had been flirting with her while demonstrating in practical classes. Not only was she a bright girl, but she was also sexually adventurous. Indeed, before going to college, she had starred in a Paul Raymond erotic revue, and had travelled in Europe with the show. Initially, I was attracted by her outgoing personality, but I discovered other delights as the relationship progressed. And it progressed very rapidly because we slept together on our first date. She introduced me to a few interesting aspects of lovemaking, and it was certainly an equitable arrangement to swap roles, with her being the demonstrator and me being the student in the privacy of our own practical sessions.

Tina and I met frequently. We went to a Jethro Tull concert at the Hammersmith Odeon and saw a few films including *Close Encounters of the Third Kind* and *Saturday Night Fever*. Perhaps it was coincidence, or maybe it was her preferred kind of movie, but we saw a succession of films dealing with love and sex. First there was *The World's Greatest Lover*, a disappointing and unfunny comedy written and directed by and starring Gene Wilder; then came *The Stud*, with Jackie Collins - say no more; and finally, a disturbing Japanese film called *Ai No Corrida*. The subject of the film was an intense and obsessive relationship between the master of the house and a wife who was formerly his servant. It was a superb film, except for the scene where you see her cutting off his penis after he dies. I secretly hoped that no-one would ever love me so much.

After Tina came Galia, or rather there was an overlap of about one week. Galia was a nurse working at St. Charles' Hospital, and I dated her in the latter half of May and most of June. There was no doubt that I was first attracted to Galia because she was a pretty Asian girl with wonderful long, black, silky hair and dark skin. Though a Philippino, she reminded me of girls I had seen in Indonesia, but not dared to approach. I was out on the town with Brian Sweet one night when I saw Galia in Thursday's Bar and arranged to meet her the next day. It was a balmy summer that year and Galia and I spent several days sunbathing in Holland Park while the city was beset with a series of strikes. Rubbish piled up in the streets and the dead lay unburied. The extent of the disaffection was unprecedented, and the situation led up to the 'Winter of Discontent' in 1978-79, and the eventual fall of the incompetent Labour government in May the following year.

As if in concert with the mood of the country, I became

increasingly discontented, a situation that led me back to the ways of my teenage years, only I was now twenty-five years old, going on twenty-six. Research took a back seat and my social life took precedence. I flitted from girl to girl, including Sarah, and between different friends in Chippenham and London. Several weekends were spent in Chippenham seeing my old schoolfriends Bernie Jones, Nick Brewer and Rob Noyes in country pubs, usually the Jolly Huntsman in Kingston St. Michael or the White Hart at Ford. And I hatched a plan with Nick to go touring across the US of A on a Greyhound bus, and we applied for Visa's.

In the meantime, my life was full of entertainment. In May, the press had reported that Bob Dylan was to perform six shows at Earls Court in mid-June at the start of a European Tour. All 92,000 tickets sold out within hours. Dylan had not performed in England since the Isle of Wight Festival in 1969, and I could not miss this rare opportunity to see the man who had made such an immense impression on me during my teenage years. I succeeded in buying tickets for three shows. In the event, I gave a ticket to my sister Diana and went twice myself, once with Galia, my current date, and once alone. At a mere cost of £7.50 a ticket, I sat close to the stage and had a commanding view of each show. I thoroughly enjoyed the new songs and rearrangements of old numbers. Presumably motivated by a need to satisfy the preconceptions of his readership, a hackneyed hack at the Daily Mail wrote that Dylan's performances 'were attended by superannuated hippies now verging on middle age, who paraded their long hair and joints as relics, remembrances of things past'. It was true that Dylan was no longer ahead of his time, but the general issues he had sung about in the sixties were still relevant more than ten years later. Yet no-one, it seemed, cared enough to write songs about the conflicts in East Timor, Ethiopia and Northern Ireland.

Four days later, Brian Sweet, Nick and I went to a Genesis concert at Knebworth Park, north of London. Brian was a big fan of Genesis and the motivator behind the trip. In the supporting line-up were Jefferson Starship, Tom Petty, Devo, and Atlanta Rhythm Section, and there were 60,000 fans in the crowd. Finally, to round off the month, on June 29th I passed my advanced driving test and was elected a member of the Institute of Advanced Motoring, at least in one respect following in the footsteps of my father.

July was no less packed with events. In the first two weeks there was a family holiday on the sunny south coast at a place named Sandbanks, near Bournemouth, and a day at the F1 Grand Prix at Brands Hatch watching Carlos Reuterman take the chequered flag in his Ferrari.

Ironically, my rock samples arrived from Indonesia just five days before I was due to leave for America. It was too late to cancel my trip, and I didn't want to anyway, so my research would have to wait another month.

CATHARSIS

It was more than eight years since Nick and I had been at school together. Nick had remained a fit rugby player, but had lost some hair and aged a little in the meantime. He was still living in Chard, and we had kept in touch, sporadically, mainly through Bernie, who periodically arranged for all of us to meet at some pub or other near our home town. And, by coincidence, Bernie was working in Dallas for oil support contractor Core Laboratories and it was in our plan to visit him during the trip to America.

At the heart of the adventure was a three-week journey by Greyhound bus across the United States. It was an ambitious plan, since we intended to stop at several places, swing down to the border with Mexico, and spend a few days in Canada. As it turned out, we travelled 5,600 miles by Greyhound, 700 miles by car, and visited seventeen states - fourteen American, two Canadian and one Mexican. We were amazed at how low the prices were in America, and managed to live on about $15 a day each. Even so, the whole trip cost me a hefty £600, including £265 for the flight and £126.50 for the Greyhound pass.

I had someone to share my experiences on this trip. Nick turned out to be a really good companion on such a long and tiring journey, fun to be with and easy going. We got on famously, despite the many points of personal stress related to excessive drinking, sleep deprivation, and uncomfortable nights spent on marathon bus journeys. And the wonders we saw and experienced! In a word, the United States was wonderful, and it was all so impressive, not just the scenery, but the courteous citizens, the first class service, the vibrant cities, the unrivalled cheesecake...

We flew on BA287 to San Francisco for the starting point of the journey. During takeoff, I reclined and switched to the rock music channel to hear Uriah Heap blasting out through the headset. Nick and I soon got stuck into the spirit miniatures; my choice was vodka with lime, Nick's was Bacardi and lime. With the score at four-all, we switched to a bottle of wine, which we shared during the meal. In travelling away from the sun, daylight was lengthened to about a day and a half. So despite a late afternoon takeoff from London, we arrived in San Francisco at six in the evening and with plenty of time to boogie. On the way, there were stunning views of glaciers in Greenland and the Arctic ice pack, as we flew over the north Atlantic towards Canada, and then directly over the ice-bound Canadian Shield.

Getting through customs presented no problems. We caught an express bus to downtown San Francisco, walked three blocks to the Winston Hotel on Eddy Street, and checked into room 315. My first introduction to an American shower left me remarking that 'downpour' would be a more appropriate description. Given the litigious state of their society, there should have been a notice disclaiming liability for any injury to the guests! We changed, left passports in the hotel safe, and went out to explore our new surroundings, finally going to bed at 3am – which was 11am in England.

Day 2. Wednesday 19th. Despite everything we managed to wake early today. Left the hotel at eight and walked to Market Street in order to find the Tourist Information Centre, which doesn't open until nine. We went to Powell Street and had three large mugs of good coffee each for $2. Caught the cable car outside, after looking in a huge Woollie's where we purchased postcards and a street map. The cable car took us north to Fisherman's Wharf. This is a popular area for tourists, judging by the shops and prices. Seafood is the speciality here, especially crab. A wax figure museum; old ship museum; helicopter flights over the bay area; boat trips. Several shops selling T-shirts, sweat shirts and underpants only. I have never seen such a range of motifs – many being humorous underpants, declaring 'German Sausage', or 'Slippery When Wet' in the form of a traffic sign, or women's briefs declaring 'The World's Most Popular Slot Machine'. Coffee again. Walked to the cable car terminal on Taylor and hopped off in Chinatown, a district with fascinating food smells. Walked to the Pyramid building and went in the lift up to the observation point for good views of Alcatraz island, Coit Tower and the wharves. Caught a bus on Sacramento and journeyed to the Golden Gate viewpoint. Unfortunately, the towers were hidden in the sea fog. Good view of the bay, Alcatraz and Downtown area. Bussed it back Downtown to Union Square. The St. Francis Hotel has five outside lifts, which buzz up and down at high speed. We asked the Doorman if the public could use them, and he said "Yeah, sure, I don't see why not. Enjoy the city." Very posh hotel. Lifts were also magic, so we rode up and down a few times. Good views, of course, particularly of the Bay Bridge (longest bridge in the world). Wasn't impressed by Macy's department store. Walked down to Market and Powell again and sat for an hour watching the people leaving work for home. A veritable mixture – very thin to exceedingly fat people, most well dressed, some colourfully so. How different to England. A few down-and-outs and nutters, including a man who didn't stop talking about Jesus. Back to the hotel by 5.30.

Needless to say, I am totally in love with San Francisco. A beautiful city, with so many attractions, not least the people, who are friendly and courteous. And so many pretty, to stunningly beautiful girls. Great coffee, plenty of entertainment, cheap transport around the Bay Area. And the city is more alive than London, especially in the evenings.

Showered, changed and back out at nine. Walked into a jazz cabaret bar on Union, where a jazz pianist made his opening number last more than an hour! The barmaid was a total knockout. At $4 a drink, we didn't want to have a second round, so we mooched up to Chinatown. Not much happening there, except on Broadway east of Stockton. This street is equivalent to Soho, but the porno laws are much, much more relaxed than in London. Bookshops, etc, and striptease joints etc, including some where audience participation is encouraged. Touts outside encouraging passers-by to 'check out' the action inside. No cover charge, but drinks are over $3 and you have to buy more than one drink. We walked into several to check out the action, but didn't stay, of course. Walked over to Union west of Van Ness and had a drink in Perry's. Not much going on in there. We both felt tired/worn out. Back in the hotel at 1.30. Sleep.

Our first full day turned out to be a typical day, packed with action, new experiences, surprise and enjoyment. We spent another day in San Francisco, managing a ferry trip across the bay, to the trendy hamlet of Sausalito, and a train ride on BART under the bay, at 80mph to Cleveland. In the evening, I fell in love with the assistant in a T-shirt shop at Fisherman's Wharf. Next day, after a late start, we sank multiple cups of coffee at breakfast, I sent seventeen postcards, and we set off for Merced on our first Greyhound trip.

Our bus took us across the Coast Ranges, a hot, dry area of low, rounded hills and no trees, only yellow grass and scattered bushes established on the thin soil. It was more than 100°F in Merced, even at 5 o'clock in the afternoon. We rented a metallic grey 1976 Dodge Aspen and drove out on the freeway towards Yosemite National Park eighty miles away. En route, or 'n rowt' as the Americans say, we were served beer at a roadside café by the most beautiful girl I had ever seen, and then continued into the park.

Yosemite is one of the premier national parks in the USA, and most of it is a wilderness. The scenery is inspiring, consisting of numerous granite peaks up to 13,000 feet high, which overshadow forested valleys. Nick and I marvelled at El Capitan, which has a spectacular vertical wall of silvery-grey granite and a summit that towers more than 3,000 feet above Yosemite Village. Dare I mention that, geologically, the park is situated in the Sierra Nevada Mountains, which formed as a volcanic arc to a Cretaceous subduction zone between the Pacific Ocean plate and the tectonic plate that carries the continent of America?

Checked out Yosemite Village and the supermarket, where we bought bread, cheese and crisps. Drove over to Curry Village and strolled into a bar. Sat drinking on the delightful terrace. Tom Collins is a fine drink. Sharon, who works in the park, came over to strike up a conversation – I'm in love for the fifth time this trip. We're going on a hike with her and her friend tomorrow. Slept OK-ish in the car, awake at 6am. Showered and went for coffee. Took the shuttle bus to Mirror Lake. A warm day under the shade of pines. Beautiful setting here in the valley, with steep granite walls towering on both sides. Sharon arrived alone, and we hiked off the main trail to a place known only to park staff. It's called Hidden Falls, and just above the waterfall were several pools that were large enough for people to jump in. The water was very cold and refreshing. Lazed about on the granite slabs, and soaked up the UV's. At about 2.30, we hiked and shuttled back to Curry, nursing many mosquito bites. Sharon is beautiful, both to look at and as a person. She has lovely black hair, dark skin and a fascinating native Indian face, a gift from one of her parents. She left to get ready for work, and Nick and I picked up the car in Yosemite Village. Cruised about 30 miles to Glacier Point, where the best view is to be had. An amazing panorama of Yosemite Valley, the villages and the forest below. A couple of dozen peaks, and beyond into the snow-capped High Sierra (13,000+ feet). Back to Curry to shower and change.

Met Sharon on the Cocktail Terrace after we'd downed three rounds of drinks. I was on my way already, but further intoxicated by Sharon's personality. Chatted to the people around the table, who got up with Nick to go to a party, leaving me alone with Sharon. At last, I got a proper chance to talk to her. Seems she likes me some. We chatted in the car for a while until Nick showed up and I walked her home. Very sad farewell, indeed I'm crazy about her, you know. I hope she makes it to London. We're gonna write anyhow. Seems like I charmed her of her feet. They just love the English accent!

I am so sad to think that I might never see her again. I was immediately involved with her. Only 19, I know, but so outward-going, so confident and relaxed. I can't face going back to England. I shall have to work and this means that I shan't be going out much, or seeing girls at all. I now have to work harder than ever, and at a time when I need to love harder than before. Compromise is not possible. It is quite impossible to be dedicated to two aspects of life – work and love. Dedication and devotion mean and necessitate total involvement and attention, and this is not possible if you have to make a choice and divide your energy, time, thoughts and feelings.

Sunday 23rd began early with coffee in the dining hall. Sharon was there, and I had a sad, churning feeling in my stomach as we said goodbye.

Back in Merced, Nick and I boarded a Greyhound taking us south then east across the Mohave Desert into Arizona, and through the night to Flagstaff, the turning point northwards into the Grand Canyon National Park. Of course, the canyon was indescribable. I found it hard to accept that I was there, and gazed in wonder at the gigantic natural spectacle that was ablaze in a medley of earthy red, orange and yellow hues. From where we sat, the canyon was 15 miles wide! A mile below us ran the Colorado River, but without trekking in to the canyon there is no way to glimpse the agent of the erosion.

A shuttle bus took us from Canyon Village to Hermit's Rest, eight miles along the rim. Walked some of the way back – between Abyss and Mohave Point, to the Information Centre and Babbit's General Store. I bought some Monterey Jack cheese with Jalapeno peppers, a bottle of orange juice, and some plums. Walked to the rim and gazed at the view for an hour or so. Shuttle to Showersville. Back to Bright Angel Hotel, and went into the bar for Budweiser and wine. After two or three rounds, Nick crashed out in the museum. And 'aza feelun ve tard y'all.' I nodded off for a while, and woke up with a wet T-shirt where I'd been dribbling! Managed to get into a crowd of people who were exceedingly friendly and interesting. About midnight, we were invited to join them for a beer. One of the guys went to his van and pulled out a crate-sized box containing ice and beer. We all went over to sit on the rim of the canyon. A guitar came along too. Things fizzled out late, and I stayed in the van with Elena. Cold night. Peace.

After a breakfast of eggs, ham, hash browns and coffee at the Bright Angel Lodge, we boarded a bus travelling to Flagstaff, changing at Flagstaff to ride south to Phoenix, where we passed an unmemorable evening and night. Tucson was our next destination, a place we instantly liked. Hotel El Presidio was opposite the bus station, so for convenience we checked in for the night before walking to the Visitor Center. After polishing off two kosher hot dogs for 50 cents, we rented a silver Ford Fairmont from Granada, and set off for Sabino Canyon. We spent the evening at Dooleys, a trendy disco-cum-bar in a converted church. I had a few beers, the music was excellent, and I succeeded in getting a couple of dances. In the morning, on Day 10, we left the hotel at 6.30 and cruised 35 miles to Mount Lemmon, which rose to 900 feet through a series of different ecosystems: desert scrub at the bottom, through chaparral, oak woodland, juniper woodland, ponderosa pine forest and to mixed conifer forest at the top. Next on the itinerary was a 45 minute tour of Colossal Cave. Finally, we drove to Old Tucson theme park, the location of many western movies and TV shows, including my favourite TV western series *High Chaparral*. We were just in time to see a bank robbery and rooftop shootout. Yeeeha!

Nick and I caught a night bus to El Paso, arriving at 7am for an interesting day across the bridge in Mexico. There was an obvious contrast in living conditions between the two countries. On one side, the cars were old and worn out, houses were small and dirty on the outside, and the shops were grubby and full of cheap and shoddy souvenirs. Whereas on the Mexican side...

We walked for miles along 16th September Street to the Rio Grande shopping center, which was almost deserted. Nick, and a Swedish tourist who was tagging along, didn't want to stay any longer in Mexico and walked back to El Paso, and I wandered by myself into the Museum of Art and History. I found some decent curio shops with leather goods and carved onyx, and went for a genuine Mexican meal of enchilada and taco. Reunited on the American side, the three of us alighted a Number 6A Highland bus to the aerial tramway, and ascended to the top of Ranger Peak on the Franklin Mountains, for a spectacular view of the countryside as far as Texas.

We boarded another night bus, this time on a journey to Dallas, a soulless and uncomfortably humid high-rise city where pedestrians seem to have been outlawed and traffic flows in a merciless stream of high speed particles, or not at all. No matter, Nick and I were there to see Bernie, not the architectural or cultural delights, and he was a well-paid chap living in a luxury apartment in a condominium on the edge of town. I was so pleased that Bernie had at last found his feet. He had spent six years getting a degree and then found it hard to get a job. Three years previously, at the end of his course, he had written to me explaining the situation.

Four rejections from quarry jobs already this weekend out of eleven sent. Did you know that if I pinned my job rejections together end to end, they'd stretch around the world twice and to the moon and back 1,754 times – well ish.

His job had already taken him on lucrative if testing assignments to Cameroon and Libya.

"Bern, who did you sleep with to get such a cushy job", I said in friendly greeting.

After further banter and a few beers, we went outside to join Clint Freeman at the swimming pool. It was really good to see Clint again. He was a tall, blond Australian who had been on the geology course at Oxford poly with me, and was now working for Core Laboratories.

Swam. Changed and went out for a meal at the Pelican. Tom Collins, all you can eat salad, rib eye steak with French fries and mushrooms, completed with a delicious strawberry cheesecake and coffee. $12 each. Cruised around town for some time. Into a bar for two pitchers of beer ($5) and then into another place for more drinks. Then, into another place – where I have never seen so many amazing women. Fell in love, twice. Several drinks, including two Bloody Mary's. Left at 2am and back to Bernie's for sleep. Up late, about 11-ish.

We went to Lake Dallas for a day of larking about in the water, playing football, Frisbee and boomerang. Beer and worldly chats. Back to the apartment to swim in one of the two pools. Laddish behaviour, skimming flip-flops across the pool and having a competition to see how long we could stay at the bottom of the pool sitting in chairs. Enjoying myself immensely.

Changed and went out to the Beggars Club for Happy Hour. $3 for as much beer and as many hamburgers as you can throw down. Was pissed a little after eight beers. Danced with a couple of girls, and went into the night club for even more drinks. I started chatting to Colleen, a fabulous and sexy girl from Fort Worth. 20 years old, married and to be divorced in a couple of weeks, tiny Derringer pistol in handbag. We smooched and kissed a little, danced a little. Back into Beggars to await the wet T-shirt contest. I didn't know they existed – it just shows you what a sheltered existence I have led in England. Nine gorgeous female contestants jiggled about on the raised dance floor, wearing dampened T-shirts and no bras underneath. The show could have been over in a flash, but fortunately, the ingenious device of having three rounds prolonged the pleasure: five semi-finalists, and three finalists. Judging was rated according the level of applause and whooping from the audience. $100 prize for the lucky and certainly well-stacked winner. Much better than opera. Dance again. Left at closing time – 2am. Pissed.

Touching farewells to Bernie at the Greyhound station, and then another night bus to San Antonio. Slept a fair amount, in stits and farts.

Nick and I agreed that the trip was getting better and better. San Antonio was the best place we had been to. It was a beautiful city, with plenty of vegetation, open spaces, pleasing architecture, excellent shops, and with a really charming riverside walk. And of course, the Alamo, the leading attraction. 187 men died there, including 29 Brits, fighting against the Mexican army. Result: Mexico 1-Texas 0. There was a somewhat interesting collection of relics at the Alamo, including Davy Crockett's gun and Bowie's knife, or so it proclaimed.

If there was such a thing as a world cheesecake contest, then the blueberry cheesecake that I had at the Kangaroo Court on Riverside Walk would no doubt have won by a country mile. It was two inches high and covered and surrounded by fresh blueberries in their hundreds; an absolute bargain at $2.

Another night journey, this time to New Orleans. It was Day 15 and we were halfway across America, and two-thirds of the way through our adventure. We arrived in New Orleans with high expectations. It was the birthplace of jazz, a city on the Mississippi River and evocative of Mark Twain, paddle steamboats, Creole cooking, and Mardi Gras.

In the town centre we entered the lobby of the Lafayette Hotel and queued for a room. At $10 a night each, it was the most expensive place we had stayed in, but it was a small, quaint hotel on fashionable St. Charles Avenue and we felt it was worth the money. After taking showers, we walked downtown to the French Quarter, the oldest part of the city. It is a delightful place where the narrow streets are lined with 18th and 19th century terraced houses, built during Spanish rule. Despite the attractiveness of the elaborate ironwork galleries that adorn the facades of the buildings, Nick and I were more interested in sampling some live music on the famous Bourbon Street, where jazz musicians play from a host of small bars. We peeped into a few to sample the atmosphere, just as many other people were doing. Topless bars, bottomless bars, exotic dancing, and so on, were available. We settled on the Paddock Lounge, where a band was playing Dixieland Jazz. It was phenomenal. I popped a couple of speed tablets, which really enhanced my appreciation of the jazz, and I didn't stop jigging about until we got back to the hotel at 2am.

Next day was full of activity too. We got up at 6.30 and had a $1.20 breakfast of egg, grits, sausage, toast, jam and coffee in the hotel. Then, a cable car ride took us to the French Quarter, where we boarded the Natchez steamboat at Toulouse Wharf for a three-hour cruise on the Mississippi river. The boat was resplendent in fresh white paint and had three decks, quaintly balustraded and with white picket fences all around the square-ended vessel. I could well imagine the poker games that went on below decks in the smoke-filled saloon, and the men who died or jumped overboard to escape a gunfight. It was a blazingly hot and humid day, and on our return to shore we walked to Jackson Square in the centre of the French Quarter, and just sat around eating butter pecan ice cream, watching people and enjoying the free street entertainment.

It was time to move on, and at 6 o'clock we caught a night bus bound for Knoxville, Tennessee. We were cruising past the Gulf coast when we spotted a fabulous beach at Biloxi, and decided to get off the bus. Within minutes, we were checking in to the Beach Motel, situated on a twenty-six mile stretch of golden sand. Minutes after that we dived into a magnificent and empty swimming pool. It was a hot, idyllic evening. After swimming, we walked to the beach for a stroll and to look for a bar, but it was about midnight and nothing was open. Back to the pool, for another swim, then bed at 2am. After a swift dip in the morning, Nick and I went jogging for a mile on the beach. We sat and watched the shrimping boats going out to sea, had a swim, then ordered a beer on the jetty bar. The rest of the day was spent beside the pool, before we boarded a Greyhound at 8.40pm to continue our journey.

This was a long, overnight bus ride, of 650 miles and 15 hours to be precise. We reached Knoxville at midday, had a coffee, and tried to find a car rental company. After many false trails and telephone enquiries, Dollar at the airport was the cheapest, and we finally rented a Ford Mercury Zephyr 7 in metallic chocolate, with a tan roof. We wanted to drive to the Great Smoky Mountains Park in the Appalachian Mountains, see some black bears, and then move on.

Stopped at a place claiming to have the world's best hot dogs. Three for a dollar. Instead, I had a deluxe hamburger with onion, tomato and lettuce. Absolutely the best I have ever tasted. Drank three coffees, and then the woman gave me her famous Chilli Dog, which must, in all fairness, be considered the world's best. Motored on to the park and up to the highest peak (6,500 feet) in the rain and fog. Motored down to Gatlinburg, a town just outside the park. We were amazed to see the main street. It was completely crammed with motels, souvenir shops, eating places – and people. Checked into a $16 room at the Ski View. A brief shower and change, then out on the town. Went to the Eagle Club and drank a few Budweiser beers. I got asked to dance by a perty lil thing called Marie. We danced, we chatted. Met a couple of the band members, who were good musicians, and then went back to Marie's house with Nick and the band, Marie's sister, and the wife of the organist, etc. I don't know what everyone else got up to, but I slept with Marie.

Saturday 5th August, Day 19. After, toast and coffee in town, we motored over the Smoky Mountains down to Cherokee, Capital of the Cherokee Reservation in North Carolina. What a let down. It was geared entirely to tourism, and in a tacky, bad taste way. Nick and I felt sad to see to that the tribe had been reduced to gimmickry, and so we left immediately, driving through the countryside back to the airport to drop off the car. Back in Knoxville, we jumped on an express bus bound for New York, We had wanted to go via Cincinnati and Cleveland to Niagara, but the schedules were bad. Neither of us slept well.

It was another long ride, 720 miles and almost 15 hours, via Washington in the middle of the night. The greyhound station in New York was housed in a huge building that was dirty inside, smelly and crowded. We sat and had coffee and experienced our first NY encounter when a man who was lurking there attempted to steal the luggage of a woman sitting beside Nick. We walked down 42nd Street to the Information Center, and then, armed with leaflets, walked on to Grand Central Station for coffee. In fact, it was a long day of walking here and there on a whirlwind tour, but we were excited about seeing all the special sights of this remarkable city. It was a rainy Sunday in New York, but that couldn't take the edge of our excitement.

First, we went to the historic landmark of the Rockefeller Centre, a complex of art deco buildings covering 20 acres of Manhattan, and home to important works of art. It was hard to grasp the fact that one man, J.D. Rockefeller, became the wealthiest man in history through producing and refining oil. Then to 5th Avenue and an elevator ride to the top of the Empire State Building, a wonder of the modern world. It was no longer the tallest building in New York, but it had a great significance as the most famous icon of the city skyline. King Kong had been there too! Then to Macy's, the world's largest department store, spread out on 11 floors. Next, we rode the subway from 24th Street to 4th, and got out at Greenwich Village. In one sense, my visit there was a pilgrimage. I knew the name 'Green Wich' village from a couple of Bob Dylan's early folk songs, and he lived there for a while in the 1960s when the village played a major role in the folk music scene. West 4th Street in the village forms the background to the cover of the *Freewheelin'* album, which features Dylan walking down the road with his girlfriend Suze Rotolo.

Washington Square Park is in the centre of the village, and that was our next destination. Drug dealing was going on and people were smoking joints quite openly, something we had not seen anywhere else on our trip. Nick and I wandered around the village, enjoyed coffee and cheesecake, then took the subway from 14th to 42nd back to the bus terminal to wash and change. At 11 o'clock that night, we boarded a night bus for Niagara Falls.

What a truly magnificent waterfall, and a unique experience to take the Maid of the Mist boat into the spray. The noise of the water falling was thunderous and deafening and the force of it plummeting down made the earth quake. We were perilously close and it was a sobering thought that the tiny boat could be smashed into matchwood in a second.

Hey, we're in Canada, and I've got a stamp in my passport to prove it. Decided to leave for Toronto. Caught a 4.30 Grey Coach and arrived at 6. Walked around. Some of the skyscrapers here are magnificent, especially banks and hotels. Stumbled across the CN Tower, the tallest free-standing structure in the world. Over 1,800 feet high, and with the world's highest observation post, at 1,460 feet. This must rank among the topmost exciting experiences I have had. Quite phenomenal. An informative board in the lobby showed that the temperature at the top was 2°C colder than at the bottom, that the visibility at the top was 47 kilometres, and the speed of the lift was 18mph. In all, we stayed two hours. Out for a beer in the Nag's Head, a dismal, Canadianised Irish pub, then returned to the terminal to catch a night bus to Montreal.

Into Montreal at 6.30. French-speaking types everywhere, and signs with French above English. Most disturbing. Walked a mile or two to the city centre for information, then into the Metro to ride to the Olympic complex for a tour of the main buildings. Took the Metro downtown again and changed lines to cross the St. Lawrence Seaway to St. Helens Island. There was an old fort there, dating to Wellington. The English defeated the French in Montreal, yet there were Scottish Pipers and French soldiers on parade. Most peculiar. But I was impressed by the well-equipped military museum. Back on the Metro yet again, this time to the Olympic Stadium to see the Montreal Expos play the New York Mets at baseball. To my surprise, I found that baseball was a genuinely interesting game, although seriously spoilt by the razzmatazz entertainment. Oh, and those pipers and French chaps were there again, even firing canon. Sacre bleu! Proud losers, I guess, or perhaps making the point that this was French-speaking Canada and a political victory in the long-run? Back to the bus terminal, and straight onto the express bus for the overnight ride to New York.

There was a one-hour wait at US customs, and enquiries

galore. All the passengers were asked to leave the bus while it was searched, and we were herded into the building. I had some speed tablets among the toothpaste and other items in my toilet bag, and was incredibly worried about getting searched. It would not be a fair outcome to find myself in an American jail, have a label attached to me for the rest of my days, or be deported and banned from ever coming again. I'd only ever taken two tablets and would probably never feel the need to have more. After all, when was I ever going to be listening to live jazz in New Orleans again!

I got searched.

"Would you open your luggage, sir", the officer said.

He rummaged around among the clothes and then picked up the toilet bag. He unzipped the bag and began feeling and looking inside. I was desperately trying to think of a story, come up with an innocent explanation. I believed it was better to be nonchalant and unconcerned, in case the officer was observing me, but had no idea how I was coming across. Was I being watched on close circuit TV, and would there be a telephone call to the customs officer whose fingers were in my bag? Presumably, they were trained to spot suspects. Was I sweating? Was I acting suspiciously? I hid my apprehension by keeping quiet. Moments felt like minutes. Then, he found the plastic bag that contained the tablets, but miraculously concluded his search, zipped the bag and put it back in my luggage. It was a close one.

It was the penultimate day of the trip. Arriving in New York at 5am gave Nick and I plenty of time to wash, change, drink coffee and devour a delicious lemon doughnut before venturing out for our second bite into the Big Apple. Or was the apple biting us? There were still a few key places to go. First, we bussed it up to Central Park, and were amazed to see so many joggers, of all ages, and certainly all sizes. Then, we bussed it to the Wharf area and took a boat to the Statue of Liberty, the bronze-clad woman more properly named the Liberty Enlightening the World. It was an impressive sight, and a good trip up to the observation room at the base of the torch. We walked all the way down, all 156 stairs, and were back in Manhattan by 10.30. Next, it was the turn of the World Trade Centre, the twin towers. We zoomed up to the observation level, which was right on the top, and the world's highest outside observation deck, eclipsing the Empire State building by a handsome margin. There were stunning views of the harbour and the skyscraper city. To round off the sightseeing, we went down to Sixth Avenue and took a tour of Radio City music hall, where many of America's great entertainers have performed since it opened in the 1930s. Back at the bus terminal, we retrieved our bags from the locker and headed for the airport, first by subway and then on a bus. To save money, we slept at the airport, and boarded the flight early next morning. ETA at LHR 9 o'clock, 11th August.

During the flight, I remarked to Nick, "I feel that I've got something out of my system, and I am going to ask Sarah to marry me."

CHANGED TIMES

How to put into words a feeling that had struck unexpectedly? I think that my resolution to ask Sarah to marry me was born of an overall realisation that it was the right time in my life and she was the right person. The PhD was well in hand; I had exorcised a need to play on the field of romance; I had seen a bit of the world; and Sarah was the person who I thought about and went back to every time.

I telephoned Sarah and we arranged to meet at her digs in Notting Hill one evening soon after I arrived back from the USA. I proposed. It came completely out of a blue sky for her, and she was at a loss to know how to respond. In fact, she had a boyfriend, though I did not know whether it was a casual arrangement or a serious relationship. What followed next was a saga that took a month to play out.

She phoned me the next day, and the postman delivered an explanatory letter of rejection from her the day after that. Come Tuesday the following week, she phoned again, and when I phoned her on Wednesday, she accepted! We met and the situation seemed to be positive, but the day afterwards, she was uncertain again. Monday the following week, I phoned again, and Sarah said it was definitely off. That night, I wrote a letter; I wrote another the next day, and went to her digs with a bunch of flowers. She agreed to meet me on Friday, but the situation was still unresolved afterwards. Another week later, we dined at a Greek restaurant in town. I had a wonderful evening, but there was no more contact for four days, until I phoned and then went to see her. I was on a fieldtrip in Llangollen all the following week, but did receive another letter from Sarah, and I phoned on the Saturday when I returned to

London, and had a 'fabulous' chat. On Sunday, we met at her digs in the evening and she finally accepted – exactly a month after my proposal. Our relationship of four years had been an on-and-off affair, all of my own doing, and it must have been an incredibly difficult decision for her to make. The next day was Monday, and we took a tube train into town, bought rings at a jeweller's shop off Oxford Street, and made the engagement official.

Dedication to love and ambition still seemed to be incompatible, but I was now ready to commit myself to the girl I treasured and needed, in the hope that a compromise would be possible.

We celebrated two days later by going to see the new musical *Annie* at the Victoria Palace Theatre, and sat in the dress circle looking forward to seeing the main stars Sheila Hancock playing Miss Hannigan, and Stratford Johns playing Oliver Warbucks. At the weekend, we drove to Chippenham to see my parents, and then to Newquay to see Sarah's Mum and Dad. It was now irrevocable.

Our engagement was announced in *The Times* and we married on 30th December in the Church of the Holy Cross in Seend. This was the place where I had been baptised, and where many generations of Earles before me had gathered to formalise births, marriages and deaths. Sarah looked stunning in her wedding dress and I looked distinctly earthy in a ghastly brown suit and scruffy brown shoes. In addition to our two families, among the guests at our reception were my old school friends Bernie, Nick, Rob, Greg, Iain, Max, and Brian, as well as Mike McMurtry from college days. The bride and bridegroom drove off in my canary yellow Ford Escort, suitably adorned with streamers and rude comments, including 'Knob It' (thank you Rob). We spent our first wedded night at the classy Bell House Hotel in the village of Sutton Benger in north Wiltshire. It snowed that night, adding a little to the fairytale beginning of our new life together. And so ended 1978.

PROGRESS

Preparations were underway to purchase our first house, and in January 1979 we signed the contract, before departing for a honeymoon on the island of Crete. We flew over the snow-covered landscape of southern England and arrived in sunshine at Heraklion Airport to spend a week in a charming little apartment. It was not the warmest time of year to visit Crete, yet there were opportunities to sunbathe and, in any case, there was the glorious history of the island to explore, especially relics of the Minoan civilisation, such as Knossos Palace with its legend of the Minotaur. We had our first marital argument when Sarah confronted me that I was taking too much interest in a girl who was in our tour group at Knossos Palace. It was a side of her that I had not seen before.

Sarah and I moved into our new home on Saturday February 3rd, and it took two trips to Chippenham to collect possessions that had been at my parents' house during my college years. 39 Wentworth Avenue was a small, mid-terrace, two-bedroom house that cost £17,500 to buy, funded by a mortgage and a deposit given to us by my parents. Wentworth Avenue was in the unfashionable part of an unfashionable town, but we could not afford to buy a place in London, and Slough was an acceptable commute into London for both of us.

Back at college, I resumed the routine of demonstrating and carrying out research. The purpose of my research was to examine critically which of the three models of the tectonic evolution and structure of Timor seemed most feasible, or whether a hybrid or new model was indicated, and to add to the body of scientific knowledge about the metamorphic rocks. Even if my interpretations and conclusions were shown later to be incorrect, there would be a legacy of data, samples and observations for the benefit of others.

A logical starting point was to assemble what was known or inferred about the metamorphic rocks of Timor and their place in the geological history, and then to assess the significance of new observations, information, data and insights provided by my research. I had already collected and read all published information that I could discover on any topic of possible relevance to my work, and so the immediate task was to review the key points about the metamorphic rocks.

Metamorphism is the solid–state recrystallisation and change in mineral assemblages within rocks subjected to temperature and pressure changes within the earth. It takes place over a range of temperatures between 120-150°C at the lower limit and 750-900°C at the upper limit, when extensive melting takes place in rocks which are rich in silica, such as granites or sediments deposited in the sea by rivers. Minerals are also sensitive to pressure, and this dual dependence on pressure (P) and temperature (T) has led to the useful concept of metamorphic facies. A metamorphic facies is an assemblage of minerals that is diagnostic of a specific range of P-T conditions. There are eight principal facies of dynamic metamorphism, dynamic in the sense that tectonic forces are operating during the transformation. Each facies occupies a specific area as depicted in the two dimensions of a graph with pressure as one axis and temperature as the other. Geologists refer to the relative conditions of metamorphism as 'grade', such that a progression from lower to higher P-T conditions is termed an increase in grade. Grade can be observed in the field, albeit approximately, from the grain size, texture and sometimes the visible presence of characteristic minerals in a rock. In Barrovian metamorphism, such as the area I had studied in Scotland, the sequence of grades increases in the order Greenschist Facies > Amphibolite Facies > Granulite Facies.

Summarising the collective wisdom in 1979, the metamorphic rocks of Timor outcrop in the core of fifteen separate mountains distributed along the length of the island and therefore parallel to the subduction zone. Termed the crystalline schists in earlier days, they were now known in East Timor as the Lolotoi Complex, as named by Mike Audley-Charles, and as the Mutis Complex in West Timor. They consist of two tectono-stratigraphic components, that is to say, two identifiable units, or components, that have distinctive differences related to one or more aspects of composition, origin and development.

One component is comprised of igneous and sedimentary rocks that were metamorphosed only once and at temperatures between 400°C and 500°C in the Greenschist Facies, in which a green mineral named chlorite is the characteristic mineral of the assemblage. Many of the rocks at this grade have not been intensely deformed or completely recrystallised during the metamorphism and therefore some of the diagnostic features of the original (parent) rocks are preserved as direct evidence of their igneous and sedimentary origin.

The second component consists of high grade schists and gneisses[3] that were metamorphosed at temperatures between 500°C and 700-750°C in the Amphibolite Facies, in which an amphibole named hornblende is one of the characteristic minerals, but the rocks have been reworked later under metamorphic conditions similar to the low grade component. With some exceptions, all original features and minerals of the parent rocks have been obliterated by intense deformation and complete recrystallisation during the initial episode of metamorphism; in some places the metamorphic texture itself has been transformed into new layering during the conversion to lower grade mineral assemblages. In such circumstances, geologists can deduce the origin of rocks from the chemical composition as expressed by the minerals. For example, igneous rocks that form oceanic crust become converted to amphibolite schist and gneiss, which are rocks consisting of alternating layers containing crystals of white plagioclase feldspar and green-brown hornblende. By convention, the high grade rocks on Timor are assumed to be older because their discernable history

---

3 A schist has thin layers, whereas a gneiss is a banded rock.

had more events than the low grade rocks of the other component.

Field relationships in several mountains revealed that the Mutis Complex lies beneath the Palelo Group, a pile of unmetamorphosed igneous, volcanic and sedimentary rocks of Late Jurassic to Palaeocene age, first identified during the 1937 Dutch expedition by Tappenbeck on Molo and by F.P van West in the Miomaffo region east of Molo. However, several generations of geologists concluded from indirect evidence that the crystalline schists are substantially older than Jurassic, namely, older by at least 100 million years and pre-Permian in age. In fact, only three years previously, Tony and Mike A-C had published an article in which they suggested that the high grade component of the metamorphic rocks of Timor consisted of slices of Precambrian continental crust perhaps more than 2.5 billion years old. According to their overthrust model, already outlined, the crystalline schists were situated on the Asian tectonic plate prior to collision with Australian continental crust, at which time they were thrust onto Timor with the Palelo Group.

I could see problems with several aspects of the collective wisdom, in part related to some of the underlying assumptions, and partly because it was contradicted by observations I had made in the field and by data that were emerging from my laboratory research. In addition, I was looking at the issue through the frame of reference of my own preconceptions, biases and knowledge, and there was plenty of latitude to make alternative conclusions from the available information. Three related issues concerned me most: the supposed ancient age of the metamorphic rocks; the grouping into young and old components; and the belief that metamorphism had taken place before deposition of sediments and volcanics belonging to the Palelo Group. In addition, it was a priority to understand in which tectonic context the metamorphism and deformation had taken place; for example, I did not agree with Tony that the high grade crystalline schists originated as continental crust.

One question I was asking was whether the identification of two components on Timor was merely an artefact, produced by the omission of sections of rock by faulting, when in fact only one continuous area of metamorphic rocks had been generated, of broadly similar age. Specifically, was the high grade component just the more-deeply buried part, which was later faulted upwards and reworked at shallow depths and lower temperatures during a semi-continuous cycle of burial, metamorphism and uplift?

In this regard, the geological relationships on Molo are instructive. When I mapped the mountain, I recognised the two principal components in the Mutis Complex, namely a retrogressed high grade component underneath and a succession of low grade rocks on top. However, my work revealed that the low grade component also consists of two units with different metamorphic grade. The lower grade unit is comprised of dark-coloured igneous rocks, such as flows of basalt lava and intrusive sheets of basaltic magma that have been metamorphosed in the Pumpellyite-Actinolite Facies, which is a grade of metamorphism lower than the Greenschist Facies, and lower than anything previously reported on Timor. This component is the filling in a sandwich between the retrogressed high grade component underneath and a Greenschist Facies low grade unit on top. I concluded that the lack of continuity of temperature conditions across the three units exposed on Molo mountain is a function of the dismemberment by faulting that postdates what was likely to have been a single metamorphic cycle.

Another key discovery that I made was that rocks belonging to the Palelo Group are also metamorphosed. In fact, they are at an even lower grade termed the Prehnite-Pumpellyite Facies, a facies whose minimum temperature requirement is 180-200°C. I was sure that the Palelo sediments and volcanics, and all the constituent parts of the Mutis Complex were metamorphosed and dismembered together on the upper, Asian plate of the subduction zone. I began to wonder whether all the low grade rocks on Timor belonged to the Palelo Group, or even were slightly older ocean floor sediments and volcanics, laid down on new oceanic crust on the margin of Asia in the Late Jurassic to Early Cretaceous period, and I published this idea in the science journal *Nature* later in 1979.

If I was correct, then there was no reason to suppose that metamorphism of the Mutis Complex began earlier than the Cretaceous or Late Jurassic, or that the high grade component was substantially older than the low grade units, at least in the sense that there were not two separate periods of metamorphism, widely separated in time and place. Geologists had assigned a pre-Permian age to the crystalline schists because they found that fragments of low grade rocks are present in sediments of Permian age exposed on Timor. Nevertheless, the fragments examined are not derived from oceanic crust and mantle rocks that predominate in the Mutis Complex, and therefore the assumption of a pre-Permian age for the Mutis Complex was just that.

Tony had described a rock from Boi comprised of plagioclase and garnet with high temperature compositions that he thought indicated metamorphism under granulite facies conditions and, by inference, a likely origin as Precambrian continental crust. However, in the absence of the diagnostic minerals enstatite and or hypersthene, members of the pyroxene group, there was no firm evidence of granulite facies conditions in Boi or elsewhere on the island. None of the samples I collected of this rock type contained pyroxenes. Undoubtedly, metamorphic temperatures at Boi had peaked in the transitional zone between amphibolite and granulite facies, but metamorphic grade was not reliably diagnostic of a geological age, and the age of the rocks on Timor could not be constrained by such an argument.

It was important to elaborate whether the geological model that I was piecing together for Molo was supported by detailed observations and quantitative data obtained from the samples of rock that I collected on Boi.

Many of the activities that constituted research for my PhD

were specific projects on different suites of rock samples, combining laboratory analysis with observation, description and deduction. I had the laboratory technician cut thin sections from my entire collection of almost 200 rock samples so that I could carry out identification of minerals and detailed description of the texture, structure and geological history of the rocks, as revealed under a high-powered microscope. A thin section is a slice of rock approximately 30 microns thick, mounted on a tablet of glass so that light can be shone through the rock, to illuminate the crystals for identification and description.

Each sample revealed several to many pieces of information that helped to construct the bigger picture that I was seeking. The most interesting rocks that I collected from Boi contained a distinctive collection of minerals known only from a few localities around the world, specifically, the assemblage garnet-sillimanite-cordierite-spinel. This type of rock has sedimentary parentage, probably as alternating layers of mudstone and siltstone, and is full of minerals that require high amounts of alumina and silica to grow. It outcrops as the lowest rock formation on Boi, and I named it the Bikmela Gneiss.

Cordierite and garnet are similar in chemical composition and each can develop from the other by diffusion of elements across the rock, principally the Fe and Mg ions. Looking at the thin section from sample TM3115, I observed that a corona or fringe of small cordierite crystals had nucleated on one side of a large crystal of garnet. The garnet had a ragged edge, and it was in the process of being consumed to form cordierite at the time the rock cooled and 'froze' the transformation. A mosaic of small cordierite and spinel crystals formed a mantle around the cordierite corona, and showed that the generalised reaction garnet+biotite+sillimanite > cordierite+spinel was taking place. From field observations and experimental data, geologists knew that this reaction takes place under conditions of decreasing pressure and, indeed, one of my samples contained relics of kyanite, a high pressure equivalent of sillimanite that would have been part of the earliest assemblage with garnet at high pressure conditions.

Validating the observations and quantifying the P-T conditions would require some hard data. Fortunately, techniques were available for this, derived from the discipline of experimental petrology, in which laboratory experiments had calibrated the P-T equilibria of many chemical reactions, and even for the specific chemistry of minerals that can vary in composition, including the main minerals in the rocks from Boi.

I was collaborating with Mike Brown from Oxford poly on a piece of research to ascertain the temperature and pressure history of these unusual rocks from Boi. I sent him three samples that were to be analysed using the energy dispersive electron micro-analyser at Cambridge University, to identify the exact chemical composition of garnet, cordierite, biotite, spinel, ilmenite and plagioclase feldspar crystals. Mike made 100 analyses, and showed that the chemical composition of garnet and biotite crystals varied from the core to their exterior surfaces, a feature termed zonation. Zonation indicated that the crystals were reacting and attempting to equilibrate to changes in pressure-temperature conditions during the main phase of metamorphism, and the data supported the visual evidence of the textural relationships between old and new minerals.

Several methods were at our disposal to estimate P-T conditions, including a garnet-plagioclase geobarometer, a garnet-biotite geothermometer[4], and the Fe content of cordierite. The data from Boi plotted on a graph at 770°C and a depth of 35 kilometres for the garnet-kyanite stage, and a temperature of no more than 700°C at a depth of 17 kilometres for the cordierite-sillimanite-spinel stage. This lower temperature was consistent with my estimate of 680°C to 710°C for the first and main metamorphic event experienced by the peridotite and

---

4. These methods use calibrations of mineral composition against pressure and temperature

metamorphosed gabbro and dolerite on Boi, and is at the upper limit of Amphibolite Facies conditions. However, final equilibrium between some of the crystals in the Bikmela Gneiss had occurred at 600°C and a depth of less than 12 kilometres. This was an exciting discovery. A decompression equivalent to an uplift of more than 20 kilometres had taken place, with minimal cooling of the rocks while they were travelling towards the surface of the earth. This was easily explained, however, because rocks are poor conductors of heat and take a long time to cool.

Rapid decompression is a common fate of high-grade metamorphic rocks, and it takes place in two different geological situations: either when convergent motions between plates squeeze them up towards the surface in the subduction zone, a process termed extrusion, or when rifting of a tectonic plate stretches, thins and then pulls apart continental crust. Rifting exhumes the deeply-buried part of the continental crust on either side of the newly-formed oceanic crust, and the old continental crust is likely to be intruded by bodies of gabbro and dolerite. The rifting model was appealing as an explanation for Boi, and I ran with it for a while. It would likely mean that when the gabbro was molten it intruded the mantle peridotite and high grade gneisses during the formation of the new oceanic crust related to the breakup of Gondwanaland in the Middle Jurassic. However, it could not explain how the gabbro became comprehensively deformed at its margins under high grade metamorphic conditions, conditions developed under compression and not under extension. I therefore preferred the alternative explanation that required subduction.

As others had commented, a remarkable aspect of the geology of Timor and neighbouring islands in the outer Banda Arc is the absence of granites. It seems that metamorphism in the region took place in the absence of continental crust, that is, entirely in the domain of oceanic crust and mantle. Tellingly, metamorphosed sediments make up less than ten per cent of the crystalline schists on Timor, and most if not all of them originated as a thin covering to oceanic crust prior to subduction. Conversely, metamorphosed igneous rocks with oceanic crust and mantle affinities, such as peridotite, gabbro, dolerite and basalt, make up more than ninety per cent of the rocks described in the Mutis Complex of West Timor.

I could infer from the arguments above that the Boi rocks had been down in a subduction zone, because a burial depth of 35 kilometres was otherwise only possible at the base of continental crust, of which there seems to have been none in the region at the time of metamorphism.

At such high temperatures, rocks are not brittle and they do not fault. They are ductile like warm toffee and they shear under high compressive stress, a process that creates a foliation or layering in the rocks because the long minerals and flat minerals align themselves to the stress field, much like iron filings orientate themselves to a magnetic field. All the rock units on Boi have a metamorphic layering, and all layers have a similar orientation, and all the long crystals point in the same direction. From this I could tell that metamorphism and deformation were taking place simultaneously in all the units, and therefore it is likely that they were together at that time.

An important discovery I made is that the gabbro-amphibolite unit on Boi was a high grade unit, but metamorphosed only once, and not retrogressed or deformed at low grade as the conventional wisdom required. All the thin sections revealed that the mineralogy preserved throughout the body of rock has an Amphibolite Facies assemblage of green-brown hornblende and a calcium-rich plagioclase feldspar, usually andesine but in places a higher temperature form known as labradorite. This discovery exposed the simplified two-fold division of the Mutis Complex and added further support for the existence of continuity of conditions during metamorphism in the Timor region.

Another important aspect of my research was to obtain estimates of the age of the rocks and therefore identify key events or better calibrate the timing of key events in the geological history. In this, I collaborated with Bob Beckinsale, who worked for the Institute of Geological Sciences in Gray's Inn Road, London.

Radiometric age dating can be performed on samples as small as a billionth of a gram using a mass spectrometer, an analytical machine that began to be used in age dating in the 1950s. Age dating relies on the fact that radioactive elements decay at constant rates, expressed as a 'half-life', which is the time it takes for half of the radioactive element to decay. Each radioactive parent element decays at its own constant rate to another element, called the daughter element. There is no way to change the rate at which radioactive atoms decay in rocks, either by heat, cold, pressure, or strong chemical reactions. The passage of time is recorded in the rock by the constant reduction in the number of parent atoms, and the constant increase in the number of daughter atoms. Measuring the ratio of elements enables geologists to estimate the length of time over which decay has been occurring.

There are more than 40 different techniques available for age dating, each based on a different radioactive isotope. Two of three commonly used methods were appropriate for my rock samples. The Rb-Sr or rubidium-strontium method measures the decay of rubidium-87 to strontium-87, whereas in K-Ar or potassium–argon dating, the potassium-40 isotope is radioactive and its decay to argon-40 is measured. Uncertainties on the rates of decay of rubidium and potassium are insignificant, no more than two percent, which makes the techniques most useful in obtaining precise ages.

I sent eleven of my rock samples to Bob, comprised of six specimens of Bikmela Gneiss for Rb-Sr age dating on the whole rock sample, and five specimens of the metagabbro–amphibolite gneiss for K-Ar age dating on the hornblende crystals. Rb-Sr data from the mass spectrometer indicated a maximum age of formation of 216 million years for the Bikmela Gneiss, much younger than the >290 million year pre-Permian or even >544 million year Precambrian age inferred by other geologists using weak and indirect evidence.

More importantly, a likely metamorphic age of 118 +/-38 million years was obtained. This placed the end of dynamic metamorphic activity on Boi squarely in the Cretaceous period, with the +/- 38 million year margin of error just slipping into the Late Jurassic on the early side. It supported my working hypothesis that the rocks were not ancient continental crust, but were being metamorphosed and uplifted during the Cretaceous period, on the evidence that grains of similar metamorphic rocks are preserved in sandstones of Late Cretaceous age belonging to the Palelo Group. Moreover, it was consistent with the concept that subduction, faulting into slices, exhumation and sedimentation were taking place at this time and involving the Mutis Complex.

Regarding the K-Ar dating of hornblende crystals analysed from the suite of metagabbro-amphibolite gneisses, there was a comforting grouping of the calculated ages between 31 million and 37 million years, that is, a Tertiary age and much younger than the age of the main metamorphic phase, which on the evidence of the Rb-Sr data was Cretaceous. K-Ar is particularly suitable for determining the age of closure or chemical isolation, which in a metamorphic rock is the age when crystals cool below a 'blocking' temperature that is characteristic for each mineral. Published research from Oxford University indicated that a blocking temperature of 250°C seemed likely for iron-rich hornblendes such as those in my samples, which compares with a probable temperature of 700°C during their initial metamorphic recrystallisation. I observed in thin sections of these rocks that low temperature minerals such as epidote, chlorite and sphere had replaced some of the high temperature minerals, and I had seen in outcrops that the rocks are cut by late fractures filled with minerals. It was evident that the low temperature adjustment had taken place in the Tertiary period and led to minor changes to mineralogy, but without deformation of the fabric or layering.

The set of samples had an average age of 34 million years, and this corresponded with the end of the Eocene and beginning of the

Oligocene epoch, when there was a major hiatus in the geology of the Banda Sea region, such that almost no sedimentary or volcanic rocks of this age are present. This timing also corresponds with cessation of sedimentation associated with the Mutis Complex. I was excited by the discovery that a low grade metamorphic event in the Tertiary period had re-set the K-Ar radiometric clock of the high grade rocks, at a time when a significant tectonic event was taking place across Timor and the entire Banda Sea region.

All researchers in the region agreed that the collision between the leading edge of the Australian continental margin and the Indonesian archipelago took place no earlier than 10 million years ago. Prior to the collision, the margin of the Australian plate was a passive one, that is, not subjected to tectonic, igneous or metamorphic events. My field and laboratory observations and data all pointed to the conclusion that the Mutis Complex and Palelo Group had been situated on an active margin where volcanic, metamorphic and tectonic activity were going on before the collision. This could only mean that these formations were on the Indonesian side prior to collision, unambiguously and unequivocally consistent with the overthrust model championed by researchers at the University of London.

All in all, I was delighted to have confirmed several key aspects of the work published by Mike A-C, Tony and our other colleagues, notably the Asian origin of the Mutis Complex prior to collision, and yet the detailed work had led to a simpler, more logical and coherent explanation. The next step would be the painstaking and thankless task of putting it all together and writing the thesis. Luckily, a catalyst for this arrived at the right time.

NO RETURN

In November 1978, the previous year, I had received a letter from the Smithsonian Institution in Washington inviting me to attend an international meeting in Bandung and give a presentation of my research. I was honoured, delighted and could not turn down the opportunity. I presumed that it was Tony working behind the scenes who had made the suggestion to the organising committee, and was grateful. More than one hundred scientists from fourteen countries would be attending, including many well-respected university lecturers and professors, and representatives from important geological organisations such as the United States Geological Survey (USGS). At the time, I had nothing to show anyone, but this commitment was important because it would spur my work on, forcing me to present something at least vaguely coherent. To give the meeting its full and glorious title, it was the ESCAP CCOP-IOC SEATAR Ad Hoc Working Group Meeting on the Geology and Tectonics of Eastern Indonesia. And it was being held between July 9th and 14th, so the effort had to begin in earnest, now that my private life had settled down.

By May I had submitted an abstract for the paper and prepared a manuscript on the Boi Massif. It contained a wealth of descriptive information, some excellent analytical data, and a coherent, if quite specialised, technical interpretation of the results. No matter that almost no-one in the audience would be familiar with the theoretical concepts, analytical techniques and jargon of metamorphic geology, I now had particular expertise possessed by few in the world, and specialist knowledge of an area that no-one else had now or at any time before. It would be condescending to 'dumb down' the presentation, but the implications should be spelt out clearly for all to understand.

I was highly pleased with the result, especially as it had given my work impetus and forced me to think of the implications of my findings. But the presentation would be another matter. Except for the lectures I gave to the students at Chelsea, I had never spoken in public before, and the audience at the conference would comprise the higher end of the distinguished peer group I had now joined at the bottom.

Margaret Thatcher swept to power on May 3rd, 1979. The country had voted for change, and the government carried the confidence (hopes) of the City, of big business, and of ordinary Britons fed up with high taxes, crippling strikes in the public sector, and double-digit inflation. There was still much trouble in Northern Ireland and with industrial relations, but the mood in the country changed for the better, and the brightening situation was mirrored in my life.

On Friday July 6th, I worked at college until mid-afternoon before leaving for Heathrow Airport to join one of the long check-in queues for the BA flight to Singapore via Bombay and Kuala Lumpur. Luckily, I had a window seat, and this time I was listening to *War of the Worlds* as the plane ascended into the evening haze over London. My trip was not an expedition in the sense of 1971, 1974, 1977, or even 1978, but I would be on unfamiliar ground giving the presentation. And there was my plan to remain in Indonesia after the meeting and travel up to northern Sumatra.

After a couple of free Heinekens, I dozed off, only to be woken for what looked like a reasonable food offering, and turned out to be the best in-flight meal I'd ever eaten. A second cycle of *War of the World's* was piped through the headset. It was one of my favourite pieces of music, especially the exquisite song *Forever Autumn*, sung by Justin Hayward. It played and I slipped into a reverie about my travels to Indonesia, America and Scandinavia; it brought on a rush of fused emotions and I now felt in the mood for another adventure.

I squinted at *Death on the Nile* showing on a screen a great distance away, but lost interest after Mia Farrow shot some fellow in the leg.

Evidently, the plot was thickening, but it was still too thin to hold my attention sufficiently to stave off the call of sleep. And then, the lights came on in preparation for breakfast. It must be BA's policy to encourage the phenomenon of jet lag in their unfortunate passengers. For goodness sake, it's 1.15am UK time!

Lunch was served at 5.50am UK time, after a short stop at Bombay, and I listened to another replay of my favourite music. I sent Sarah a postcard during the stop at Kuala Lumpur, and bought some perfume for Jan's wife at Singapore airport before continuing on Garuda Airways flight GA989 to Jakarta. Three miracles happened to me at Jakarta airport, which I hoped was a portent of favourable circumstances to come: I cleared immigration quickly, my luggage was whizzing towards me as I approached the luggage belt, and my bags were not searched.

Definite déjà vu hit me during the trip into town. Nearly two years ago I was doing the same journey to Jakarta and Bandung. But so much water has passed under the bridge since then. I'm happily married to Sarah and we have our own house. The work for my thesis is drawing to a close instead of just beginning. And in the meantime, I have spent five months in Indonesia, visited Crete on my Honeymoon, plus the US, Canada and Mexico.

I spoilt myself and booked into the Sheraton for $27 plus tax. I needed to get clean after such a long trip, so stripped and got into the shower. But just as I was fully-soaped, the water dried up and I had to climb into the sink to sluice myself down. This was more like the Indonesia I knew.

On Sunday morning, while queuing for a ticket at Gambir Station, I recognised Professor Charles Hutchison and introduced myself. I didn't get a seat on the train, and spent three exceedingly uncomfortable hours sitting on my rucksack in the corridor. Reunited with Charles on reaching Bandung station, we strode expectantly forward in search of accommodation and other known attendees gathering for the meeting. After checking in at a hotel, we ambled off to a Padang restaurant for dinner. It was wonderful to have Indonesian food and Bintang once again. Afterwards, we bumped into an American contingent at the Grand Hotel Preanger, including Dr Peter Jezek from the Smithsonian Institute, who had sent me the invitation, and Professor Eli Silver from the University of California in Santa Cruz.

Well, all the top people are here, so I'd better do myself justice at the meeting. I must start planning the talk sometime, otherwise I'll never finish in twenty minutes.

Next morning, having arrived at the meeting and registered, I opened my Delegate Pack and discovered to my horror that my presentation was scheduled for that afternoon. Controlled panic gripped me momentarily, before I decided that it would be better to listen to the other presentations and 'wing' my own, hoping that it would flow out in a logical, coherent sequence. After all, I was thoroughly familiar with the details, and the sequence of slides would lead me through. As it turned out, I had no nerves whatsoever, my talk was controlled, and I fielded all the questions without problem. But I did overrun, and I had to deliver the last part at breakneck speed, so probably no-one was able to follow what I was saying. I felt relaxed afterwards and sat back to enjoy the rest of the proceedings. Full credit to the Geological Survey, because their organisation was impressive and the conference ran smoothly.

Representatives from more than twenty-five universities, research institutes and government institutions attended the meeting, and the topics of research included an impressive range of techniques and specialist disciplines. Chief among these were geochronology, which uses the decay of radioactive isotopes to estimate the age of rocks; marine seismology; gravity measurements; palaeomagnetism; field mapping; metamorphic petrology and geobarometry; volcanic petrology and chemistry, and many instances of tectonics, the principal topic of the meeting. It was clear from this level of interest, the range of opinions and models, and the sparse coverage of data across Indonesia, that research in the region was not only exciting and rewarding, but would remain the focus of considerable interest and debate for many years.

I was delighted to see Fred Hehuwat and Jan Sopaheluwakan at the meeting, and went to see Fred and his wife Dolly for tea at their house. Jan turned up at seven in the evening and we went with Tony for another superb Indonesian meal. Crab claws, king prawns about six inches long, fried rice and vegetables, Bintang.

On the second day of the meeting, Untung and Barlow presented a compilation of gravity data from the region that showed that the Timor Sea is underlain by continental crust. This confirmed the conclusion of earlier work based on deep-penetrating seismic refraction data. Both pieces of research also showed that Timor is separated from the continental margin of Asia by a patch of oceanic crust that lies beneath the Banda Sea north of Timor and the present inner volcanic Banda Arc. Taking all the evidence together, it seemed likely that the rocks with Asian affinities that outcrop on Timor formed a small block of crust detached from the margin of Asia, that was then propelled southwards towards Australia by the creation of oceanic crust in the Banda Sea. In other words, the present structural configuration of Timor was the result of a head-on collision! Because of my research, we could now say with some confidence that the Mutis Complex and Palelo Group were components of that detached block. The mystery of the 'missing' granites on Timor and the outer arc was solved, because they are situated in Borneo where the detached block had originated.

Dutch geologists on the 1937 expedition pointed to the similarity between the geology of the mountain massifs of Miomaffo, Boi and Molo, and rocks of the same type and age exposed on the islands of Sulawesi and Borneo, a connection strengthened by later work carried out by Tony and his colleague Neville Haile. In all areas there is an association of crystalline schists, including components of oceanic crust and mantle, together with radiolarian cherts and Cretaceous to Eocene sediments and volcanics. The similarities with the Palelo Group are striking, not just the types of rock and their environment of deposition, but their common age and the fact that they are sliced up by many faults and associated with a range of metamorphic rocks, as on Timor. The correlation was more evident to me after I sat in on the presentation given by Marius van Leeuwen, who worked for Rio Tinto, and described the geology of southwest Sulawesi. It was highly probable that the exotic Asian rocks on Timor were situated in the arc-trench gap environment adjacent to Sulawesi and Borneo, before being detached in the Eocene-Oligocene by the formation of the Banda Sea and propelled southwards and eventually on to the continental margin of Australia.

While I shuffled along in the buffet queue, I talked to Dr Warren Hamilton of the USGS and to British geologist Dr Neville Haile from the CCOP office in Bangkok. Alerted to the fact that photographs of the meeting were posted on a big board outside the meeting room, I bought all five in which I appeared. I shared a meal of Rijstafel with Tony at the Mitra Restaurant that evening, and had a good chat and a few beers. I was really enjoying the whole experience, although at the end, I had not developed any leads for future projects I might get involved in after the PhD. There were cocktail parties and cultural events to attend, including an evening of Indonesian folk dancing, which was entrancing, especially the Dance of Sangkuriang from West Java. Indonesian dances are religious tales, adapted from India and performed with stylised movements and in fabulous costumes. Tony had a bit of a dance, too, arms akimbo, knees bent, bum out and lips pursed in concentration.

On Saturday, I joined the party going to the Tangkuban Prahu volcano, where I had been with Fred and Suparka two years previously. On this occasion, I walked part way around the rim, and down to a thermal spring where many people were bathing in the hot water. Later in the day, I joined Tony and the Japanese contingent from the meeting for dinner at Fred's house, and enjoyed an amusing evening, my last in Bandung.

Next day, I took flight GA461 from Bandung to Jakarta Airport, a twenty-minute journey, and then went to check in for flight GA402 bound for Polonia Airport in Medan, the capital town of North Sumatra. I wanted to go to the island in the middle of Lake Toba caldera and see the traditional Batak culture. The catalyst for taking the diversion was Bona Situmorang, a LIPI geologist being sponsored to study at Chelsea and who wanted me to deliver a letter to his parents in Medan.

I joined the queue at the check-in. After a while, I realised that no one but me was queuing at all. Hopeful passengers had formed a triangular-shaped phalanx and were besieging the hapless check-in staff sheltering behind the vulnerable fortress that was their counter. Men pushed in from the side and the front, and agents passed bundles of tickets over the heads of the crowd to get further ahead in the queue. When in Rome, I thought, and pushed my way to the wide mass of people at the front. I am only 5 feet 9 inches tall, but I had the in-built advantage of being taller than everyone else in the country. I waived my ticket high in the air and caught the attention of an assistant, who obliged by taking it and quickly issued my boarding pass.

It was July 15th, and four days earlier, a Fokker F28 on the same route had crashed into a mountain near Medan, with the loss of all sixty-one passengers and crew. A recent volcanic eruption had poured dust into the air and somehow caused or contributed to the crash. And it was not the first time that a Garuda Airways plane had crashed approaching Medan. We took off at 3.50pm, after a two-hour delay that made it likely we would arrive over Medan in the dark. The passengers were tense.

We are nearing Medan, we are enveloped in dense cloud or fog, and we are being buffeted quite strongly by thermal currents. The fasten seat belt sign is on and the passengers are somewhat agitated. We are now descending and reducing speed. It has become deadly silent. The cabin lights are on. The boy opposite has taken the emergency position. We are out of cloud now, I glimpsed the ground. The engines are very quiet and we are still descending. Continued buffeting. The nose is slightly up. Slower. Back in cloud. Can hear engine noise now – approaching to land? Nose steeper. Buffeting quite pronounced. Gasps. Must be coming in to land. But the No Smoking sign is not on. This could be a totally blind landing. Glimpse of sunshine above, but thunder and lightening outside. Very slow now. Can see into the crew's cabin – door is open. Hostess is on the PA. Can see outside again. We're just below cloud level. Landed. Relief all round.

I deliberately chose the best place to stay, the four-star Hotel Danau Toba on Jalan Iman Bonjol. It had been a long, sweaty day and I felt considerably refreshed after checking in and taking a shower. I dined at the Japanese restaurant on the 8th floor and then walked outside in the warm rain to have a look around. I found the Jungle Bar, and stopped to watch the news: there were details of President Nixon's visit to Mexico, and Clay Regazzoni had won the British Grand Prix in a Williams at Silverstone. I watched some American TV, but got bored and went back to the hotel to go to bed, wishing that Sarah was there with me.

At the checkout next morning, I rued my decision to choose the best hotel. The bill came to $55, which would leave me with only $50 for the rest of the trip. But I was short-changed by 1,000 Rupiah and complained, which is not normal behaviour, but I wasn't going to be taken for a ride just because I was a foreigner. After some discussion and re-calculation, the receptionist seemed to be quite confused, but it worked in my favour because I walked out $10 ahead, a reasonable reward for my trouble.

I caught a motorised Becak from the hotel to the bus station, and hopped on a bus that was about to depart for Perapat, my destination on the edge of Lake Toba. On the journey, mile after mile after mile of virgin rain forest flashed past my eyes. I had never seen such a vast expanse of trees. It evoked images of a prehistoric setting that would contain mysterious and frightening beasts, the ruins of lost cities and a host of tribes that would shrink your head and boil you up for dinner.

After a change of bus at Siantar, the final 45 kilometres of the journey was very crowded, and there were several white tourists on board heading for the same cultural experience. There were lovely views of the beautiful lake, the island and the mountains as the bus descended into the caldera and down to the lakeside. I found it genuinely awe-inspiring to see and go into the largest caldera in the world. It measures 30 by 100 kilometres, and was created by a series of gigantic explosions, the most recent one about 75,000 years ago. I found it truly humbling to consider that the knock-on effect on the climate almost wiped out the entire human race.

On Jalan Joseph Sinaga, I found a decent place to stay for 750 Rupiah a night. The Pension Aurora seemed to have no other guests and I was given an enormous room with three double beds and an Indonesian style bathroom with invigorating cold water. Oh, the memories of 1977.

Walked into the village. Not much of a place. Had a small meal in a Padang restaurant. Back to the hotel at 7.30. Bored, bored, bored. I wish Sarah was here. Plenty of mosquitoes about. Several bumps have appeared already. It looks as though I'll be going to Samosir tomorrow to join hundreds of 'Hippy' type characters. What a pity.

I walked into town next day and bought a ticket for the 10.30 ferry. It was hot, the air humid, and the sky overcast and threatening rain. There was a pleasant vista across the lake, and the island looked beautiful as the boat approached the village of Tuk Tuk on the shoreline. It was a remote spot in a remote country, yet the place was crawling with white tourists. German, French, American, Australian and English voices could be heard in the cafés, restaurants and on the beach. Disgusted, I walked east from the harbour area in search of the countryside and passed people going about their business in the fields before arriving at a different point on the lakeside. As the water looked inviting, I asked a local man if it was safe to swim, then changed and waded into the warm water. A French family appeared on the scene, and the man engaged me in a conversation; yet again, all the mystique of the faraway experience disappeared.

The problem of where to sleep that night was solved when I spotted a traditional Batak house, with its roof in the shape of an upturned boat and the floor elevated above ground level on stilts to keep out rats and other unwanted creatures. A Batak man was lounging outside, and I negotiated to rent a spare room for 250 Rupiah. This was a bargain for 20 pence, even taking into account that the room measured 6 feet by 6 feet. It had walls made of tree trunks and the monotony of the room was relieved by scattered newspaper and magazine cuttings nailed here and there on the walls as decoration. Slung diagonally across the room was a line of rough twine that was meant to be for hanging up clothes.

Out of necessity, I went in search of a place to spend the evening, since there was no form of lighting in my room – indeed, no electricity on the island. I joined a group of three Australians, barely illuminated under the light of the hurricane lamp in the restaurant, and later chatted to the French man I had met at the lakeside. Jacques was a maths teacher who lived near Toulon. France was too crowded for him in the summer, and it was cheaper to come to Indonesia than to rent a villa on the Cote d'Azur. I felt out of place having a normal conversation in the depths of a tropical rain forest in the crater of an extinct volcano, and was relieved when I found myself alone.

It's nearly 10pm. Nothing to do; bedtime I suppose. I am missing you my darling Sarah. I do so hope that you are well and happy. I cannot wait to be with you again. In one week, I hope I will be with you. Flight from Singapore not confirmed, so I might have to stay over a day or two. Money is running out and I can't use my credit card here. I suppose I shouldn't be bored – maybe I'm not, but I'm not exactly excited. I have no-one to share the experience with. Have I changed that much? It seems such a long time since I left England, but it's only 10 days. I wonder if Anglo has written offering me a job? How will I be able to choose between industry and academia?

Early to rise, I was already tucking into a breakfast of papaya, pineapple, banana and coconut pieces as the sun made its appearance above the rim of the caldera the next day. In the restaurant the Aussies recommended that I to go to Tomok to see the interesting headstones on the Batak graves, some of which were 400 years old. I headed south, the sun burning my exposed arms, and reached Tomok after half an hour. It was not so much a graveyard as a craft market. Stalls brimming with handicrafts and textiles from all over Indonesia were jammed between the headstones. Twenty or more tourists were crowded around the graves on the receiving end of some bullshit about Batak traditions from a guide. I'd had enough. There was no sense of adventure here.

It was a brisk walk back to Tuk Tuk to try and catch the 2 o'clock boat to Parapat, but the ferry had already left when I reached the mooring. I sat down and offered a smoke to the Batak men minding the wharf. The ticket man offered to buy my tobacco, but I gave him about half of what was left in my tin. Ticket Man sold me a ticket and I relaxed as I waited for the 3 o'clock ferry.

Another night in Parapat. I returned to the Aurora losman. It had electricity and a fridge to keep water cold, and I felt glad to be back there; perhaps it was the familiarity of the place, or that it provided confirmation I was returning homewards, or at least away from the spoiled experience of my pilgrimage to see the unique Batak culture. A young couple behind the reception asked to have their photograph taken and I obliged, taking two shots. Not in the mood for a stilted conversation about which country I came from, and so on, I said I needed a shower and went to my room to relax. I had just started to unpack some clean clothes when there was a knock on the door. The young girl from the reception came in bearing a towel and made a hand movement indicating she would turn down the bed; or that is what I thought at first. I looked at the bed. It had a single cotton sheet on top and it did not need turning down. I looked back and was just about to tell her not to bother, but she had put down the towel and was advancing towards me.

Moments later, we were kissing and undressing each other. A rush of signals and chemicals took control of my mind and eclipsed any external perspective. We lay naked on the bed and I caressed her taut brown body and proud breasts. I delighted in the sensation of her smooth young skin and I drank her dark beauty and became intoxicated.

As I contemplated consummating the relationship, a clear voice somewhere above and behind me spoke, breaking the spell. What was I doing? What about Sarah? Was it a setup, and would her husband/father/brother/uncle come in wielding a machete and demand money? What if she did this with all passing strangers and had some horrible disease? It was a close call. I got up and said that I was married, feeling conspicuous and foolish standing naked with a rampant hard-on pointing longingly at her in defiance of my rational state of mind.

Thursday came. It was raining again. I packed, walked into the village centre and caught the 10 o'clock bus to Medan, a gruelling five-hour journey. I delivered the letter to Bona's parents and left with a big parcel to take back to Bona. Three days later and I was back in London, after a stopover in Singapore to do some sightseeing and shopping.

Landed at 6.45am. Lovely Sarah there to greet me.

FREEDOM ROAD

My NERC grant ran out at the end of August. Now Sarah was supporting me and I was anxious to complete my thesis as soon as possible. I wondered what I could have achieved if I had gone to Timor at the beginning, instead of having to wait a year. What if there had been a second trip to find answers to all the questions raised by my first trip? There were too many 'what-ifs' and nothing could be changed now. The facts were that I had plenty of excellent analytical data to incorporate into my thesis, I was formulating ideas about the bigger picture, and was starting to publish results and ideas into the scientific literature. And in addition to being a Fellow of the Geological Society (FGS), which was a relatively simple matter, in October I was accepted as a Fellow of the Royal Geographical Society (FRGS), an altogether more prestigious position, not that I would, for a minute, equate myself with past fellows such as Darwin, Livingstone, Scott or Shackleton! My situation looked bright and it provided a satisfactory ending to 1979.

Fortuitously, my research on Timor provided important evidence in support of earlier work carried out by Mike A-C, Tony and other researchers at the University of London, including evidence that the geology beneath the Asian thrust sheets had an orderly and predictable structure. By corollary, the evidence contradicted the model developed by Flinders University and that of Warren Hamilton of the US Geological Survey. However, I thought that Hamilton was right in claiming that the exotic rocks on Timor were a stack of sliced components produced in a subduction zone, at least, this seemed true for the metamorphic rocks and Palelo Group. Aside from the scientific value of the work, the results supported the conclusion that the predictable structure beneath the complex near-surface geology of Timor might provide favourable conditions for the accumulation of oil, especially as there are active oil seeps on the island and discoveries of oil and gas beneath the Timor Sea.

My first publication came out in *Nature* in November, and a paper I had submitted in August was in press with *Tectonophysics*, an influential journal published by Elsevier. Together with the proceedings of the Bandung conference, I was assured of having at least three publications to my name, and I was working on a fourth with Mike Brown at the poly. It felt good. These were tangible achievements, representing acceptance of my ideas into the arena for scientific debate. They provided data and insights that might help other researchers on their journeys of discovery. I was particularly proud of the *Tectonophysics* paper, since it was a general concept I had developed about metamorphism in subduction zones, and was nothing to do with my work on Timor.

1980 was going to see the culmination of my research, and I would need to consider my next move, taking into account the fact that my wife also had a career. Sarah was now working for Getty Oil. Her office was in Surrey, in a grand stately house once lived in by Henry VIII. However, the commute from Slough was difficult, and we were planning to move closer to her office. We decided on Woking, which had good rail connections to London, so that I could get into college, and bought a house in Heythorp Close on a new development.

And what of the future? I had been offered a Post Doctoral position with Alex Grady at Flinders University. It was a highly attractive proposition, giving me the opportunity to live in Australia, continue my work on Timor, and develop my friendship with Alex. I was bursting with excitement at the prospect, but the position would not materialise until January 1981, and it looked as though my thesis would be completed months before then.

Sarah proposed a solution.

"Why don't you try to get a job with an oil company, and then you'll have the option of choosing between two career paths?"

She suggested BP, since it was a British company with a good reputation for training geologists. This might have been an insight gained from her last boyfriend, who was a geologist with BP. It sounded like a reasonable idea and I contacted BP in London and completed an application. The company had a formal programme of graduate recruitment and I was asked to attend a full day of events with other hopeful candidates at the Great Eastern Hotel near Liverpool Street station, in the city area of London. BP assembled some of its most-favoured geologists, geophysicists and engineers from a pool of about 400, to tell prospective employees enticing tales of life inside the world that was BP Exploration. The crucial test was an interview with Dr David Jenkins, BP's Chief Geologist, for which I was not prepared, because I had not prepared at all.

I was offered a job. I felt lucky and amazed, and I accepted. Somehow, I had landed a well-paid job with one of the world's largest and best oil companies, having applied to only one company. It vindicated the decision to move to Woking, and Sarah and I moved into 7 Heythorp Close three weeks before I was due to start at BP at the end of June.

BP had made me an incredibly attractive offer. In addition to a salary of £5,000, there was an uplift of £1,200 for having a PhD, there was a London weighting, free rail travel – first class – and a chauffeur-driven limo to and from Woking Station. This was not a normal situation, but a special arrangement I had made through Dr Jenkins. The usual career path for graduate geologists began with a two-year stint in Aberdeen as Rig Geologist. New recruits were allocated to the 'Rig Pool' and their time was split between working offshore and onshore to learn the basics. However, I explained that I wanted to work in London, otherwise I would have live away from my wife or she would have to give up her job.

So the agreement was that I would be listed as being based in Aberdeen, but on secondment to London, a situation that BP viewed would entitle me to compensation for the disturbance to my personal life. However, to make the arrangement kosher, I was required to spend the first two weeks in Scotland on the oil industry accredited Fire-Fighting Course in Montrose and Offshore Survival Course in Aberdeen. These were the two mandatory training courses for working offshore, not that I ever did go offshore. Highlights included sitting in a helicopter simulator, and being dunked upside down in a swimming pool to make an emergency exit underwater; entering a smoke-filled bunker in full breathing apparatus, to find and rescue a trapped victim; and advancing against a wall of fire with a hosepipe and seeing flames go over my head and lick around the side.

Monday 14th July 1980 was the day that the chauffeur arrived and took me to Woking Station, timed to get there five minutes before the 7.48 train to Waterloo Station. From Waterloo, the next leg of the journey was on a special underground train known as The Drain, which ran only between Waterloo and Bank Station in the city. The Drain offers a unique travelling experience in three respects: it is the only British Rail underground train; conditions are cramped inside the carriages, because the train runs in a small-bore tunnel, and, by unwritten convention, to board, passengers are expected to join one of the long, orderly queues that lead to each carriage door. However, the platform is so crowded that there is no space between the queues, and on my first day at work I did not realise that there were queues. A few of the legion of pin-striped stockbrokers that morning puffed, muttered and scolded me in harsh tones when I mistakenly joined the front of a queue. There was a satisfying sense of symmetry later that day on the train back to Woking, when the pin-striped brigade told me off for opening the window without permission in *their* carriage.

Living in the commuter belt around London exposed me to daily surprise. What time will my train eventually arrive? Will the service be cancelled? Will I be able to find a vacant seat? Standing in the corridor meant that I would be squashed against the man with a blocked nose and bad breath who was breathing out of his mouth directly into my face. Perhaps it would be the man in a dark suit who had large flakes of dandruff on his collar and was standing upwind in a draft. Or perhaps it would be the man with a gigantic, overpressured boil on his neck, pulsating at me as a warning that eruption was imminent.

From Bank, I walked to BP's Head Office near Moorgate station and arrived on the right side of 9 o'clock. Britannic House was a towering block of impressive proportions, with a grand entrance patrolled by a doorman, and inside was a large atrium guarded by a security desk. However, BP Exploration was housed across the road in Britannic House North, a dark, dingy building with beige and brown décor and rows of closed doors on either side of the long corridors, conjuring comparison with a Victorian mental institution. Size of office allocated to the individual depended upon seniority: indeed, the higher I rose, the more status symbols I would be accorded, such as a carpet, a bigger office, a corner office with windows on two sides, and so on. Further up the chain, and I would be entitled to have morning tea and afternoon coffee brought to me on a silver tray. And, if I ever progressed from my present Grade 7 to reach the dizzying heights of Grade 11, I would qualify to dine in the Senior Restaurant alongside managers and directors. It was a different world with its own culture and customs, but at that point, I only cared whether the work was interesting and fulfilling. The hazards and hardships of going through the minefield of performance assessments and office politics were yet to come.

Derek South was head of the Africa and Southern Europe Group and was my first manager. Derek was a likeable boss: he listened with interest, was not aggressive, and had a good sense of humour. However, I hardly had time to settle in to my completely new environment before Dr. Jenkins told me that I was being posted to Norway at the end of the year. I didn't mind at all. It would mean lots more money, free housing and an opportunity to go back to the country I knew well from my travels in 1971 and 1974.

By this time, I was certain, but sad that I should not pursue the opportunity in Australia. I was going to be living abroad anyway, but with the benefit of a secure future with BP, and much more money than the two-year Post-Doc in Australia could offer. More than this, it was the right time to join the oil industry. Exploration was entering a boom period, stimulated by war, risk and uncertainty in the Middle East. In 1979, Ayatollah Khomeini took over in Iran, after the US-friendly Shah was deposed. Then the US Embassy in Tehran was attacked and 52 hostages held there. Oh, and the Russians invaded Afghanistan. Oil went to $24 a barrel and the price of petrol rose steeply.

Though it seemed that the posting to Norway was going ahead, Derek South casually announced one day that I would be going to Singapore instead. Even better! I had formed a good impression of Singapore when I had visited for a day at the end of my trip to Indonesia the previous year. It also meant that I would be working on the geology of Indonesia, with which I was familiar through my research. My only proviso to BP was that I could not leave until after my external examination, the Viva interview, which was scheduled for 5th January, 1981. And so it was agreed. An added bonus was that Sarah was offered a job in Singapore. We put our house in the hands of a letting agent and set in motion the complex preparations needed to vacate our home and move abroad.

There was one final test: the Viva with an external examiner who had read my thesis and came prepared with searching questions. I thought about the time when I had been interviewed for a place at Chippenham Grammar School, which had been a prerequisite for my opportunity to study geology. It was seventeen years ago, and so much had happened in the intervening years: from bottom of the class at school to top of the class at college; from wayward teenager to respectable scientist; from shy virgin to married man; and from long-haired pupil in school uniform to long-haired and bearded Petroleum Geologist in a business uniform.

I passed the Viva, and next day Sarah and I boarded a flight taking us from the tame, safe and predictable commuter belt society in Surrey, to the steamy equatorial climate of an exotic island in Southeast Asia, inhabited by ethnic Chinese, Malays and Indians. I was putting distance between my present and past, but I hoped that I would not lose touch with my school and college mates. Nick was now manager of the Transport Department in Chard; Brian was working in IT in London; Bernie was in a supervisory position at Core Laboratories; Dave West was working for a copper mining company in Zambia; and Mike McMurtry had finished his PhD and started a career with oil company Texaco. And Rob, who I had always admired for his intellect, had taken a degree as a mature student and was going on to start a PhD in astrophysics.

At BP, I was on equal terms with my peer group, most of whom had good bachelor's degrees or even higher degrees from the best universities in the UK, such as Oxford, Cambridge and Imperial College. Now I could hold my head high, now the healing was complete, and now I was ready to face the outside world. What I didn't know then was that my fight for recognition and acceptance was just beginning all over again. But that is another story.